An Introduction to the
Canterbury Tales

Reading, Fiction, Context

Helen Phillips

St. Martin's Press
New York

AN INTRODUCTION TO THE CANTERBURY TALES

Copyright © 2000 by Helen Phillips

St. Martin's Press, Scholarly and Reference Division,
175 Fifth Avenue, New York, N.Y. 10010

First published in the United States of America in 2000

This book is printed on paper suitable for recycling and made from fully managed and sustained forest sources.

Printed in Hong Kong

ISBN 0–312–22739–6 clothbound
ISBN 0–312–22740–X paperback

Library of Congress Cataloging-in-Publication Data
Phillips, Helen.
An introduction to the Canterbury tales : reading, fiction,
context / Helen Phillips.
p.   cm.
Includes bibliographical references and index.
ISBN 0–312–22739–6 (cloth). — ISBN 0–312–22740–X (pbk.)
1. Chaucer, Geoffrey, d. 1400. Canterbury tales.   2. Christian
pilgrims and pilgrimages in literature.   3. Tales, Medieval—History
and criticism.   4. Storytelling in literature.   I. Title.
PR1874.P48   1999
821'.1—dc21   99–22268
                                                              CIP

#4158042Y

Contents

Preface

I hope this book addresses the needs of students of Chaucer, as well as the interest of readers and critics generally, and that it conveys something of the complexity and enjoyment of the *Canterbury Tales*. This is only one interpretation of Chaucer; there will always be others. The *Canterbury Tales* is a work, more than most, which is different and new on every reading. This book tries to show some of the reasons which make this so. It aims to introduce and discuss a range of approaches to Chaucer, some from the past as well as those of today. Formal, stylistic, political, gender, psychological, religious, historical and historicist approaches are all employed, though often not in strictly separate compartments, since in literature form is meaning, and Chaucer, in particular, is adept in writing in styles which seem to inhabit several different worlds simultaneously. Certain aspects of Chaucer and certain issues about the *Canterbury Tales* have special prominence. These include: a sense that the tales offer a cumulative and many-faceted exploration of authorship (which includes the author's readers and the creation of meaning between them); explorations of Chaucer's polyphonic uses of stylistic register, and of spoken and narrative forms; the question of how this narrative, often seen as politically conservative or evasive, may represent tensions in the economic and social England outside the story; and, in addition, critical issues concerned with Chaucer's long-famed, and by now long-disputed, handling of realism and character.

This book owes a great deal to friends and colleagues. For help, inspiration and advice, I would like to thank particularly Catherine Belsey, Derek Brewer, Helen Cooper, Alfred David, Linda David, Douglas Gray, Stan Hussey, Sarah Kay, Stephen Knight, Mike McCarthy, Alison McHardy, Derek Pearsall, Miri Rubin, Meg Twycross, and Jocelyn Wogan-Browne. I am grateful to the University of Nottingham for a sabbatical semester, and to students in Lancaster and Nottingham for discussions about Chaucer, and especially to Dee Dyas, Sally-Ann Harding, Jill Seal, Michelle Wright, and (for technical help) Adam Quesnell and Matt Hassan. Thanks go to Margaret Bartley at the publishers for all her help and patience, to Valery Rose and Jocelyn Stockley for their help with the copy-editing. Nicola Phillips helped with checking and cheerfulness and Hugh Phillips with the computer. And to two people who have given me most over the years, Gwen Phillips and Graeme Segal, this book is dedicated with love and gratitude.

1

Chaucer and the *Canterbury Tales*

THE CANTERBURY TALES –
CHIVALRY, LOVE, LUST, THE BLACK DEATH, RAPE, DECEPTION AND
CHICKENS

That is how the promotional material for the 1998 animated film of
The Canterbury Tales sums up its contents.[1] Surprising juxtapositions
and variety are certainly the most obvious characteristic of the *Tales*.
They are also the source of the most interesting critical questions the
text asks. To the film-makers' list we could add such topics as saints,
martyrs, students, mechanical flying horses, Islam, pacifism, the fairy
queen, the Anglo-Saxons, chemical experiments, Mary, miracles,
Amazons, sex in trees, profiteering on European exchange dealings, and
geometrically divided farts, and still leave much of the diversity of
Chaucer's subject-matter out. The *Canterbury Tales* also offers great
diversity of styles, moods and genres: from epic and religious lyric to
parody.

The most challenging aspects of its diversity, however, are the
conflicting moralities that seem to be present within the text, and the
diversity of interpretation that Chaucer's writing invites. At times the
narrative itself acts out multiple reader-response, by showing the
pilgrims divided in their reactions or expectations concerning the tales
they hear and tell. This, for example, is the response of the pilgrims to
the bawdy *Miller's Tale*:

> Diverse folk diversely they seyde,
> But for the moore part they loughe and pleyde.[2]

From his mixed band of pilgrims, varied in both their social status and
their levels of morality, who are both the fictional narrators of his tales

1

and a fictional audience, Chaucer creates a many-voiced narrative which lacks both the limitations and the safety of a single focalization.[3] The first-person narrator, the main narrator in one sense, does not organise the story-telling: the pilgrims themselves are given, in the fiction, control over the ordering and content of the series of tales; they quarrel about them and dispute authority. When the narrator does get to speak, they soon refuse to listen to what he has to say. In this way, and others, it is a polyphonic text: no one viewpoint is allowed to preside over the story-telling. Though the first-person narrator in some sense represents the author, as the source through which the story is told to us, another authorial function, control over the order and design, is displaced from him and formally vested in a different character: Harry Bailey ('Herry Bailly', I, 4358), the Host of the Tabard Inn. Chaucer presents Bailey's authority too as contested, by other characters who insist at certain moments on having their own way about what happens next in the proceedings. Chaucer's decision to paint his pilgrim company as a socially variegated group, full of rivalry and internal tensions has several different effects; it creates narratological complexities which intrigue the critic; it raises deep questions about the text's overall moral standpoint; and it could also be an image of Chaucer's awareness of his own late fourteenth-century context as a society of rapid economic and political change and movement, bringing classes into new relationships of rivalry and conflict, with challenges to established authority – from the rising power of the merchant classes, from the economic frustration and ambitions of artisans and peasants, and from discontent among reformers and laity about the state of the Church.

The *Canterbury Tales* is presented fictionally as a composite text, a randomly created collection of stories without an organising plan or unifying principle, yet Chaucer offers us a structure which constantly seems to promise unity. The story-collection, for example, occurs within the device of the pilgrimage, a frame-story which suggests a purpose and a goal – though the extant narrative never shows the pilgrimage reaching Canterbury. And the collection begins with the tale of the socially most authoritative pilgrim, the Knight, rich but dedicated to his fellow-Christians, and ends with that of the man of most spiritual authority, the holy Parson, poor but dedicated even more crucially to their spiritual salvation. The positioning of these two tales might imply that the *Tales* are conceived within an integrated social vision, and a vision of life that integrates the worldly and the heavenly. Other elements in the work similarly draw on models of human life and society which contain diversity and conflict within reassuring assumptions of benignly designed order. Yet diversity and conflict remain major characteristics of the *Tales*, and the text itself, in the extant physical form in which it has been left to us, is in fact a fragmentary one, unfinished and full of gaps. The text Chaucer left is one that can never give readers a clear unified plan, even if he had envisaged eventually producing a completed work which would have done this. Material fact and the internal tendencies of the text itself thus work together to deny any easy sense of closure.

As readers of literature we tend to assume, unless shown otherwise, that first-person narrators broadly represent the author, though, of course, writers frequently challenge that assumption by creating unreliable, ignorant or even deceptive narrators. Here the first-person narrator can certainly not be taken as an adequate representative of Chaucer's own authorial control over what we are shown in the text. This is not just because he himself is constructed as an unreliable narrator (though much twentieth-century criticism read him primarily as an example of the type of narrator who is ironically constructed as a naive observer), but also because the whole narrative is structured to disperse any sense of authoritative organisation: authority for the organisation and the evaluation of the story-telling is dispersed among different characters. The diverse group of pilgrims is also used by Chaucer, as we see in their diverse reactions to the *Miller's Tale*, above, to represent a heterogeneous audience, with equally heterogeneous readings of the narratives.

Diversity, then, is central to the *Tales* both on the obvious level of the social mix of the pilgrims and the range of genres, subjects, styles and moral seriousness in their stories, and also at a deeper level in the way the text permits disparate worldviews and incompatible readings to co-exist, without subjugating them conclusively to one controlling vision, and the *Tales*' management of its dual impulses, towards unity and towards diversity, raises issues about how the multiplicity of human experience, desires and goals relates ultimately to the concept of a divine order. The variety in the *Canterbury Tales* thus presents us with some issues which are critical and others which are ultimately moral and theological questions about the design of human life and society. Politically, the stance of the *Tales* may seem at first conservative or apolitical, serving the interests of the ruling class for whom, and among whom, Chaucer worked as a courtier and civil servant, and yet subversive forces and problematic elements are also discernably present in most of the tales to a degree it is hard for the critic to ignore, and the whole miscellany of narratives, juxtaposed with each other, ensures that no single tale can create its own world of values without being challenged by the often incompatible values of other tales around it. The vulgarity, lawlessness and celebration of physical pleasure in the *Miller's Tale* is not accommodated in any way – by anything within the fictional narrative of the *Tales* – to the very different values of the *Knight's Tale*, which precedes it; similarly, the Man of Law's condemnation of the miseries of poverty in his Prologue contrasts completely with the praise of poverty as a spiritually and even practically advantageous state expressed in the *Wife of Bath's Tale*. Nothing in the *Tales* provides any way of reconciling the two. In his company of pilgrims, brought together both by holiday spirit and by religious purpose, Chaucer creates an appropriately dialectic frame for the stories: a chattering and quarrelling assembly of *diverse folk* with *diverse* reactions, who comment on the tales they tell and hear, and offer a bewildering variety of inter-pretations and assumptions about their purpose and meaning during the so-called 'link' passages of pilgrim conversation between tales, thus foregrounding for the critic the issue of individual reader-response to literature and its meaning(s).

Aspects of the *Tales'* diversity have been discussed, in different forms, by critics over a long period – indeed, the pilgrims' diversity of opinion about the *Miller's Tale* could stand for the diversity of critics' readings of Chaucer's work. The critical, political and religious dimensions of the *Tales'* provocative structure will be central topics in this book, together with an aspect of its diversity which has been relatively little explored: the ways in which the text offers a many-faceted examination of the nature of authorship, including related issues about language and interpretation. Tale by tale, as well as in many of the links between tales, Chaucer brings to our attention such matters as authorial intentional-ity, the role of a text's audience in the creation of meaning, the question of whether tales should be read literally or symbolically, the medieval secular writer's socially authorised functions – as traditional minstrel or advisor to princes – and the uses to which skill in language and rhetoric may be put, whether as praise to God, as moral instruction, or to earn money. Some of these questions are universal, others – such as the ques-tion of whether secular texts should be read allegorically to yield a moral, and whether the secular author has to define and justify his role, within fairly narrow traditional limits – were of special importance for medieval authors and readers. Among Chaucer's pilgrim-narrators are some, such as the Lawyer and the Pardoner, who offer disconcerting parallel images of other professionals who, like authors, use skill with words to win money. Just as disconcerting for the medieval secular author, the *Prioress's Prologue* declares the supreme power of the unlearned, even inarticulate, tongues of infants in praising to the Lord:

a vision of how speech should be used that Chaucer sets just before his own tale in the sequence of stories. At times these themes appear in explicit terms, as when the Nun's Priest tells us we can choose whether to read his tale allegorically or literally, or the Shipman warns that a Lollard may present a sermon that will spread religious dissent – a sharply contemporary, controversial view of one of the uses to which verbal skill may be put. More often aspects of authorship are presented in oblique or fable form, like the Manciple's caged crow who sings to please its master and faces danger if it speaks the truth: surely a metaphor for the court poet.

As the pilgrims' reactions to the *Miller's Tale* illustrate, this is also a work of laughter and *pley*, of entertainment 'for the moore part' – though modern criticism has revealed how much Chaucer's post-medieval reputation for quaint, harmless jollity misrepresents the social and political complexity, the intellectual depth and the problematic aesthetics of the *Canterbury Tales* – and its comedy. Chaucer remains one of the world's funniest writers, whether of satire, farce or of social and domestic sitcom, skilful in the comic writer's most important arts – of revealing speech and gesture, narrative pace and timing, the social dimensions of conversation and interpersonal conflict, verbal ingenuity, and all the pitfalls that lie ahead for the pretentious, the obsessed, the naive and those who are too clever for their own good. As a highly theatrical writer, specialising in dialogue, and as also a very visual writer – more interested usually in catching the appearances and actions of human behaviour than in painting natural scenery – and as a writer who mingles together gods and humans, humans and talking animals, in their different dimensions, it is not surprising that Chaucer created a text that responds so well to recreation as an animated film.

The *Canterbury Tales* was probably written between the late 1380s and Chaucer's death in 1400. His other surviving works are *Troilus and Criseyde* (*c*.1386), four dream poems (the *Book of the Duchess*, *c*.1368–75, *House of Fame*, *c*.1374–80, *Parliament of Fowls*, early 1380s?, *Legend of Good Women*, *c*.1386–*c*.1399), and a number of lyrics, prose works and translations.

Of the twenty-four *Canterbury Tales*, the *Cook's* and *Squire's* are unfinished. The *Monk's Tale* and Chaucer's own tale of *Sir Thopas* are cut short by other pilgrims' objections to them – as too gloomy and too badly written respectively. The *Canterbury Tales* contains narratives which have been cut short deliberately and other parts of the text which have been left unfinished, though whether by accident or design is not always certain. At his death Chaucer seems to have left his composition in ten fragments, each containing one or more tales. While the obvious conclusion is that he would have completed a smooth final version, had he lived, it is just possible, as the discussion of the incomplete *Squire's Tale* in Chapter 12 shows, that he deliberately decided to leave at least some of the elements in the text unfinished. This could be a daring aesthetic that matched the refusal of his narratives themselves to provide simple resolutions to contradictions and tensions revealed in them. The fragments, and the tales within them, do not always appear in the same order in the manuscripts, including manuscripts which have important textual authority: some of the variations may represent Chaucer's own changes to his design, others are probably scribes' attempts to reorganise the text.

The story-tellers are pilgrims journeying from Southwark, on the south bank of the Thames opposite Westminster, to the shrine of St Thomas à Becket at Canterbury Cathedral. Chaucer says there are twenty-nine (at I, 24), though the *General Prologue* portraits do not tally with this number, a minor discrepancy no doubt resulting from the fact that he never finalised the plan. They are joined by his own representative, the narrator, by Harry Bailey and later by a Canon and his servant. They are young and old, male and female, of different ranks and from various parts of England. Most of the tales are in iambic pentameter couplets, the major English verse form that Chaucer appears to have invented, some in a seven-line stanza rhyming *ababbcc*, the so-called Rhyme Royal stanza, also Chaucer's invention. The exceptions are three tales which stand apart for other reasons: Chaucer's 'own' tales and that of the Parson, who refuses to tell a tale, in the normal fictional sense, at all. The *Parson's Tale* and Chaucer's *Melibee* are prose, and Chaucer's *Sir Thopas* is in the 'tail rhyme' stanza traditionally used for popular minstrel romances (see pp. 173–5).

The first-person narrator, traditionally labelled 'Chaucer the Pilgrim' by critics, tells two tales, *Sir Thopas* and *Melibee*, which are known by those titles rather than by their teller's profession since Chaucer leaves the narrator's profession and other details about him intriguingly blank. It is important to recognise that Chaucer does not use the device of a first-person narrative voice in any consistent, fixed way. Indeed, we are only intermittently aware of the text as one narrated by a character. Chaucer the Pilgrim does function for short passages as a consciousness through which the narrative is focalised, or with which other personalities interact dramatically, but much of the narrative could just as well be regarded as third-person impersonal narrative (the other pilgrim-narrators' voices and personalities are similarly only occasionally introduced into the tales attributed to them). Moreover, this narrator, when his presence is felt as a character or observer, is emphatically not in charge of what is presented to us, but rather is passive: at the mercy of Chaucer's other characters and their stronger wills. Despite Harry Bailey's, and on occasion the Knight's, attempts to steer the story collection along, the individual wills and moods of others often pull the order of events in different directions. The functions of the author, recording and ordering his material, are thus dispersed among several different characters. One of the many issues Chaucer explores through this decentralisation is that of the relative authority of secular and religious literature. After the Knight's preliminary tale, the Host wants to get the highest-ranking religious man, the Monk, to tell the second tale, but his plan is disrupted: the secular Miller follows. The powerful Knight begins the tales but the poor Parson – rich in heavenly qualities – brings them to an end. The Parson's refusal to tell a *story* at all seems both the final rebellion against Harry Bailey's authority and the replacing of that power with a higher authority, that of spiritual priorities.

Harry Bailey's original plan, (I, 790–801), was for each pilgrim to tell four tales, two while going and two returning from Canterbury. Chaucer completed less than a quarter of this design and there are signs within the extant text of an alternative plan: the text apparently presents only the outward journey, ending on the outskirts of Canterbury and with a religious conclusion, the *Parson's Tale*, not with a jolly dinner back at the Southwark inn, as the Host envisaged. (Of course, this shorter Southwark-to-Canterbury design may have been Chaucer's own original plan; see Pearsall 1997 on the two plans and the question of which came first.)

Chaucer, born in the early 1340s, was the son of a rich London wine-merchant who had been at times in royal service: for example, from 1347 to 1349 as deputy chief butler to Edward III. Chaucer's own career was as an employee in royal households, an administrator and civil servant, during the reigns of Edward III, 1327–77, and Richard II, 1377–99 (on biography, see Pearsall, 1992, and Dillon, 1993). He began as a page in his teens, rising to the rank of esquire in the king's household, a title which brought him onto the lowest rung of those who were *gentil*: esquires ranked below knights or aristocrats. Advancing socially thus from a merchant background into the world of the royal court and into the symbolically important class of the *gentil*, but through government service rather than through the older qualifications of *gentil* ancestry and landowning, Chaucer typifies the increasing interpenetration in late fourteenth-century England between the rich bourgeoisie, with money made from commerce, and the *gentils*, whose wealth came traditionally from feudal estates (see Strohm 1989: 23). In his administrative posts in government service he similarly typifies the increasing importance, in this era, of the secular rather than priestly administrator.

This upward mobility, and his familiarity with both the world of commerce in the powerful City of London and the courtly world of aristocratic society and the royal palaces, are reflected in the social variety, and variety of values, depicted in his *Canterbury Tales*. His aggressive Wife of Bath, a businesswoman who believes everything has its price; his brutish Miller who will not lower his hood to show deference to anybody; the alchemist making money out of nothing by false and diabolical-seeming contrivances; the ruthlessly successful Reeve, a low-born rural administrator running the estate of a lord and building up his own well-stocked residence in isolation from the community: these are literary creations which capture contemporary socio-economic developments, while working frequently within conventional literary satiric models. The negative thrust in these particular portrayals dramatises a hostile, apprehensive attitude towards new economic and social forces such as growing commercial individualism, a developing cash and profit economy, greater freedom for employment and enterprise in both town and country, and less rigid distinctions between ranks – and the consequent fear of less respect, and of new wealth and power for enterprising members of the lower classes. In contrast, Chaucer's crusading Knight, using warfare only to defend the Christian community, and the selfless Parson and Plowman working to serve their neighbours, are idealised projections of the bonds of mutual service and fidelity which, in theory, underpinned the traditional feudal economic structure with a fixed and hierarchical relationship between classes in a rural community. His use of an idealised, iconic style for them, however, suggests awareness of changing structures and realities as much as does the sharp caricature in the portrayals mentioned above.

Chaucer and his wife Philippa, a lady in waiting, were attached to several households of the royal family during their lives. Typical duties would include being an attendant and companion, a general assistant in the organisation and provisioning of these large and expensive organisations, a clerk, tutor or secretary, and for male retainers the possibility of military service (Chaucer was captured in a campaign against the

French in 1360, with Edward III paying his ransom), as well as contributing to entertainments: music, hunting, games, jousting, dancing, performances and literature. Richard II, unlike his predecessors, was reluctant to undertake military campaigns; with no need for a large military corps his court became more civilian, with more of its staff engaged in administration. Historians have disagreed about how far Richard brought a new court civilisation into being, something approaching the Tudor concept of the court as the apex of culture and elegance, but his tastes seem to have made his court sophisticated, luxurious and – imitating French practices – more hierarchical in its rituals than that of previous English monarchs (Saul 1997: 327–65).

London (population about 40,000), close to the centre of royal government at Westminster, was a rich, cosmopolitan, in many ways independent city, a centre for trade by sea and land, ruled by a powerful merchant oligarchy (Keen 1990: 108–28). Chaucer was familiar with the London mercantile elite. His friends included Nicholas Brembre, an important merchant and Lord Mayor in 1383. His two major administrative posts involved varied commercial contacts: Controller of Customs on wool and leather, 1374–85, and Clerk to the King's Works, 1389–91, overseeing royal building operations (Richard II was an indefatigable builder and refurbisher of his many residences) and also the installations for the king's magnificent Smithfield Tournament of 1390. The *House of Fame* refers to long hours working at his accounts, presumably for the Customs. Perhaps we can see an oblique self-portrait of Chaucer's two careers in the Manciple, the able low-born administrator – cleverer than his masters – who tells a tale which can be read as a fable about how the court-poet has to keep his mouth shut (see pp. 213–18).

Chaucer visited France, Spain and Italy on government service. He was widely read in contemporary and classical authors, science and philosophy. His friends included Ralph Strode, an Oxford philosopher; he may have met Italian poets including Petrarch, and certainly became acquainted with their work. He is the first English author to respond creatively to the Italian Renaissance and to the new status it gave to vernacular literatures (see pp. 46 and 18–20). His contemporary John Gower wrote in Latin, Anglo-Norman French and English. Anglo-Norman was only just beginning to decline in Chaucer's England. Chaucer, nevertheless, wrote apparently only in English, although fashionable French (Parisian French – not Anglo-Norman) literature was enjoyed at court and Chaucer's lyric and dream poetry imitates contemporary French styles with brilliant success and creativity. *Sir Thopas* suggests a certain impatience with traditional English styles (pp. 173–5). Chaucer's use of English was clearly not an automatic or conservative decision: he may have been consciously creating for English a language of styles and forms which could equal the best Italian, French and classical Latin literature. The anthology of genres which is the *Canterbury Tales*, with their enormous range of European and English literary sources and affinities, suggests a desire to explore, extend and establish the resources of English poetry and prose.

Before the advent of printing in Britain in 1476, a patron was the chief source of payment for a book. There is no record of patronage for any of Chaucer's works. We do not know how far he was renowned at court as a poet rather than for his other services, nor how close he was personally to members of the royal family, though his *Book of the Duchess* was probably composed for Edward III's son John of Gaunt, Duke of Lancaster, as a memorial to his first wife, and the *Legend of Good Women* perhaps for Anne of Bohemia, Richard II's first queen.

At times the *Tales* project a conservative, aristocratic perspective, like that of the landowning class whose world Chaucer had entered and served: it can be suspicious of money made through commerce or financial dealing and of artisan wealth, associating these at times with vulgar pride, duplicity or even impiety – in the *Canon's Yeoman's* or *Reeve's Tale* – while conversely the traditional rural feudal economy may be bathed in a sentimentally benign light, with a contented peasantry – like the *Nun's Priest's Tale* widow – or villeins happy to work free for the common good, like the *General Prologue* Plowman.[4] But Chaucer does not simply endorse the status of inherited wealth. He writes, for example, powerfully of the idea that true *gentilesse* is virtue, and in his rejection of aggressive economic individualism, Christian morality mingles with a sense of communal values. An abhorrence of tyranny, oppression and arrogance by lords, and concern about the responsibilites of those who rule others, are recurrent themes. He writes fiercely of clerics, like the *General Prologue's* Friar and Pardoner, who fleece the trusting poor. The design of the *Tales*, its surprising juxtapositions, many narrators, and the comments and reactions expressed in the Links – variegated, irreverent or irrelevant – ensure that no one view or voice dominates (see Rigby's discussion of 'Monologic versus Dialogic Chaucer', 1996: 18–77). The Host's plan was for a competition; and conflict and rivalry, rather than hierarchy and harmony, often characterise the relations of the pilgrim group and juxtaposition of tales, a characteristic explored particularly by Knapp (1990). The very clarity with which Chaucer's fictions capture the complexities of social and personal relationships militates against a single or complacent vision. His writing illustrates well the way that clarity, depth and perceptiveness in narrative depiction of society can expose the weak points, omissions and conflicts inherent in a dominant ideology at the same time as the text ostensibly endorses it. The *Tales* create a narrative world of variety and contradictions, one with the potential for multiple critical interpretations.

Appropriately, for a writer whose work cannot be pinned down to a single message or set of values, and shows conflicting attitudes co-existent in the same experience, Chaucer's career shows him as a political survivor – though there may have been fluctuations in job security and finances since records show him occasionally in debt and moving his activities at periods of political crisis prudently away from the centre of things (see Pearsall 1992: 143–51, 202–9). He was a Justice of the Peace, 1385–6, and 'Knight of the Shire', i.e. Member of Parliament, for Kent in 1386. In the 1386 and 1388 parliaments Richard II's opponents forced the dismissal of royal supporters and favourites (medieval parliaments did not sit regularly but were summoned when monarchs needed to raise money). The young king, threatened with deposition, acceded to his opponents' will and some of his supporters were executed. Chaucer, a royal servant, probably identified with the king's party in Parliament, survived unharmed, though several victims of this political purge had been his associates.

His enemies saw Richard as headstrong, pleasure-loving and extravagant, preferring the advice of lesser and younger men to that of older princes who saw themselves as the proper navigators of government. In the 1390s Richard provoked more opposition. His quarrel with the City of London over money and the City's independent power was only assuaged by the City's payment in 1392 of vast sums of money. Richard raised money from his subjects by dubiously legal methods which aroused resentment. Unjust extortion was one of the chief definitions of a tyrant in medieval theories of kingship, and the last years of Richard's reign were denounced by his critics as a tyranny. In 1397 he took delayed revenge on some lords who had opposed him in the late 1380s, including John of Gaunt's son Henry of Lancaster, who was exiled and subsequently deprived of his inheritance. Henry returned in 1399 to lead a successful rebellion against Richard, who was deposed. Henry of Lancaster became Henry IV and Richard died in prison, probably murdered.

Throughout his career Chaucer kept the favour of both the king and the increasingly powerful Lancastrian dynasty (his wife Philippa was in the service of John of Gaunt's second wife and her sister was probably

Catherine Swynford, Gaunt's mistress and later his third duchess). Chaucer survived the Lancastrian coup of 1399 with his annuity continuing to be paid by the new king. He rented a house in the grounds of Westminster Abbey and was buried in the Abbey in 1400.

The *Canterbury Tales* and Late Medieval English Society

The English economy and society experienced major, sometimes violent, changes during Chaucer lifetime.[5] The population, already declining earlier in the century, was reduced by at least a third by the Black Death, 1348–9. Resultant labour shortages produced wage rises and increased labour-mobility, and landowners, including ecclesiastical landowners, now saw the advantage of insisting on villeins' traditional services and on the ancient fines, payments and monopolies that custom let them impose on their villeins, but which had been in decline as a wage economy developed before the plague. Government attempts to help landowners put the clock back through the Statute of Labourers 1351, which tried to peg wages to pre-plague levels and forbade villeins to leave estates, failed but caused discontent. In the post-plague economy some people of peasant origins did well for themselves: we see financially successful, confident peasants in the *General Prologue's* Miller and Reeve, and Thomas in the *Summoner's Tale*.

Unpopular military campaigns and the taxes squandered on them fuelled discontent. The imposition of heavy Poll Taxes led the English Rising of 1381. Despite its popular name 'Peasants' Revolt', the Rising had widely based support which included local community leaders, tradesmen, artisans, and clerics – solid citizens goaded finally into action by a series of government acts and extortions that seemed to deny justice, dignity and modern social realities. To many villeins (roughly 50 per cent of the population) the whole concept of their unfree status had become unacceptable. The revolt, though nationwide, was strongest in the south-east, and from 12–15 June the rebels invaded London and the centres of government and commerce, powerless to act, were potentially at their mercy. The young king and his lords were trapped in the Tower of London. Finally Richard, advised by lords and City leaders, fronted a successful manoeuvre to outflank the rebels, kill their leader Wat Tyler, and persuade them to return home. Some were pardoned, some executed. Though order had been restored, the Rising created a fear among the governing classes that ran through the next decades.

Chaucer lived in the City: his house at Aldgate was directly over the rebels' route into London yet, apart from scattered allusions on violent disorder as an aspect of rebellion (especially VI, 3394–6), he makes no direct comment on 1381 as a political event. Absence of direct discussion does not mean that the text cannot in its own literary way present Chaucer's awareness of, and responses to, the challenge the rebellion represented to the ruling classes. Patterson (1991) sees the insubordination with which Chaucer's Miller pushes into the story-telling sequence after the Knight as Chaucer's dramatisation of that challenge and the social conflict that produced it. Stephen Knight observes that 'The world of the *Canterbury Tales* is the world of conflict that generated the Peasants' Revolt', though Chaucer's own position did not make him sympathetic with revolution, and the text reveals signs of strain and restraint over its own recognition of social oppressions, tensions and aspirations; the fiction of the pilgrimage neutralises these and subsumes secular conflict and variety into an ultimately spiritual purpose (1986: 69).

Other forces were at work in the period. The century saw the beginnings of modern banking and credit systems: the *General Prologue* Merchant and the *Shipman's Tale* businessman who plays the exchange markets for profit, both making their money through credit and exchange, illustrate this. Lay literacy was increasing. Literacy, like computing skills today, meant a whole range of skills, from minimal ability to decipher some written words up to fluency in reading and writing Latin, the language of education and power, though in an age where much information, education, and religious teaching or discussion was oral, illiteracy did not necessarily mean ignorance. Poetry was written to be performed orally as well as read privately. Chaucer talks of his audience as both reading and listening in I, 3176–7. Books were produced by commercial booksellers as well as monastic scriptoria. Education was in the hands of the Church: *clerk*, from Latin *clericus*, meant both priest and educated man. Priests were clerks in 'Major Orders', but students, university scholars, doctors, lawyers and clerical assistants like Absolon in the *Miller's Tale* were also technically clerks, in 'Minor Orders': without vows of celibacy or the right to celebrate sacraments.

The Church provided education, hospitals, and much local and national administration. Church courts dealt with wills, tithes, marriage, and moral offences like fornication or adultery (summoners summonsed people to answer charges in these courts). In many ways the medieval Church and medieval society were the same thing, yet there were separate spheres and deep tensions. From 1337, the 'Great Schism' – the spectacle of two rival popes and an associated Europe-wide power-struggle – bred cynicism. Clerics' incomes varied enormously; in contrast to Chaucer's poor parson, men with powerful friends might acquire lucrative livings or bishoprics. Absentee priests neglected their pastoral duties. Many people wanted reform or abolition of religious houses, which often had rich land-endowments and ran enormously successful farming enterprises (see the monks in the *General Prologue* and *Shipman's Tale*). A whole range of superstitions and beliefs without sanction in the Bible or the Early Church had developed over centuries, flourishing partly because few could read the Latin Bible and also because of the superstructure of often bizarre and biased interpretation laid over its statements by centuries of exegesis. Many who loved the Church most wanted reform. Chaucer's anticlerical satire belongs to a long tradition of such writing, much of it penned by clerics. The leading reformer, the Oxford theologian John Wyclif, and his followers, sometimes called Lollards, advocated vernacular translation of the Bible, a return to more Bible-based Christian doctrine and practice, a reduction of the Church's financial, judicial and administrative power to what was needed to run its religious mission, and the subordination of the Church's organisation to the king; they opposed pilgrimages, devotion to relics, religious orders and the celibacy of the clergy. Sympathy with Wycliffite ideas was quite widespread. Secular lords, including John of Gaunt, supported some of Wyclif's ideas – not least because reducing Church wealth and jurisdiction would remove what was virtually a second political power in the country and increase the freedom of secular government. A group of Wycliffite sympathisers at court, the so-called 'Lollard Knights', included friends of Chaucer. Nothing in his writings suggests his piety was anything but orthodox; his religious writings centre on saints' lives and prayers to the Virgin, but contemporary religious controversies and Wycliffite ideas appear in the *Tales*, including the *Wife of Bath's Tale* and *Parson's Prologue* (pp. 94, 102 and 220). The Parson that Chaucer presents as an ideal of gospel-based goodness is labelled a Lollard by Harry Bailey (II, 1170–7) for reproving blasphemous swearing.

Texts and Criticism

Eighty-four *Canterbury Tales* manuscripts survive, some merely single tales, fragments or extracts. The order of the tales varies in different manuscripts. The two most important are the Hengwrt and Ellesmere Manuscripts, both *c*.1400. Most modern editions follow the Ellesmere order. This may only be a scribe's or compiler's order, though it and Hengwrt are generally believed by scholars to represent orders for the tales devised by Chaucer. We cannot therefore automatically assume that in Chaucer's plan, for example, the *Man of Law's Tale* followed the *Cook's*, nor can we assume he only had one design: it seems likely he changed his mind in the course of composing the tales. Manuscript variations and the *Tales'* unfinished state have crucial bearing on critical debates about the work's design and meaning. An influential early twentieth-century critic, Kittredge (1915), writing in the golden sunset of the realist novel, saw the *Tales* as a drama of realistically conceived characters: the central subject is the pilgrims, and their tales are mono-logues revealing their characters (pp. 154–5). He proposed that the *Wife's*, *Clerk's*, *Merchant's* and *Franklin's Tales*, in that order, form a 'Marriage Group' (pp. 185–211), with the Franklin's providing the answer to problems raised by the other three. Many manuscripts, however, do not give the tales in the sequence Kittredge's theory requires, though it is the order found in Ellesmere and a number of other manuscripts. Thus Kittredge may be right that Chaucer designed a 'marriage group', but there is no certainty.

In contrast to the emphasis on the *Tales'* diversity at the beginning of this chapter, several critics, including Baldwin (1955), Robertson (1962), Jordan (1967), and Olson (1986), see the whole work as propounding a monologic, Christian message, with the *Knight's* and *Parson's Tales* representing a divine design within which all human life, and all the intervening tales, fit: for them the work is ultimately about spiritual pilgrimage to the heavenly Jerusalem, taking us from Southwark to Canterbury and allegorically from earth to heaven. This hypothesis only works with the extant, fragmentary, sequence of tales, ending with the Parson and Canterbury, for Harry Bailey's original plan, had Chaucer completed it, would, of course, wreck the hypothe-sis. It would take us from earth to heaven and then back again! How do the bawdy tales, which seem to celebrate physical desire and selfish aggression, fit into such monologic critical readings? For Olson (1986: 70–84) they illustrate what happens when moral and philosophical control, symbolised by *governour* Theseus in the *Knight's Tale*, is absent. The most influential criticism of this type was that of the American 'Princeton' or 'Exegetical' school between the 1960s and 1980s, which drew its inspiration from D. W. Robertson Jr. For them, all medieval literature teaches Christian doctrine, based on St Augustine's dual model of humanity either dedicated to the heavenly Jerusalem and a worldview of *caritas*, desire for God's will, or dedicated to the life of this world and *cupiditas*, worldly desires. For them those tales which do not directly teach such a lesson do so allegorically. Thus adultery in the fabliaux tales is read symbolically: for Robertson (1962: 374–5), the *Miller's Tale* symbolises the betrayal by the worldly of their true spouse, Christ. Opposition to this type of criticism centres on perception of the dialogic character of the *Tales*. Though he begins with the Knight and ends with the Parson, Chaucer's structure and language simultaneously invoke ideas of unity and hierarchy and present challenges to them. Another counter-argument is Chaucer's rejection of his sinful tales in the *Retraction* that ends the text in twenty-eight manuscripts. If tales like the Miller's could be so easily subsumed into a monologic, didactic message, simply by reading them allegorically, then this retraction of them makes no sense: there would be nothing to regret.

Exegetical criticism itself arose in opposition to earlier twentieth-century 'dramatic', character-based criticism. It provided salutary reminders of the Christian parameters of medieval aesthetic thinking and its deep penetration with symbolic and iconographic concepts. Its short-comings are a tendency to ransack Christian allegorists randomly to support its readings, and its one-sided view of medieval literary tastes: ambiguity and tension, especially about the role of the sensual and secular, are central to many great medieval works, including the romances of Chrétien de Troyes, the *Romance of the Rose* and *Canterbury Tales*. It is, in fact, fairly common for medieval writers to present their readers with opposed or unresolved views, whether by offering material in debate form, or by using dissonant juxtapositions, or with texts whose conclusions contradict the directions taken earlier in the composition, or by deeply ambiguous writing styles. With the *Canterbury Tales*, whose variety of pilgrims necessitates a broad social canvas, this aesthetic tradition gave Chaucer a precedent for acknowledging social and political tensions.

The story collection is a form common to many cultures. Examples particularly relevant to Chaucer's design are Ovid's *Metamorphoses*, the voluminous medieval *Gesta Romanorum*, Gower's *Confessio Amantis* (1380s), and Boccaccio's *Il Filocolo* (1336), *Decameron* (*c*.1350) and *De casibus virorum illustrium* (1350–74?). Chaucer eschews the options of choosing a single narrator, as Gower, for example, does, or designing the series of tales to a pre-ordained theme, as Ovid and Boccaccio do, or keeping to one genre, as Boccaccio does in the *De casibus*. Boccaccio's story-tellers in the *Decameron* and *Filocolo* are all upper-class young people; Chaucer has varied ranks and ages.

Chaucer's popular image is as a comic writer – especially of bawdy and irony – and as a realistic writer, or at least a proto-realist, especially in the creation of characters, and also as a writer who gives us a portrait, a panorama, of the medieval world. For many readers, especially in the USA, he also portrays an organic community, a theocentric society. For English readers he has long stood as the Father of English Poetry, at the beginning of the canon – the earliest literature that can still be read without a dictionary and enjoyed – reflecting back a pleasing image of the supposedly English characteristics of humour, tolerance and enjoyment of spring rain.[6] There is some truth in all these popular impressions but they will limit and distort our study of Chaucer if we approach him with them too confidently and exclusively as our guides. That is a danger partly because they correspond so readily to long-held stereotypes of the Middle Ages. All of them are valid only with crucial qualifications. His bawdy, as bawdy – the enjoyable introduction of taboo subjects into the text – is more nuanced than his reputation indicates, and is often also used for complex, serious purposes (pp. 109–11). His irony is by no means ubiquitous: assumptions about Chaucer's constant irony go with the unfounded assumption that we find consistent characterisation between the pilgrims and their tales. Chaucer's realism and psychological acuity are actually manifested more in his style than in his structure: he is a supreme master of realist technique, particularly in depicting speech, reactions to speech, and gestures, but these tend to be local effects. We cannot expect the *Tales* to give exactly the same pleasures as a Victorian novel, with coherent characterisation maintained over the whole text, and the creation of an illusion that the events of the plot spring out of character or from the interaction of an individual with the environment. Chaucer's image of society, we have seen, is not straightforward realistic reporting: it is deeply indebted to literary conventions and political ideologies. As for the theocentric Christian society, while there seems no reason to doubt the sincere faith of the *Retraction*, or that Chaucer, like many medieval writers, was purturbed by the role and justification for secular literature, we should be aware that there was no calm uniformity in fourteenth-century society or Church: Chaucer's was a period full of controversial new ideas about what constituted the Christian social order – cleric or lay? Church practices or biblical precepts? The text often puts these controversies to creative use, and the tales that convey Christian hegemony in most triumphalist form, the *Man of Law's* and *Prioress's*, are the two that contain the most troubled verbal dissonances. And these tales elicit from Chaucer, if not Victorian character-consistency between teller and

tale, disturbingly deep penetration into the psychological roots of patriarchal authority and racist cruelty.

For what audience was he writing? Was it, as some 1980s studies
argued, primarily that highly educated, masculine and middle-class or
knightly group of his fellow government clerks and knights in the royal
household? Or is there some truth in the older assumption that he
wrote for princes and courtiers? (See the discussion and references in
Pearsall 1992: 178–85.) The imagined audience, the one inscribed in
his text, seems wider than either, and it includes women (Riddy 1993:
104–5). The *Tales'* social spectrum, combined with its lack of single
viewpoint, suggests that, whatever his personal and ideological prejudices, he is writing in his deceptively ungrandiose way potentially for a
national readership rather than a clique. Though the lower echelons of
those he includes as story-tellers – millers and plowmen – would have
had little opportunity to read or hear his *Tales* in his own day, the
number of manuscripts and the alacrity with which early printers
brought out editions, shows an ever-widening audience from his death
onwards. Wordsworth found Chaucer an inspiration in his humanity
but also in his ability to use a clear, natural and shared *spoken* form of
English to create great poetry.[7] Surprisingly for a medieval poet, the
popular image, even today, of Chaucer – whether people have read
anything of him or not – is as a national cultural asset but also as an
amusing writer, an entertainer: a writer it might be fun to read, not just
an educational duty.

2

The *General Prologue*

'From every shires ende of Engelond to Caunterbury they wende'

The *Canterbury Tales* begins with a beginning and with movement: April, the start of spring fertility and growth, birds unable to sleep, and then, juxtaposed as if just as much part of Nature's stirring, humans' urge to go on pilgrimage. The opening lines also mimic the state of the reader beginning to move into the new text and, in keeping with the whole of the text we are about to read, it is impossible to decide in this first paragraph whether the overall picture is secular or religious. It starts with the quasi-sexual movement of rain piercing down into the earth, ends with people journeying with a religious aim: to seek 'the hooly blisful martir'.[1] The human impulse is poised in the middle of the long sentence –

> Thanne longen folk to goon on pilgrimages
>
> (I, 12)

– an impulse belonging, the sentence's design suggests, to both the natural processes and the religious purpose. Chaucer's syntax offers two different causations: the first line's 'Whan that April . . .' is picked up at line 12 with 'Thanne longen folk' – as if they are cause and effect, where the cause is a natural instinct; yet the continuing sentence gives a differ-ent, spiritual, cause in line 17:

> The hooly blisful martir for to seke.

A similar ambiguity, if it is ambiguity, about whether everything in the pilgrimage is ultimately subsumed by its sacred destination, and how we interpret the relationship between the sacred and secular in Chaucer's narrative, will remain throughout the *Canterbury Tales*.

19

After the initial, vertical movements, down from the sky into the earth and back up, with the growing flower, again towards the sky, followed with the sun's movement across the sky in the sign of Aries, the human part of the first paragraph, after line 12, takes a great horizontal geographical sweep on earth, as Chaucer first visualises pilgrims to Jerusalem visiting foreign shores on the very edge of medieval Christendom, then in a centrifugal movement, the pilgrims travelling from every shire's end towards the south-east of England, until the narrative comes to rest on the 'I' who is to be the story's narrative voice. Our focus narrows down to one day, one man, one inn, and the evening of that day. And at this point, from line 23 on, there begins another opening up of the fictional perspective, as we are shown the 'Wel nyne and twenty' pilgrims, 'in a compaignye / Of sondry folk'.

Despite their social diversity, Chaucer takes us into what is, in many ways, a closed world after he introduces his 'sondry folk': the social micro-world of their temporary companionship together. The whole narrative of the *Canterbury Tales* now leaves the wider English society, 'every shires ende / Of Engelond', from which Chaucer's social, economic and regional miscellany of people have come. From now on, they and we are within a new unit, of the fictional pilgrim company and of the text itself. The pilgrim group, riding together and talking along the road, resembles many similar unifying fictions familiar to us in books and films – the island, the train, the snow-bound hotel, and so on – and it symbolises and facilitates the unity and exclusivity of the fictional narrative. Though there will be some references to placenames along their route and though the pilgrims often quarrel, they are for the most part presented as if both isolated and unified within that company until, towards the end of the extant *Tales*, the scattering of references to the outside world and the passage of time accelerates; a stranger, from that outside world, rides up to the group and departs from it, and we begin to sense that our immersion in this magical, enclosed world is about to end.[2]

The narrative enters into this shared world in the *General Prologue*, soon after the company is introduced, when the voice that speaks the narrative, the *I*, becomes the recorder of *we* (line 29), rather than the *they* of line 26; he is one of their 'felaweshipe' now and their journey becomes 'oure wey' (lines 32, 34). The transition of pronouns marks the submersion of narrative consciousness into the travelling pilgrim group.

The problems and conflicts in late fourteenth-century England, that wider contemporary context outside the pilgrim company, from which the pilgrim group has come – *every shires ende* – are largely ignored by the *Canterbury Tales* narrative on a direct literal level and yet more present in it than first appears, often in indirect, disguised forms. Chaucer's representation of society is in this sense a paradox. There is less explicit reference to the historical context than modern readers might expect from his social mix of 'sondry folk' and from an author who lived at the centre of national life during a turbulent period; his contemporaries Gower and Langland both allude more to the historical events of their time. Of course, much of the detail in Chaucer's writing derives from literary tradition and many tales have exotic or ancient, rather than fourteenth-century English, settings – that is unsurprising in a medieval author whose priorities were by no means limited to realism – yet Chaucer is also frequently a superb practitioner of the realist style, and adept at representing colloquial conversation, verbal conflict and class-based mannerisms. None the less, even where settings are contemporary, there is a virtual absence of allusions to late fourteenth-century history and politics. It seems as if a habitual, cautious self-censorship is at work. A reference to topical religious controversy in the Man of Law's Endlink seems to have been cancelled, perhaps after official opposition to heresy became fiercer at the close of the century (see pp. 77–8), and the allusion to the 1381 Rising in the *Nun's Priest's Tale* is so frivolous as to appear contemptuously dismissive (see p. 193). Contemporary political issues and controversies are, however, explored in the tales, but indirectly. It can be argued, for example, that the political conflicts within London guilds are implicitly a subject in the *Cook's Tale*, that the *Canon's Yeoman's Tale* is as much about fear of incipient capitalist commerce as about alchemy, that the *Wife of Bath's* antagonism to clerical views of monogamy are as much an indirect expression of Lollard attitudes in contemporary England as of the fictional Wife's rampant sexuality, or that the *Monk's Tale* reflects the causes of Richard II's downfall.[3]

Certain general themes, political in essence and with particular resonance in the period, recur throughout the text: the need for authoritative order to be imposed – however painfully – and obeyed; a vision of social relations as prone to conflict; low-born men and women rising economically and acting assertively; an apprehensive perspective on commercial money-making as a potentially wild, immoral and unnatural force. Many tales end leaving the reader with a sense that disturbing tensions or irreconcilable conflicts of outlook have been revealed; many go to the heart of issues born of a changing, transitional late medieval world: for example, the relationships between the urban professional and landowning *gentil* caste in the *Franklin's Tale*, or the diametrically opposed views of poverty and deprivation expressed in the *Man of Law's Prologue* and *Tale*. The *General Prologue* does not just show eternal human virtue and vice, but includes specific examples of some recent social phenomena which did not fit into inherited moral and social criteria: the skill of an uneducated administrator such as the Manciple, or the Merchant's maintenance of an impressive lifestyle on credit. For all its benign laughter the *Tales* presents a world where chaos and lawlessness could easily break through the social fabric. The qualities Chaucer holds up against social and moral evils are usually individual contentment and stoicism, and a voluntary obedience on the part of those who are ruled, together with virtuous service – a voluntary self-restraint from 'maistrie' – on the part of those who rule. Chaucer ends the extant text of the *Tales* not by showing his travellers arriving at Canterbury at the close of a spring day, and not by returning them to the inn at Southwark, nor by showing them disperse to ride back out again into 'every shires ende / Of Engelond', the society from which they came into his fiction, but by abandoning his depiction of human society entirely and turning the reader's mind to eternal verities, and finally taking leave of his readers neither as a social being nor as an author, but as a soul caught between sin and salvation, facing the final judgement.[4]

The Pilgrims: Traditions and Contemporary Context

Chaucer's opening description of spring (I, 1–11) draws on a wealth of classical and medieval literary tradition: the fertilising showers, Zephyrus, flowers and birds appear together in Virgil's *Georgics*, 2.323–35, and Guido delle Colonne's *Historia Troiana*, 4.34–5, described the April sun in Aries, moisture rising up to the tree-tops, and people enticed out by spring into the open air.[5] Chaucer's passage seems fresh and dynamic primarily because of the movement running through it: it is a description rich in verbs and the camera-eye of the narrative moves around over a large scene, up and down and across wide spaces. Spring openings are common in medieval texts, especially in love lyrics and dream poems. The story proper begins at the Tabard Inn, line 20, but with his seasonal preface Chaucer prepares expectations for the canvas to be a larger, more general one, encompassing heaven and earth, the natural and the spiritual, English shires and 'straunge strondes', the world of ancient learning, myth and poetic tradition, humour (those insomniac 'smale foweles' and the humans so like them), and the divine design in the heavens, on earth and in humans souls.

Moving on to his pilgrim portraits, the poet's eye stays general and generic in ways that the modern reader, used to the novel and its individual characterisation, may miss. As Knight (1986: 72–3) observes, Chaucer writes of *a* Knight and *a* Prioress – representatives of their rank, even though his treatment moves towards some individualisation of them too. Mann (1973) shows that the *General Prologue* portraits and Chaucer's design of listing a miscellany of people according their work are rooted in the medieval tradition of 'estates satire'.

Estates satire is a modern term for a broad range of medieval writings describing representative members of different 'estates' (ranks or professions) and the sins to which each social rank was prone. There are passages of this kind of satire in texts which Chaucer knew, including Gower's *Vox Clamantis*, *c*.1380, and *Mirour de l'Omme*, *c*.1377, and the anonymous *The Simonie*, *c*.1320, which concentrates on ecclesiastical evils – 'simony' is the sin of abusing clerical office – but includes wider satire too. The range of professions varies from text to text but most estates satire began with clerics (for example, popes, cardinals, bishops, priests, monks, nuns, and sometimes other educated professions like lawyers and doctors), moved on to those who rule and govern (kings, barons, knights, etc.), and then those who work (merchants, burgesses, peasants, etc.). Married people sometimes constituted a distinct estate, as do women, who were often subdivided into married women and nuns. In medieval social theories and models generally women are often defined according to marital status rather than the types of work they did, though in actuality, since medieval work was often household-based, women were involved in a wider spectrum of labour than in later centuries. Chaucer's portraits of one married woman, specifically labelled the 'Wife' of Bath, and one nun, the Prioress, reflects this categorisation of women by marital status in estates tradition. Chaucer concentrates in the *General Prologue* on society's middle ranks, with a Knight as the highest-ranking person: within the *gentil* class but not an aristocrat.

Estates satire was a literary tradition and its moral analysis is essentially religious rather than sociological, visualising each rank's sins in relation to its specific duties. Chaucer's own handling of a group of figures defined by profession extends to interests far beyond this relatively narrow range, and he frequently indicates his pilgrims' faults more indirectly and ambiguously than estates satire does. Each pilgrim is defined primarily by profession but that is not merely a peg on which to hang characteristic virtues and vices; another strand in the *Prologue* is an interest in the distinctive worlds and jargon of the professions in themselves – perhaps a reflection of Chaucer's tendency, in the *Tales* as a whole, to present human social relations as a conglomeration of separate and incompatible purposes and viewpoints. His decision to designate his story-tellers by profession also signals an interest in society, social identities and social relationships, not just in individuals; though Boccaccio also used multiple narrators in *Il Filocolo* and the *Decameron*, they are identified by names and personalities but socially all of the same rank.

Chaucer's group of professional figures does not simply represent ranks in society: he locates it in the geography of his own world. The Knight and Squire, though archetypal chivalric figures, are associated with specific places where English armies and mercenaries fought in Chaucer's lifetime. For other pilgrims the range of named locations extends from Norfolk, for the Reeve, to Bath and Dartmouth, for the Wife and Shipman; the Clerk is from Oxford and three of the pilgrims live and work in the City of London, the Lawyer, Cook and Manciple; the Pardoner is based in the London hospital of Roncevall, the Host is from Southwark, and the Prioress from the wealthy convent of St Leonard's at Stratford, just north of London. The places indicated by name are either contained within an area from the Wash to the Severn or are extensions beyond this part of southern and south-eastern England looking outwards from Britain, to the continent: to Flanders and specifically Middelburg (the port through which English wool was exported) in the case of the Merchant; to Bordeaux (situated in the English territory of Gascony, the centre of the English–French wine trade) and along the coast from Gotland to Spain, for the Shipman; and in the case of the wealthy Wife, to Ypres, Ghent, and fashionable continental pilgrimage shrines. In as far as the context from which the pilgrims have come are intermittently brought into focus by these placenames, it is contemporary *economic* England that Chaucer visualises as their social context – the most wealthy, productive and populous segment of Britain together with the overseas destinations with which it traded: it is a territory of contemporary commercial activity rather than simply a geographical territory. Some of the military concerns indicated by placenames had themselves powerful economic motives: the 'keeping' open of the commercial lanes between Orwell and Middelburg, the English expeditions to Artois and Picardy in 1383. Chaucer's inclusion of a Shipman, a figure rare in the tradition of literary satire but central to fourteenth-century England as a trading economy, and his decision to make his representative married woman not merely a wife but a businesswoman trading in England's premier product, wool, are symptomatic of the extent to which his social imagination is a contemporary, commercial one. We are aware everywhere, except with the 'manorial family' of Knight, Squire and Yeoman, of the economic basis of these figures and their activities: the Lawyer's and Doctor's fees, the funding on which the Clerk's studies depend, the tithes the Parson forgoes. Economics are not as dominant in Chaucer's social imagination as they are, say, with Defoe but they are a recurrent element in his fictional creations in the *Tales*. For Chaucer, as for Jane Austen, it is the moral issues in social relationships which are paramount, but both authors are always aware that these relationships are also economic ones.

Shifts and complexities in the manipulation of the narrative voice remove Chaucer's portraits far from the single moral viewpoint and unambiguously condemnatory attitude typical of satire. Estates satires, for example, often criticised monks for laziness, and for their fine food and clothes (especially furs and comfortable shoes) and sometimes expensive horses and hunting. Chaucer's portrait of the Monk includes details of this kind but the narrative simply states or praises his Monk's attributes, and at I, 173–88 and 200 the narrative voice loses any independence, entering into the Monk's own view of things and thus leaving it to the reader to form any moral judgement.[6] Estates satires attributed fraud, dishonesty and usury to merchants, but if Chaucer's portrait of the Merchant implies these, as some critics have believed, it does so ambiguously and many readers will find no condemnation at all in the references to his credit and exchange dealings.[7] The focalisation of the text here neither praises nor condemns the trading on credit and the unrevealing demeanour of the businessman: it is as poker-faced as its subject. The avoidance of clear condemnation here perhaps indicates Chaucer's acceptance of the fact that contemporary merchants did, of necessity, buy and sell on credit. The need for credit was a fact but late medieval society's models for social ethics had not yet caught up with it. Aers (1986: 17–19) suggests a similar reading of Chaucer's unjudgemental presentation of the Monk's worldly perspective – his work as an *outridere* for monastic estates, and his landowner-like lifestyle; when Chaucer asks 'How shal the world be served?' (I, 187), it is possible to read in it the Wycliffite view that fourteenth-century monasticism was neither keeping the old rules nor helpfully serving contemporary Christian society. This does not mean the Monk is a Wycliffite, but

Wycliffite background means the question is a serious one for the late fourteenth century as it might not have been in earlier medieval culture. It also means the narrator's question is not simply an example of naivety, to be read ironically. While a few portraits, like the Parson's, are unambiguously positive and a few, like the Friar's, unambiguously negative, critics have disagreed greatly about how far details in most portraits are meant to be condemnatory. This may suggest that Chaucer is on occasion raising issues rather than offering clear moral judgements.

The sequence of pilgrims does not follow any obvious princple of order: the pilgrims are not arranged strictly in rank nor grouped into virtue and vice. A number of different types of classification, social and moral, can be discerned mingled together, with thought-provoking and unexpected juxtapositions. This denies the reader any simple formula for interpreting society. One ancient model of society that seems to play a small part in the design of the sequence of figures is that of the Three Estates. This theory visualises society as three mutually dependent classes of knights, priests, and labourers, with the knights' duty to fight for everyone else, the priests' to pray for everyone and the labourers' to work for everyone. This ancient model, always more theoretical than realistic, bore even less correspondence to actual socio-economic forces and divisions as a 'feudal' economy gave way to a more commercial and even proto-capitalist one in the late Middle Ages (see Strohm 1989: 1–23; Keen 1990: 1–26; Rigby 1995: 17–103). Chaucer seems to invoke the Three Estates theory provocatively in the series of portraits: hinting at its tripartite scheme at some points while clearly not using it to delineate the picture of society the series presents.

Whereas estates satire produced negative views of estates, each estate seen in terms of its characteristic sins, the Three Estates model offered a vision of social divisions as an interlocking network of mutual service. Unlike the looser tradition of estates satire this model cannot absorb new professional groups, urbanisation, or changing economic forces and it was a myth which disguised the actual indebtedness of landowning and clerical classes to the labours of those who, in traditional agrarian society, would always have remained poor. As a wage-economy, a market economy and labour mobility developed, from the thirteenth century on, and came to appear to challenge social relationships in the later fourteenth century, the old Three Estates model seems to have been promulgated with fresh vigour by some conservative writers.[8] It presents the relations between classes as those of loyalty and duty rather than of conflict. Many of Chaucer's portraits are negative or morally ambiguous but three are completely idealised, the Knight, Parson and Plowman, and these represent the Three Estates. Each serves the community: the Knight fights to defend Christendom against its non-Christian enemies; the Parson serves God and his parishioners perfectly; the Plowman works diligently, and serves his neighbour and the Church. All are loyal to their associates and their traditional callings: the Knight loves 'trouthe and honoure' and is loyal to his own feudal overlord; the Parson teaches the gospel 'trewely' and is a trustworthy priest; the Plowman is a '*trewe* [loyal] swynkere'. They appear uncontaminated by commerce, personal greed or the worlds of towns and trade. Despite the conservative tendencies of any invocation of the Three Estates model, Chaucer's choice of a poor peasant parson – rather than a virtuous bishop, monk or friar – for his ideal cleric in the trio, reflects an ideal of gospel simplicity, and perhaps also contemporary (and Wycliffite) disapproval of the wealth and power of the Church hierarchy and the well-endowed religious orders. The Parson's and Plowman's brotherhood itself symbolises the Three Estates' model of mutual service between fellow-Christians, just as the father–son relationship between Knight and Squire symbolises the authority of inherited *gentil* identity which gave such men their special position in medieval society. In contrast to these kinship bonds linking the idealised figures, the Summoner and Pardoner, the least idealised, seem to be portrayed as homosexual partners, (I, 670–9, 688–91). Since medieval homophobia conceived homosexual relations as an unnatural state, Chaucer is using a stereotyped caricature of homosexuality to cast an aura of barrenness and unnaturalness over the Pardoner's and Summoner's financial practices and ecclesiastical abuses.[9] A sense of fear and a sense of the bizarre is injected into both portraits; both men's offices give them frightening power over others, and both their tales deal with subjects of deep fear – fear of hell and of death – and centre on an unperceived danger.

The Clerk, though less spiritual and idealised than the Parson, is another positive portrait of the clerical estate, representing a second type of virtuous and dutiful medieval cleric other than the priest: the clerk as scholar. Similarly, the Franklin is a further positive portrait of the landowing estate, representing the upper class in their role as actual landowners, an element omitted from the portrait of the crusading Knight. The Squire and Yeoman provide two other positive, though not totally idealised, representatives respectively of the warrior and labourer, both presented in obedient relationship to the Knight. Knight (1986: 73) calls this first trio the 'manorial family'.

Chaucer's second trio, the Prioress, Monk and Friar, represents religious orders. Their worldliness dramatises contemporary criticisms of the wealth, comfort and temptations of that life. The Monk, running estates for his order, an 'outridere', illustrates the extent to which many monasteries were essentially agricultural businesses as well as centres of spiritual life dedicated to God. This type of late medieval monk, running an estate and enjoying his hunting, good food and fine clothes, had much in common with the secular landowner, which is perhaps one of the points implied by Chaucer's juxtaposition of an 'outridere' monk, and the upper-class Madame Eglentyne, with the 'manorial family'. The Friar typifies not just the individual abuses of friars who turned begging into financial enterprise but the problem of a whole religious organisation, founded to re-create gospel poverty, which had become very wealthy. The Prioress, resembling a lady as the Monk resembles a lord, exemplifies the contemporary situation where only women from relatively wealthy backgrounds could become nuns. While nothing suggests actual impropriety in the Monk's and Prioress's portraits, Chaucer's language conveys a sexuality at odds with their celibate calling. By using a variety of worldly registers in their portraits Chaucer creates a disconcerting contrast between these three members of religious orders, vowed to poverty, chastity and obedience, and the secular Knight, subject to none of these vows, who is as meek as a virgin, serves 'oure feith' with his life and hastens zealously to perform his pilgrimage. The constrasts, while they may be directed at bad members of religious orders, could be seen also as projecting a perception of a society in which the traditional divisions between the monastery and the world no longer seem to guarantee a satisfactory division of prayerfulness and worldly business.

Subsequent *General Prologue* portraits include many examples of just those areas of commercial, professional, administrative and entrepreneurial activity where the most fluid opportunities for profit and social advancement were to be found in Chaucer's society. The Three Estates model had no place for an upwardly mobile peasant who acquired the powers of the Reeve, for the rich Merchant's *bargaynes* and *chevyssaunce*, the Guildsmen's civic ambitions, the lord-like Monk or grand Sergeant of the Law – nor for the socio-economic roles of such men and the wealth and influence they represented in contemporary England. The social origins of the final seven pilgrims are low and the last five are all cheats, exploiting others for financial gain, in what seems to be descending order of wickedness down to the Pardoner, whose deceit hits at the basis of people's faith and hope for eternal life. Though we begin with the highest-ranking pilgrim, the Knight, and these last few figures are socially and morally low, no single consistent principle decides the order of the portraits as a whole and the juxtapositions between them involve both parallels and contrasts, as do the tales. It is up to the reader to discern connections, rather than being given a single scheme onto which all the figures are mapped, whether of hierarchy or the estates satire conventions, or virtue versus vice, or the Three Estates model. Parson and Plowman, tirelessly and faithfully working for others, are obvious parallels to each other, and the Plowman then contrasts with the next peasant, the brutish, aggressive and fraudulent Miller. The Doctor seems inappropriately lowly positioned, after the Shipman, but both consult the stars in their professions and both, like the preceding Cook, are dangerous to their clients. Chaucer spreads his ideal figures among the others; Aers (1986: 17) comments that in his series of portraits he alludes implicitly to the Three Estates but 'in a context which destroys the estates ideology, within . . . a mobile, dissonant social world penetrated by market values and pursuits'.

'And at a knyght than wol I first begynne' . . .

Chaucer sets first the knight whose adult life has been that of a crusader, defending Christendom against the infidel: north, south and east, on the borders of medieval Europe—with the Teutonic Knights, at Alexandria, in Turkey, and so on. The crusading theme and its accompanying placenames almost completely fill the text. The portrait has only two other elements: one is a set of key terms, *chivalrie*, *trouthe*, *honour*, *fredom*, *curteisie*, *worthynesse* and *gentil*, which convey virtues that in the ideology of chivalry comprise the mind and heart of an archetypal ('a verray parfit') knight; the other a scattering of details implying a corresponding lack of outward ostentation or materialism: the knight's eschewing of *gay* splendid clothing, his unpretentious demeanour, 'as meeke as is a mayde', and his rust-stained tunic.

The passage is studded with historically realistic detail – English forces did fight at all the places mentioned; many knights of Chaucer's time went on crusading expeditions; and the crusading ideal was still, despite criticism, quite widely revered.[10] That does not make the Knight's portrait any less ideological. What Chaucer depicts is not at all the life of the landowner of his time as the modern social historian Christopher Dyer describes it:

> They ruled over estates and manors which provided a flow of money and labour from tenants. They wielded extensive powers of

jurisdiction by holding courts, and they exercised much control over unfree slaves and serfs. At their behest the landscape was reorganised for more efficient production in compact demesnes, granges, mills and reclaimed wastes, or mainly for pleasure in the case of parks, pools and gardens. They channeled trade through the boroughs and markets that they founded and protected. And by their own spending power, they were able to mould the trading system, encouraging the concentration of rich merchants in large towns to supply their specialist needs.   (Dyer 1994: xii)

Chaucer and Dyer both give an overview of knights' activities over a geographical terrain but those are almost the only points of similarity. The management of estates was a business; for the great magnates very big business. England was still primarily an agricultural economy. Dyer shows the *gentil* class as key controllers of economic and social organisation at local level (they also had important local judicial authority, as the Franklin's portrait illustrates) and as central to developments in urban production, commerce and consumption. Knights expected to be paid for military service and some were mercenaries, providing military support for campaigns (the gap between this reality and Chaucer's portrait led Jones 1985 to suggest the portrait was ironical, a picture of a mercenary).[11] By the end of the fourteenth century, knights' socio-economic status and influence in society was in reality equalled by that of wealthy merchants; a knight's *gentil* lineage and his duty of providing military service to the king remained the only concrete distinctions between the two groups of rich and powerful men. The boundaries dividing merchants and *gentils* were being crossed: some important merchants were knighted, a process that accelerated in the fifteenth century; marriage alliances joined *gentil* and merchant families; knights took part in a widening range of commercial activities (Keen 1990: 14–23).

What kind of text, then, is the *General Prologue*'s first portrait and how does it relate to the series of portraits that follows? Clearly it offers an ideal, based on traditional religious and political theories, rather than contemporary actuality, an ideal which had been enshrined in the ancient Three Estates model: justifying the power of the warrior caste in society in terms of their service as defenders of the rest of the community, the clergy and laity, against external threat. Langland's *Piers Plowman* contains an allegory of society (A VI, 25–56) in which the knights are commanded to guard the field of working people (European Christian society) from external predators and internal criminals, and treat their villeins well. Chaucer's portrait of the Knight establishes service to others as a moral criterion we shall find implicit through the *General Prologue* portraits and some tales. Yet it can also be seen as exemplifying a political myth which concealed and mystified the unequal power and wealth commanded by the knightly class: the military campaigns mentioned in the portrait, after all, depended on the financial and structural power the landowning classes commanded, yet Chaucer's portrait never alludes to these background factors, whereas Dyer's focuses entirely on them. This first portrait also establishes a religious dimension to the *Prologue*'s portrayal of humans' varied activities in this world, and that dimension itself enhances the key position of the knight as the cornerstone of society. Unlike the estates satire norm, Chaucer begins with secular, not eccesiastical, authority, yet he includes spiritualised aspects of the Knight's worldly power and identity: they are skilfully balanced, as is the whole *Canterbury Tales*, between secular and spiritual perspectives. A knight represents traditional feudal authority and this knight's portait, as a classic and wholly virtuous warrior, also casts a kind of blessing over that model of society at the outset. The inappropriate worldliness of the Monk and Prioress stands out by contrast with the unostentatious authority, earned by Christian service, possessed by this paragon of the knightly class whose lifestyle they ape. Chaucer does not depict a bad knight or *gentil* in the *Prologue*: possibly because he is a conservative whose upbringing and career have allied him with the *gentils*, but alternatively perhaps because the Knight represents social order itself, a vision of authority as benign service to the community. The *Knight's Tale* (and later the *Man of Law's Tale*) will present lordship as a necessary, if sometimes painful, good: a force for order regulating society, personal relationships and psychology which has cosmic and divine sanction. The portrait mirrors ideology more overtly than Chaucer's usual styles of writing. Critical examination of it is salutary preparation for reading the *Canterbury Tales* precisely because it provides so clear a warning to modern readers against too readily assuming Chaucer's text either offers the kind of naturalistic character-creation – the illusion of individual personality – that is the glory of nineteenth-century fiction, or provides a simple and direct historical record of late fourteenth-century England.

The Descriptions of Pilgrims

The details in the portraits have a miscellaneous air that artfully suggests real individuals lie behind them. These details are drawn from contemporary fact about professional and social life and from literary, learned and artistic traditions. The Wife of Bath's portrait reflects anti-feminist literary polemics in items like her headgear, her jealousy over the Offertory procession, and enthusiasm for travelling rather than staying in the house (Mann 1973: 121–7). The allusion (I, 475) to Ovid's misogynist *Remedies of Love*, a satire about women's predatory attitude to men, makes both her widowhood and sociability seem a man-trap. More original (though just as revealing as a male projection) is Chaucer's addition of bold, masculine touches: *Boold, bokeler, targe, spores sharpe*. She is independent both in running her own business and in lacking the curb of a husband: a free-wheeling traveller, who is both relaxed – with her comfortable foot-mantle and her 'felawshipe' jokes – and successfully aggressive, getting ahead of Flemish businesses as determinedly as she gets ahead in Offertory processions.

Many portraits reflect contemporary social and economic reality as well as literary tradition. The Wife's flourishing cloth business, exemplifies the most important trade in the English economy. Wool and cloth were to England what oil is to modern Texas. Textiles represented the most important large industry, already developing post-medieval characteristics like capital investment by merchants, separation of different processes, moves away from merely household production, a large and international market, and complex transportation servicing the individual processes and industries that, in different parts of the country, contributed to the finished products (see Bolton 1980: 153–6). That Chaucer gives prominence to the cloth trades and presents their representatives (Wife, Merchant, Dyer, Weaver, Haberdasher, Tapestry-weaver) as thrusting and ambitious, imposing on others a sense of their own consequence that might not have been automatically given, indicates how sharp, despite the political conservatism and evasiveness often seen in his writing, were his social antennae in discerning the really significant changes in the power structures of his own world. The Guildsmen are, apart from the Carpenter, all in textile trades. In larger towns, leading trades guilds (not traditionally those of the trades from which these men come) dominated town councils, regulating and ruling civic life and business (see p. 70). These men are guildsmen in an alternative sense: members of a parish guild or fraternity, which was a religious and social association, rather like a mutual benefit society. Unlike the trades guilds these parish guilds included men from a variety of professions. The *General Prologue* Guildsmen may dream of becoming aldermen, but do not belong to the politically powerful and exclusive trades guilds such as the Victuallers' or Vintners' guilds, from which aldermen were generally chosen.[12] These men's clothes and accessories, and their pretentious hiring of their own cook, indicate their social climbing (on the portrait of the Cook see pp. 71, 74). The passage's emphasis on externals like clothes, girdles, pouches and mantles suggests superficiality, a lack of traditional civic standing to match their ambitions. This connects with the typically Chaucerian ambiguities we find in his statements of the reasons why they might be suitable to be aldermen: the reasons are their 'wisdom' and their income and rents (lines 371–4). As often with Chaucer's satire or social comment, we do not know from whose point of view these rich men seem to have the wisdom to be civic leaders; here the parallel linking of wealth with this 'wisdom' implies that it is the guildmen's own viewpoint that is being represented and mocked. Chaucer's provocatively unstraightforward syntax right through lines 366–78 suggests that in these tradesmen's limited understanding their clothes, lifestyle and incomes seem reasons enough for them to break into the highest circles of the established urban merchant oligarchy, to which Chaucer's father as a rich vintner, of course, had belonged.[13] Chaucer's dismissive attitude towards the guildsmen's ambitions is encapsulated in his phrase 'shaply for to been an alderman', for, as Gastle's illuminating article on the portrait's contemporary social references shows, 'shaply' means not only 'suitable' but 'appropriate . . . [regarding clothes]: well fitting on' (1998: 211). The word does not endorse but rather ridicules such ambitions: 'Chaucer's aristocratic audience most probably found such sumptuous dress subject for derision . . . They were dressed like aldermen, but could never be aldermen' (Gastle 1998: 213). Yet it is also typical of the complexity of Chaucer's presentation of contemporary society that this passage does not merely reproduce the upperclass's traditional condemnation of *nouveau riche* aspirations as pretentious folly but it accurately pinpoints one of the pressure points of economic and political change: the growing wealth but exclusion from civic authority of successful tradesmen and their associations.

As in all eras, clothes provide the author with a language of social definition and comment, but aspects of medieval society gave them special sharpness as vocabulary for a social saririst. Very fashionable clothes and materials or furs were hugely expensive; robes often formed a substantial part of salaries and allowances (the lawyer's portrait twins 'fees and robes' as indicators of his success, line 317); medieval economics and social assumptions meant that the clothes of poor and rich differed markedly in colour and style as well as quality, and that those who dressed above their traditional station met hostility. In a patriarchal society women's dress is liable to be satirised both because of the traditional dichotomy of men's attitudes to attractive female clothes and because husbands' rising fortunes are typically expressed in fashion by their wives. Women's expensive headgear was a traditional target of misogynist and snobbish disapproval: the amount and quality of the Wife of Bath's 'coverchiefs' therefore says enough to condemn this member of the rising trade classes (lines 453–5). Long trailing clothes were, similarly, regarded as the privileged sign of *gentil* class, so the Guildsmen's wives' dreams of 'roialliche' borne mantles have an absurdity that helps to discredit their husbands' manifest wealth as baseless pretension. Just as ideologically biased, of course, is that absence of any hint of criticism, implicit or explicit, against the Squire's extravagantly embroidered clothes, wide sleeves or curled hair (though the lower-class dandy Absolon's fashionably styled clothes and hair are mocked in the *Miller's Tale*, lines 3314–38).

The Wife of Bath's wealth and confidence reflect the extent to which this was the era of the rich widow: widows typically inherited a third of the joint estate and before the sixteenth century widows often continued to run or be active in their late husbands' businesses. The Shipman reflects the enormous contemporary trade, especially in wine, between London and Bordeaux. Here is another pilgrim running a commercial business, and one concerned with exchange and trading, not with primary production, and Chaucer treats this representative of trading with a mixture of praise, for his professional skills, and savage accusation: commercial competitiveness here is transmuted into outright robbery, piracy and murder. Sergeants of Law were the group of lawyers from which the judges of the King's Court were chosen, and if the reference to his 'purchasing' and 'fee simple' implies that Chaucer's lawyer is judiciously buying up land for himself, he typifies the movement (even more marked in the next century) of top lawyers beginning to cross the boundary into the landowning class. As with the Franklin's, this portrait reveals Chaucer's acute sensitivity to what might be called sociological forecasting: he is aware of groups who are beginning to move into new areas of power, influence or authority. If there is criticism of the Sergeant, it is not made explicit in the text. It is for the reader to assess, lying in the choice and balance of words: 'wys' and 'excellence' seem unequivocal praise until we weigh them besides 'war' and 'riche' (I, 309, 311), suggesting that calculation and avarice drive the lawyer's exercise of his abilities. 'Semed' and 'renoun' imply a hollowness in his 'excellence' and 'reverence', confirmed by the admission:

> And yet he semed bisier than he was.
>
> (I, 322)

If there is something suspicious about the lawyer's profits, it is hard to detect, and the style of the passage, appropriately, uses a matching discretion and lack of showyness in its satirical elements. Whereas the Doctor's magnificently lined silk robes are a blatant giveaway, in tune with the heavyhanded style of Chaucer's jibe that he loves gold in medicines, nothing in the lawyer's clothes awakens suspicions of profiteering: his 'medlee' coat is respectable but downright 'hoomly'; its sobriety, like the Knight's unconsidered dress, causes surprise in the context of a rich man and it draws the reader's questioning attention to its significance for just the same reasons.

The Merchant's fine clothes (his hat reflecting the importance of Flemish–English trade at this period) and his self-controlled, dignified demeanour are described in respectful terms: he is 'worthy' (twice), 'estatly of . . . governaunce', impressive in his way of speaking, obsessively intent, like the *Shipman's Tale* merchant, on business. His opinion about Middleburg and Orwell introduces the real-life interweaving of English commercial and military policy (I, 276–7). Stylistically the portrait provides examples of Chaucer's use of forms of Free Indirect Discourse: narrative saturated with a character's words or thoughts. His 'chevyssaunce' [lending or borrowing on interest or securities], 'eschaunge' [exchange dealings, especially using 'shields', a coin of account to facilitate international deals] and his state of debt were all normal practices of late fourteenth-century commerce. The Church's age-old condemnation of usury, interest, led to morally ambivalent attitudes towards the necessary use of credit deals, interest and banking. The narrator's reference to hidden debt may be less a condemnation than acknowledgement of the habitual confident exterior of a successful dealer. It is hard to know whether Chaucer is criticising, or merely registering as a contemporary problematic phenomenon, the presence of debt and interest in contemporary commerce. This unspoken credit-dealing virtually symbolises contemporary culture's failure to come to terms with, or find a moral language for, its own commercial and financial methods (compare the emotive attack on Jewish money-lending, a more ancient source for gentile credit, in VII, 491). The *General Prologue*'s stance of tolerance or neutrality towards such modern phenomena as credit-based commerce, monks acting like estate-owners, the rich independent widow running a business, and the non-*gentil* Franklin running local government – or at least the absence of unambiguous condemnation – means the text often gives us a glimpse of new social and economic forces as they existed in Chaucer's England, side by side with more traditional moral and religious discourse about society that frequently cannot encompass them. An analogy to this mingling of liberal and condemnatory representations of new economic trends is the contradictory tendencies in Chaucer's presentation of the independence of the Wife of Bath, here and in her later *Prologue*. The language of anti-feminism in the portrait of the Wife of Bath, with its somewhat sniggering suggestion of her as a sexual threat to men, may indicate not so much that Chaucer was rabidly anti-feminist as that his culture gave him no other language for envisaging a financially independent woman who enjoyed travel. As we have seen, many details in the portraits come from literary tradition and should not be read simply as realistic observation of society, and in general Chaucer's language for describing individuals as social and economic beings tends to be one with inherited moral perspectives, whether these moral criteria come from ecclesiastical strictures on worldliness or from estates satire. Yet his frequent use of the jargon of trades suggests a real relish for the actualities of physical work, and a sense of the professional worlds and their languages as key elements in personal identity. As Mann shows, while belonging to the large, amorphous tradition we label 'estates satire', with its bias towards a moral assessment of professional activities, Chaucer tilts portraits somewhat towards observation of professions in their own right (1973: 15).

The Miller's portrait certainly draws on traditional satire against millers as liable to commit fraud, but also reflects resentment against upwardly mobile peasants in the decades after the Black Death. The 'golden thumb' accusation (of millers' false measurement) was proverbial, but the animal similes (I, 552, 556) may draw on a specifically post-1381 mode of belittling upstart peasants by comparison to unreasoning brutes (Justice 1994: 193–223). In reputation the second-hand car salesmen of their day, millers were distrusted not only because it is hard to ascertain exactly how honestly corn has been milled, but also because they could be used by landowners to impose monopoly milling on peasants on their estates, and also, conversely, because some millers set up as independent entrepreneurs.

The Manciple and Reeve represent the uneducated but successful administrator at this period: both low-born and *lewed* ['lay' and 'uneducated'], they have carved out their own lucrative empires while in the employment of socially superior but less able masters – learned lawyers and an estate-owning lord. The *sclendre colerik* Reeve's unsociable position behind the company of pilgrims, the image of the hermit-like solitude of this rich miser, twinned with his total control over everything and everybody his work brings him into contact with, present avarice as a failing in communal as well as spiritual values. Yet the attack on the Reeve is above all in religious terms: his avarice and exploitation of others and drive to amass money are externalised into a frugality and spareness which make him like a priest or friar: a false ascetic, dedicated to his own enrichment. His lonely, shaded house on a barren heath, his rusted blade, and the death-like manner of his dealings with other people (I, 605–7), all imply that obsessive private 'storing' of wealth (I, 609) is both a social wrong, because unfruitful to the community, and a spiritual wrong, leading to death of the soul.

If the first portrait represents one aspect of the myth of chivalry (the landed class as warriors fighting for God and Christendom), the second portrait represents another aspect of the same myth, embedded in courtly literature: the landed class as romantic lover. This Squire is created out of literature; he *is* a work of art, described in terms of decoration and art: prettily dressed, singing and playing the flute, writing songs and composing poems. He is depicted as being himself an artist: he can draw ('purtreye'), and the activities attributed him are classic activities of lovers in literature – fighting to please his lady and staying awake like a nightingale. He is more a metaphor or simile than a man: apart from the comparison with a nightingale, he embodies two other poetic love-images: the month of May, regularly associated with love in medieval lyrics, and red and white flowers, ubiquitous metaphors for ladies' beauty and for love. The portrait operates in combination with those which flank it to express the principles of loyalty, service and obedience that validate the feudal model of society. Just as his father is, for all his implicit wealth and power, wise, humble and unshowily dressed, so this young *gentil* is modest and obedient, showing respect to his elders by the symbolic etiquette of carving for his father. Continuing this series of ideologically rather than realistically or historically conceived portraits of the feudal hegemony of the inherited landowner, the Yeoman (a word which can mean 'employee' at this period, so here perhaps an estate servant), represents an obedient tenantry. As both personal attendant – a kind of batman – and gamekeeper combined, this figure brings into the picture a reminder of the Knight's estate, so decisively absent both from the Knight's own portrait, with its concentration on faraway crusading duties, and from the pretty literary images in the portrait of his heir. As (probably) a free peasant, he is represented as personally bound to voluntary service, as feudal retainer to master, and exemplifies management of the land for the traditional and exclusive, almost iconic, knightly sport of hunting. His efficient *takel*, shining equipment, superior peacock-feather arrows 'bright and kene', and great bow indicate the same solid good quality in practical matters as do the Knight's fine horses.

Critics are divided as to whether the Franklin represents a *parvenu* class of non-*gentil* landowners (with his opulent catering showing up a lack of taste) or whether, as the archaic term 'vavasour' (I, 360) suggests, established country squires (see Pearcy 1973–4 and Saul 1983). The truth may involve both elements: franklins, as substantial farmers and landowners, may have had long-established local standing, but the kinds of dominance in local goverment and lucrative office-holding Chaucer's Franklin illustrates (magistrate, Member of Parliament, Sheriff and county auditor) were perhaps new spheres into which such non-*gentil* landowners were moving. The Franklin's interest in food is hardly heroic, but the elevating reference to Saint Julian suggests it fulfils the ancient, hallowed, role of the lord as hospitable host and householder.

The apparent mingling, in Chaucer's visualisation of his Franklin, of *nouveau* and deeply traditional messages may be illuminated by a comparison with the substantial houses upwardly mobile 'yeomen' landowners were building in the fifteenth-century. It has been remarked that these newly wealthy men designed houses with traditional high halls for public dining rather than private low-ceilinged chambers, as if yearning to step into the role of the hospitable lord of cultural and literary tradition.[14] Chaucer's presentation perhaps creates his Franklin, similarly, as *nouveau riche* precisely in his ready adoption of the duties of local government and public hospitality traditionally undertaken by the gentry. The trestle-tables in his hall, always standing ready, sum up a powerful cultural self-image as benign squire, not just personal greediness. As in all cultures, food is a powerful and complex repository of symbolism and communal meaning in the social vision of the *Canterbury Tales*.

Clashing stylistic registers are used with peculiarly sharp satiric effect with the Prioress. Her 'ful plesaunt, and amyable' manner (I, 138) is undercut by the word 'countrefete' in the next line. The description of her table manners echoes a memorable misogynist passage in the *Romance of the Rose*, lines 13355–444, where an old woman reveals, to men, how she instructs girls about the arts of captivating men. Even if it is the elegance not the immoral associations that are echoed here, Chaucer's lengthy emphasis on so superficial an example of the Prioress's self-command and 'curteisie' suggests those qualities of hers are devoted to inessentials. There are also details reminiscent of a heroine in courtly verse: her name Eglentyne, her soft, red, 'ful smal' mouth, and the phrases 'symple and coy', 'nose tretys', 'eyen greye as glas'. The worldly element in the portrait, the sense that the woman vowed to God, and administering a convent, cultivates the airs and graces of an upper-class, sexually attractive lady, is encapsulated in the ambiguity as to whether the all-conquering *Amor* of her brooch's motto is heavenly or earthly love. Yet there is no doubt Chaucer's figure shows us also someone who has mastered the difficult social skills required of a woman in a position of authority, as a prioress was: the skills of being both 'ful plesaunt, and amyable' and at the same time commanding 'reverence'. The three priests and *chapeleyne* (personal assistant) indicate that Chaucer envisaged her as the head of an important establishment. Is there something sexist, a hatchet job, in the way he first devises an unmarried woman with some independent authority, analogous to a headmistress or college principal, and then undermines her dignity, implying that her air of having a position in life is false and what she really – naturally – wants is to attract men? He stresses her femininity rather than her spirituality as the locus of the problem he perceives in her. The same *Romance of the Rose* passage that is used to make this woman seem silly, is used in the *Wife of Bath's Prologue* to make that other independent woman seem aggressively predatory: two ways of destroying what may be perceived as a threat, or alternatively an example of how the available, male-dominated, discourse of the time could not encompass female independence except by constructions such as the *Romance*'s unsavoury old woman. Chaucer may be giving a sexist twist to the Wycliffites' opposition to institutions of celibate monks and nuns. This pilgrim has no serious sins and the portrait is actually filled with her gifts and virtues (though these do not include any socially powerful ones) – she is *symple and coy* [sincere and quiet], 'semely', 'plesaunt', 'charitable', 'pitous' and so on. Most of these are then undercut, but primarily from a worldly, class-based viewpoint – she has a large figure, her courtly elegance is a little too punctiliously laboured, her French is unfashionable, and so on – with only the lightest of religious elements to it. The implication is a suspicion that her charms and virtues are misapplied and hollow. Riddy (1993: 105–6, 117) suggests one of Chaucer's targets may be the development, popular particularly among upper- and middle-class women, of new kinds of devotional practice and literature, centred on a mystic theology of love and affectivity (deeply emotional religious responses, including weeping). The Prioress's ready tears and 'conscience [sensitivity] and tendre herte' focused on dogs, may be a caricature of this 'affective' style of devotion, as well as ridiculing fashionable ladies' fads for spoiled small dogs. Some negative touches in the description seem less the fictional Prioress's sins than Chaucer's prejudices: Anglo-Norman had long been the language of devotional literature for nuns and devout laywomen, not educated in Latin – Chaucer's jibe about Stratford French reflects the hauteur of an educated male and a fashionable courtier. Nasal chanting was one standard way of singing services. The mockery of the relatively important woman whose elegance can be undermined by her physical size uses exactly the same masculinist requirement, that women must be pretty and small to win male acceptance, that the Prioress herself is pilloried for observing in her manners, and the stress on small dogs here and 'litel' schoolboy in her tale. A modern animal-loving reader's agreement with the Prioress's concern for mice and beaten dogs, her 'conscience and tendre herte', may therefore not be just an anachronism: it perhaps reveals a tension in the text between what Chaucer shows and the effort he puts into undermining it. The language of this portrait remains unresolved between positive and negative (see David 1982).

With the Summoner and Pardoner, both professions attracting odium in satirical tradition and contemporary complaints for abuses associated with them, there is no ambiguity about the main sins being attacked. The Summoner uses blackmail and bribes to make money. His own sin involves playing on other people's sins – emptying of all moral substance the archidiaconal system of moral policing: a perversion symbolised by his meaningless parroting of legal terms. He operates through fear ('awe', 'drede', 'daunger') and a dangerous intimacy ('gentil', 'kynde', 'bettre felawe', 'privily', 'good felawe', 'knew hir conseil'), and the face that terrifies children externalises both his inner corruption and that fear, though his own joke about equating 'purs' with 'helle' is, in its very funny outrageousness, a reminder that his own personal lack of fear of the Lord will lead to damnation for him. Whether the Pardoner's appearance and voice, and the comparison to a gelding or mare, implies that he is homosexual or a eunuch is unclear (see McAlpine 1980; Dinshaw 1989). Medieval attitudes to homosexuality saw it as an unnatural state because infertile, and also as effeminacy – which in a man was seen as unnatural. The Roncevall hospital had been associated with financial scandals, and the falseness of his 'pigges bones' and pillowcase is quite explicit (I, 694–700). The *recherché* Latin term 'ecclesiaste' suggests the Pardoner's love of the rituals – especially the Offertory singing which precedes the Collection. Pardoners, as fund-raisers, might be lay or clerics: this one seems a cleric and his empty performance of the Mass summarises his perversion of Church office.

The portraits make occasional use of medical lore, like the Franklin's sanguine humour, and references to names or places, ornaments, food and drink, and music. They rely more heavily on clothes, physical appearance, and a variety of horses – social, economic and psychological indicators as revealing to contemporaries as types of car are today. Throughout his work, Chaucer shows a skill in using and mixing sociolinguistic registers that has never been surpassed by any writer in English; we see this everywhere in the *Prologue* descriptions, notably in virtuoso shifts between incompatible registers, employed for satiric purposes.[15] The pilgrims' styles of speech are often differentiated: *simple and coy*, *short and quik*, lisping, solemn, laughing and carping (chattering), and so on, as well as the technical jargon or obsessive professional subject-matter that make each pilgrim above all a representative of a type of work. There is a tension between the traditional and generic nature of much of the material in the pilgrim-portraits and an illusion, aided by the kind of details we have been considering, of the pilgrims as individuals. The impression of random order conveys the illusion that there is a person, out there beyond the written text, as does the device of suggesting a personality with inner life by quoting pilgrims' own opinions or using Free Indirect Discourse.

The Friar's portrait shows Chaucer's language offering the reader opportunities for moral judgement, without explicit condemnation from the narrative voice. The methods include incongruous verbal juxtapositions: 'wantowne' and 'solempne' in I, 208–9; incongruous rhymes: 'penaunce'/'pitaunce', 'vertuous'/'best beggere in his hous' (suggesting that the house's criterion of virtue is also money-making) I, 223–4, 251–2;[16] lexical sets unbefitting the man's vocation: 'wantowne' ['waggish' as well as 'flirtatious'], 'marriage', 'wommen', 'strong', 'champioun', 'tavernes', 'vittaille', 'profit', 'rage', etc.); words with potential *doubles entendres*: 'wantowne', 'dalliaunce', 'post'; denials of precisely the qualities expected in a friar ('nat lyk a cloysterer . . .'). The plethora of such devices makes every use of positive terms, 'solemne', 'noble post', 'biloved', 'swetely', 'plesaunt', 'curteis', 'lowly of servyse', 'beste', 'worthy', 'honest', etc. strike the reader with negative

force. Showy preaching and unrigorous confession, used to win donations, were the chief contemporary complaints against friars (Williams
1953). Chaucer uses the subject's own words, 'As seyde hymself', (I,
219), for the most controversial area: friars' exploitation of official
licences and *limitations* to displace parish priests' authority, hear confessions and give easy penance; this one takes money without concern for
contrition and saving souls (I, 223–32). Stylistically Chaucer's most
original device is the Free Indirect Discourse that captures the Friar's
own topsy-turvy values in the disdain for sick lepers (I, 244–7).

All these devices are used with the Monk: incongruities ('manly'
with 'abbot'); lexical sets ('lord', 'pulled hen', 'grehoundes', 'huntyng',
'ful fat', 'gold', 'fat swan', 'rost'); discordant rhymes ('cloistre'/'oystre',
'greet estaat'/'prelaat'); possible *doubles entendres* ('venerie', 'huntyng for
the hare'); denials of asceticism ('nat pale . . .'). Chaucer exploits the
capacity words have to possess multiple senses: the primary sense here
of 'greet estaat' ['fine condition'] relates to the horse, but another sense,
the aristocrat-like lifestyle, enters the reader's consciousness too, in relation to the lordly Monk; the link of 'venerie' with *Venus* does not necessarily imply this Monk is lecherous: rather it brings another,
incongruously sexual, sense to tangle with the reader's mental assimilation of the primary sense of 'hunting'. Chaucer subtly wields multiple
senses of a word simultaneously, juxtaposing discordant registers. This
contributes to the polyvocal, many-voiced, richness and dialectic which
is arguably his most powerful characteristic as a writer. In this portrait
we also hear literally two voices, as the text enters into Free Indirect
Discourse, conveying the Monk's own attitude to regulations (I, 175
on), with a suggestion of his own disrespectful phrases, 'yaf nat of that
text . . .', 'nat worth an oystre', 'Lat Austyn have . . .', and then inserts
the narrator's:

And I seyde his opinion was good.

(I, 183)

This is perhaps the most famous line in the history of critical examination of Chaucer's management of the narrative voice. In context, of
course, it disabuses us of assumptions that the narrative will provide
unequivocal directives on how to judge the Monk. The question
format that follows continues that feeling that the Monk's attitude,
and the conflict between the needs of secular society and traditional
religious values, does call for some kind of examination (so does the
question about the Manciple in I, 573–5). Whether the reader's

answer is traditional values or, like Aers (see pp. 25–6), some acknowledgement of society's new needs, is – like the interpretation of the Prioress's brooch – left entirely up to the reader. The narrator's statement in I, 183 is passive, accepting of the pilgrim's own worldview. The lordly Monk has squashed the narrator's capacity for independent opinions. The line stands out both for the unexpected expression of a narrator's voice – an intradiegetic voice, speaking as if within the fiction – and its total endorsement of outrageous *opinion*, going against traditional morality, and against the tenor of the rest of the portrait, which depicts the Monk as fulfilling exactly traditional moral definitions of bad monks. A narrator's voice like this is actually rare in the *Canterbury Tales*, and, apart from the Links round Chaucer's own tales, it appears when the text touches controversial areas: here the possible opinion that many monks might be better employed serving the world with their talents. Before the *Miller's Tale* the undeferential peasant's insistence on breaking hierarchy and literary decorum elicits the narrator's 'Blameth nat me', abjuring responsibility for his text; again, the narrator's srance is passivity. An equal mix of prominence and evasiveness is achieved with 'I trowe he were a geldyng or a mare' (I, 691).

Some critics have seen a thorough-going, consistently characterised narrator: a passive, naive creature. Kittredge (1915: 48–53, 181–5) proposed that an artless narrator is created in all Chaucer's narratives; Donaldson (1954) defined this character as humble, easily impressed, admiring extremes, whether of worldliness or virtue. It is true that the narrative often takes these stances – and others, including omniscience and explicit moral judgement – towards what it describes – the question is whether we apprehend the consistent presence of a narrator. In the mid-twentieth century it became almost axiomatic that Chaucer creates a narrative 'persona', a fictional character with his own limited vision, in the manner of Victorian novelists like Wilkie Collins in *The Moonstone*, so that other characters and the plot are filtered through a fictional consciousness. In fact, nothing so consistent takes place, and Chaucer employs a range of types of narrative, changing sometimes over a few lines. He certainly uses at times the fiction of the mere reporter, the man who has only just, casually, encountered what he describes: I, 726–46 is one such moment. It is an art which disguises art (but draws attention to that disguise): the excuse that this speaker has not ranked the pilgrims in 'degree' wittily dissembles about the fact that Chaucer's *General Prologue* invokes complex and multiple criteria for social, economic and moral ranking. The intermittent picture of a naive narrator, dominated and pushed around by his own characters (like Pirandello's *Six Characters in Search of an Author*) is one of the comic pleasures of the *Canterbury Tales*. It serves, however, not merely realistic character-creation, but also draws attention to two mysteries: one the issue of the moral and political standpoint (if there is one) of this text, the other a more general enquiry into the nature of authorship which runs right through the *Tales* and Links, raising questions of the author's role in medieval society, the relation of author to text, and of text to meaning, to reception and to its readers.

One problem with the 'persona' theory is that there are so many narrative stances in the text: moments of omniscient narration, ostentatious moments of un-omniscience ('I noot how men hym calle', I, 284 (a statement revealing much about the professional cageyness of a Merchant and nothing about 'Chaucer the Pilgrim'); explicit praise and explicit condemnation. Chaucer's text uses, in short, the narrative stances and devices it requires at different moments, unconstrained by any need to maintain a plausible narrator-character over stretches of text: how could the narrator know the Merchant was in debt or the Clerk had twenty books in his bedroom? Another problem, if we take the 'persona' theory too far, is that it all too easily leads to ubiquitous ironic readings (see Pearsall 1984). Many problematic elements in the text can be dismissed as the perceptions of an inadequate narrator, whether Chaucer the Pilgrim or one of the story-tellers. Donaldson – far more nuanced than some later adherents of the 'persona' hypothesis – warned against the notion that moral ambiguities in the text can be explained by assuming a 'tongue in cheek' reporter who presents evil as good so that the reader can then read the report ironically. Most of the time the reader's sense that Chaucer's text frequently offers multiple readings is due not to a clash between events and a naive reporter of them, but to multivalence inherent in Chaucer's word-choice and stylistic juxapositions. Classic critical examinations of these issues include Muscatine on shifting narrative stances (1957: 96), Lawton (1985: ix–xiv, 1–16) on narrators and the 'persona', and Pearsall (1984: 79–89) on irony.

Occasions when a narrator's voice is heard are rare enough to be striking. They do express passivity, but the result is less to create a single character's perspective than to help to remove expectations of authoritative or single viewpoints in the narrative. The narrator's voice at I, 727–36 divests the narrator of responsibility for the *Tales'* variety of style and morality; at I, 3167–85 it proposes that it is the reader who decides the order and selection of material; and at VII, 707–9 it disclaims any skill as a narrator at all. Just as no voice consistently or reliably conveys authorial control or judgement over the material, so another aspects of authorship, the design, is displaced onto the Host ('governour . . . juge and reportour') assisted sometimes by the Knight. Yet the Host's design is itself subverted from within the text, as pilgrims interrupt, insist on their own vengeful designs, or get too drunk or angry to co-operate. The ending of the *General Prologue* with its show of hands and lottery continues to dramatise the notion of absence of design or control.

3
The *Knight's Tale*

Chaucer's *Knight's Tale* is a reworking of Boccaccio's epic *Il Teseida*, *c*.1340, itself based on a first-century Latin epic: Statius' *Thebaid*. The ancient saga of the Greek city of Thebes, little used by modern writers, also provided the subject for one of the greatest of the medieval romances dealing with classical subjects, the *Roman de Thèbes*, *c*.1150. Romances on the tales of Troy, Greece and Rome were popular from the twelfth century on and their heroes, as warriors and lovers, provided models and cultural expression for late medieval myths of chivalry: the nobility as the embodiment of courage, honour, *courtoisie*, and national leadership.

Chaucer had written about Thebes already in *Anelida* and an early, lost version of the story of Palamon and Arcite mentioned in the *Legend of Good Women*, and he alludes to the tragedy of Thebes in *Troilus and Criseyde* and *Complaint of Mars*. Scattergood (1981) and Patterson (1991: 172–98) show the *Knight's Tale* may reflect political anxieties in later fourteenth-century England about the nature of war and the role of the knightly class, in the face of the costly, inconclusive Anglo-French conflicts of the 1380s and the often unedifying aims and conduct of contemporary crusading campaigns. If the tale does this, it is through its exploration of wider concepts: love, mutability, conflict, good rule and tyranny, suffering, chivalry and order; it raises questions to which Chaucer's poetry constantly returns – Why is love so painful? Is mortal life potentially glorious or hopeless? Do we have free will or any power over what happens to us? Is there a loving order behind the universe?

The *Knight's Tale* is about order and sadness. Some might see it, rather, as a tale of love and war, and it is that too, but order and sadness come closer to its overall effect. First, because human love and war in the tale are related to larger cosmic patterns of harmony and antagonism, to the planets, the gods, and the whole created order of the universe. Also because, above the human characters, we have the impression always of higher powers, a celestial design to which the

46

human love and war are small parallels. The theme of order in the universe will be raised later, in the *Franklin's Tale*, when Dorigen questions the design of Providence, but it dominates this first tale, in style as well as content, to a degree fitting its position at the head of the tales and its teller's status as the man with most authority in the pilgrims' social hierarchy. Order comes closer to the tale's subject than love, because there is less of human passion and affection here than of more abstract concepts like harmony, respect, honour, or union. Sadness, too, is more prominent than war itself. War and conquest can, indeed, be a cause of social harmony, bringing order and good rule: this is the dominant message of the first two episodes.

Suffering is the tale's other subject and Chaucer makes suffering the text's other polarity, whether he is writing of war or of love. It takes three forms: pain, the breaking of harmony, and loss. His general presentation of war in terms of glory, honour and chivalric brotherhood, and of conquest as the bringer of social order, help to make war seem more like harmony. War can have a positive side, except in as far as it involves disorder (between the quarrelling young lovers) or tyranny (as with King Creon). The figure who represents the positive aspect of martial power is Theseus, military commander, governer, arbitrator, and maker of marriages. Yet Chaucer also includes details that show the brutality of war: for example, battlefield pillaging, Mars's malign influence, or Arcite's death agonies (I, 1005–8, 1975–2039, 2690–810). A tournament occupies the centre of the narrative, and it begins with a description of a May morning full of *plesaunce* and thoughts of love (I, 2483–91), in a splendour of *riche*, *brighte*, *golden* equipment, and music; yet even in the music Chaucer gives a sudden reminder of bloodshed:

> Pypes, trompes, nakers, clariounes,
> That in the bataille blowen blody sounes.
>
> (I, 2511–12)

It is a tale founded on opposites. Love involves both harmony and suffering; war brings both honour and destruction. The narrative presents the world in terms of polarities, rivalries and contrasts: Thebes and Athens, Venus and Mars, man and woman, youth and maturity. Yet it is also about parallels. There are two blood brothers, captured together, falling in love on the same day with the same woman; each has a champion in their battle; they both, in a sense, win (I, 2667–70). There are three gods and planets, three temples, three set-piece descriptions of planetary powers. There is frequently symmetry in the narrative: set-piece passages match set-piece passages, whether of speech or description. This textual symmetry implies the reconciliation of opposites within union, of order over-ruling diversity, and of harmony issuing from conflict. Despite the pervasive sense that tumultuous and conflictual human experience has been ordered in this tale into large symbolic forces and neat divisions, that thematic style of narrative is also used to explore some of the ambiguities of experiences like love and war, marriage and conquest, or kingship and tyranny: they prove at times very similar. Muscatine (1957: 181) characterised the tale as one in which 'order and power are always being opposed by chaos, disorder, pain and destruction'. Besides the dualities on which the plot is built – marriage and war, sexual love versus knightly brotherhood, Venus and Mars, Thebes and Athens, Palamon and Arcite – there are associated third forces, disconcerting presences which interrupt the simple oppositions: Diana alongside Mars and Venus, Theseus overruling Palamon and Arcite, time alongside the forces of love and conflict. These help to create a sense that polarity and conflict are not everything: there are alternatives and resolution, though the answers they offer are not clear-cut. Beyond the turmoil of the plot's action are the figures of old Egeus and his celestial equivalent, Saturn, and they speak – if not of answers – of a further realm of greater reality, beyond death and time.

Chaucer begins his version of the story with the marriage of Theseus and Hippolyta; Theseus' war against the Amazons has already happened.[1] Theseus is introduced in the first four lines as *duc*, *lord*, *governour*, *conquerour*: as a power, a ruler. These are terms appropriate to the Knight as fictional narrator, but the tale is also concerned thematically with these ideas in both social and celestial terms. Theseus is called 'conqueror of Femenye', Feminia, the name from the *Roman de Thèbes* for the female kingdom, the Amazons. The syntax of I, 866–8 suggests symbolic linking of conquest and marriage:

> He conquered al the regne of Femenye . . .
> And weddede the queene Ypolita.

In this sequence of verbs, 'conquered . . . and weddede', we could well see the inception of the topic of *maistrie*, domination in marriage, which will recur in the *Canterbury Tales*, but here it has a wider, almost symphonic range of meanings: marriage as man's control of woman, political domination as the source of social harmony, and the psychological hierarchical harmony resulting from the proper subjugation of sensuality and emotion (deemed to be feminine in medieval thought) to mature rationality (deemed to be masculine).[2] This message about the benign potential of power to bring order is encapsulated in the phrase 'with victorie and with melodye' (I, 872). There is perhaps a contemporary ideal here: Richard II, whose style of rule brought accusations of tyranny, had a vision of himself as a peacemaker.

The second episode shows the alternative, negative, potentiality of power: tyranny. The encounter with the grieving widows introduces two themes which recur in the tale and throughout the *Canterbury Tales*: mutability ('Fortune and hire false wheel', I, 925) and the pity which characterises a truly noble heart (I, 953–5; on Chaucer's conception of tyranny and pity, see Burnley 1979: 29–63). Theseus' defeat of the tyrant Creon also introduces into the plot Palamon and Arcite, 'yonge knyghtes' in contrast to the mature king, and identified immediately as a pair, brothers in every respect, as their first description indicates: 'Bothe in oon armes . . . two . . . highte . . . highte . . . they . . . hir cote-armures . . . hir gere . . . they that weren of sustren two yborn', etc. (I, 1012–21) – the passage treats them verbally as a unit.

As Kolve (1984: 85–157) shows, the prison in which Palamon and Arcite languish comes to symbolise major themes in the poem; 'prisoun' and words like 'fre' and 'romynge' recur, underlining two philosophical questions: how far emotion, desire, is itself a bondage (see I, 1224), and whether humans have free will in a world ruled by Fortune. The planetary gods are shown controlling the three young people's destinies, and more generally Theseus teaches (I, 3039–44), that there is no point in humans rebelling against their fates in a mutable world. Arcite's death is described as an escape from 'this foule prisoun of this lyf', (I, 3061). The thematic symbolism of this text is often spatial: the prison, garden, opposed cities, triple temples and the amphitheatre all illustrate the parallels and contradictions in human experience which the whole narrative explores.

The immediate alternative to the princes' life-long misery in the literal prison is the sight of Emily, with whom they both fall in love. The first description virtually identifies her with the beauty of the springtime garden. But when this love comes to the prisoners it comes as pain:

> [Palamon] cast his eye upon Emelya,
> As therwithal he bleynte and cride, 'A!'

(I, 1077–8)

Arcite says her 'fresshe beautee sleeth me sodeynly' (I, 1118). Love also brings conflict to the brothers-in-arms. From now on the terms on which the narrative has been constructed begin to overlap and contradict each other. Love is like war, bringing wounding and conflict. Love, says Arcite, is a law (I, 1164–6); but it is a law which threatens to overturn any other type of *decree*, 'regulation', or *degree*, 'social hierarchy'. Far from uniting them it makes each man self-seeking:

> 'And therfore, at the kynges court, my brother,
> Ech man for hymself, there is noon oother.'
>
> (I, 1181–2)

Throughout this speech the word 'brother' ironically recurs. This quarrel is the beginning of a theme of rivalry between men which will run throughout the *Tales*.

When love leads literally to battle, the descriptions of the *oratories* of the three gods emphasise how much this is a drama of ideas, with the characters representations of forces in human life.[3] It is not just that the planetary gods represent the three young people; the gods and the characters, their speeches and actions, together represent three concepts: Venus (passion and harmony), Mars (conflict and aggression) and Diana (chastity). The descriptions of the gods draw on centuries of literature, learned commentary, and artistic representations of the classical deities, during which they had acquired many symbolic, philosophical, astrological, medical and psychological associations. Chaucer, even more than Boccaccio, in these descriptions mingles positive and negative aspects: Venus, for example, produces the miseries desire brings, and deceit and folly, as well as beauty, pleasure, music and dance (I, 1904–66). Appropriately in this tale of a military man, concerned with the nature of power, Mars gets most attention: Mars's colour is red, his metal iron, his place the North, and he is responsible on the one hand for 'Conquest, sittynge in greet honour', for the deaths of famous leaders like Julius Caesar and Mark Antony, and also for felony, tyranny, towns destroyed, 'The smylere with the knyf under the cloke', and the 'open werre, with woundes al bibledde', and humbler horrors: the pickpocket, the cook scalded, barns burnt in civil unrest, the carter run over with his own cart (I, 1967–2050). It is the cruel, savage and destructive side of Mars which receives most emphasis. Diana's triple aspects are depicted: as the moon, as 'shamefast chastitee' with lowered eyes, as the goddess of childbirth, and especially as a huntress, who takes ruthless revenge on any violation of her modesty (I, 2051–88): the tale stresses the most violent aspects of this deity too. In this drama of predominantly masculine themes, Diana represents Emelye's role as the marriageable virgin, a projection of masculine desire, though the motif of her reluctance to wed at all (I, 2304–5) could be seen as a displaced representation of her absent female subjectivity and free will (on gender issues in the tale see Crane 1994: 15–23, 169–85). None of the characters is depicted as having much subjectivity, however, and Chaucer increases the polarity whereby Palamon is a Venus-type and Arcite is a Mars-type, by making, for example, Arcite's first reaction to Emelye the cry 'A!', as if from a wound.

Both men win, and in his initial victory-moment, Arcite's death comes not from Palamon but from a Fury sent by Saturn to even up the victories granted to Mars and Venus. The long, magnificent description of Arcite's hero's funeral symbolises a balancing too: he gains the honour and fame of a successful warrior, though losing the satisfaction of a lover. At I, 3047–56 Theseus says it is best for a man to die thus at the peak of his chivalric honour. Falling, literally, when at the height of his success, Arcite also represents the theme of Fortune's wheel and mutability. And the text now begins its long final task of exploring whether, behind the unevenness of earthly experience, there is an ultimate order and wholeness. The first stage is Egeus' speech and that gives a perspective which is confined to life in this world and seen from its end-point, death: 'wo' and 'transmutacioun', mutability, are its nature (I, 2837–49).

Theseus' speech (I, 2987–3066) looks beyond the world: it invokes not the Christian God, but the Aristotelian concept of the First Mover, the force which, itself unmoved, started all the motion of the universe. The speech has echoes of Boethius's *Consolation of Philosophy* (AD 524), which teaches that though Fortune causes mutability and undeserved adversity, she is the servant of a benign providence and her greatest good is to turn human minds towards the stable reality and eternal truths of the eternal realm. Theseus posits a benign parallel between the order of the universe, as a 'faire cheyne of love', and human life. Time and change are the conditions the deity laid on this world: to 'grucchen', grumble, against them is folly and rebellion against God 'that al may gy', God the supreme *governour*. What lay ahead of Arcite in this world was a less glorious old age; what lies beyond this realm of time, imperfection and change is a reality which 'parfit is and stable' (I, 3009). Theseus' conclusion is

'Thanne is it wysdom, as it thynketh me,
To maken a vertu of necessitee,
And take it weel that we may nat eschue . . .'

(I, 3041–3)

The marriage he urges on Palamon and Emelye is that solution: knowing the imperfection of life, 'to be merye . . . er that we departen from
this place' (I, 3068–70; *place* having a double sense of 'here' and 'in this
world').

We are told nothing of their reactions but that conveys the fact that
this wedding and its subsequent harmony (I, 3101–6) are primarily not
individual experiences but symbols of the wise solution to recognition
of the nature of life: to create order and benevolence. The long period
of sorrow that precedes the marriage, similarly, indicates less the incon-
solable nature of Emelye's or Palamon's sorrow than the theme of time
itself as an element in this final lesson. Time brings sorrow, and sorrow-
ful recognition of the nature of transient life-experience; the solution is
the deliberate cultivation of order and benevolence, symbolised here as
marriage.

Whatever the claims made, on the literal level, for its happiness, this
union is the closure imposed by Theseus: on the couple, and also on the
philosophical questions of why life seems random, unfair and doomed
to disappointment. It is also the closure imposed on the whole text by
the (knightly) worldview that maintains that conquest and control are
necessary for social and marital benefits, and that chivalric myth and the
concept of knightly honour make glorious the loss and destruction of
warfare. In parallel ways both Theseus and the text subdue women: at
the beginning the challenge of Hippolyta's independence, her role as an
Amazon queen, is conquered – conquered as literal defeat and in the
form of marriage; after that, all appearances of women in the text are
subjugated to the same hollow level. Lacking all elements of subjectivity, they are emblematised to convey a series of male projections: as that
which is desirable (the linked ideas of Maytime/garden/Emelye); as
intercessors, in I, 1748–61 ('wommanhede' eliciting mercy from
masculine justice and authority); as passive virgin (even Diana cannot
alter Emelye's marital fate, I, 2348–57); as fickle (woman as Fortune,
I, 2681–2); and as tender wife (I, 3103). Marriage at the end of the
Knight's Tale symbolises one of Chaucer's foremost philosophical
themes, that of 'suffraunce', the willing acceptance of whatever vicissitudes life sends: this wedding is not, finally, presented as a union of
passionate desire, but as a philosophical theme, that of rational reaction

to a long experience of loss. Similarly, the anti-feminist observation that Emelye, like all women, followed Fortune (I, 2680–2), though typical of the emblematic presentation of the females in this text, is primarily a way of introducing the theme of Fortune into this section of the tale.

Nolan (1992: 250–5, 272–81) suggests that the *Knight's Tale* presents a Stoic philosophy, rather than a specifically Christian one: it would thus present an appropriately secular counterpart to the religious answer to recognition of life's transience presented in the *Parson's Tale*. It certainly sets human life in both a philosophical and a cosmic context, and insists that there is stability, order and a plan beyond earthly change and misery. It has a dignity and a vision of order in multiplicity that are appropriate to the first tale in the pilgrims' sequence. The form and style of the tale suggest that the structures and values of benign authority are integrated throughout the cosmos, in microcosm and macrocosm alike, and that oppositions can be reconciled within such order; Chaucer's magisterial evocation of that vision is without peer in English literature. Yet what stays with the reader, as the most original feature of the text, the one that raises the most profound philosophical and ethical questions, is the recurrent reminders of pain, disorder, loss and unresolved desire. While this aptly takes the exploration of military power beyond conventional parameters within this particular tale, it provides also, in another and deeper way, the appropriate pattern for the first tale in the pilgrims' sequence, for pain, loss, destruction and desire will follow in future tales, refusing easy assimilation into a master narrative or programme. The immediate form that rejection of a master narrative takes proves to be the far from sublime drunken obstreperousness of the Miller against the Host's plan, but this can be read as a fable of the same provocative pattern as we contemplate in the disturbingly unreconcilable elements in the *Knight's Tale*.

4

The *Miller's Tale*

Seven of Chaucer's tales, the *Miller's*, *Reeve's*, *Cook's*, *Friar's*, *Summoner's*, *Merchant's* and *Shipman's*, are fabliaux. Chaucer's fabliau tales are richer and more complex than the general norm of the genre and it is helpful before considering how he used a fabliau plot in the *Miller's Tale* to look at the genre as it existed before the *Canterbury Tales*.

Fabliaux were particularly popular in twelfth- and thirteenth-century France: medium-length comic narratives, often in octosyllabic couplets; and in a looser sense the term is used of humorous tales in prose or any kind of verse, which centre typically on sexual escapades and cynical tricks. Fabliau plots often use motifs that can be found in folktales, anecdotes and jokes all over the world, from many ages up to the present day. The *Miller's Tale*, for example, uses two plot motifs known as the Girl with Two Lovers and the Misdirected Kiss (on the fabliau genre in general, see Hines 1993: 1–70).

Like farce, fabliaux stand or fall on the strength of their plots and the arts of telling a story: selection of details, pace, suspense, economy, dramatic irony and surprise. Everything moves towards a climax, a comic dénouement (or often linked dénouements), which typically involves a trick, joke or insult. Any extra pleasures they provide in the way of characterisation or background are typically limited to those which help the plot: if the plot requires a window, a tree, an abbess or a prim girl, there will be those things, but generally details are sparse and the lines of the mechanism of the plot are left clear, though many French fabliaux show subtle expertise in socially observed dialogue. The typical characters are those the plot requires and tend to be stereotypes: lecherous clerics, faithless and cunning wives, stupid husbands or miserly peasants. They are primarily counters to be moved round by the plot towards the comic climax. The motivations that get them moving towards it are of the lowest: lust, lust for money, and lust for revenge. Fabliaux, like many folktales, frequently celebrate the trickster rather than morality, yet there is often an evening-out of aggression and requittal in these dénouements which substitutes for the absent morality a sort of aesthetic justice or balance. Fabliaux often ended with a moral, whose connection with the tale might not always be completely serious. *Heile of Beersele* (Bryan and Dempster 1941: 112–18), a Flemish fifteenth-century fabliau, which is an analogue to the *Miller's Tale*, illustrates many of the characteristics:

> Heile arranges to let three men visit her at different times on one night. While she is in bed with the miller, the priest comes. She sends the miller to hide in a tub in the rafters. While she is in bed with the priest, the miller overhears the priest talking about the Flood. When the blacksmith comes and knocks at the door, begging at least to kiss her, she persuades the priest to stick his bottom out of the window. The blacksmith, having kissed it, returns with a hot iron and, in a repeat of the window-scene, burns the priest, whose cries for water cause the miller to cut himself loose and fall from the rafters. The moral is that injury and shame come to those who consort with whores.

Although the setting of fabliaux is typically an everyday one of a street or small house, the action, as here, is far from realistic. One of the pleasures of fabliaux is of entering temporarily into a world where normal morals, normal sanctions and normal consequences are removed. Bizarrely ingenious strategies and bizarrely unexpected dénouements are part of the enjoyment. This plot is one of high artifice and symmetry: we have three men, three times, a triple dénouement and triple punishments. The everyday milieu led early critics to label fabliau a bourgeois genre, but they seem to have been widely enjoyed, with clerics among the authors (and prominent among the heroes), and they often use ingenious verbal games (see Hines 1993: 22–7).

The *Miller's Tale*, like all Chaucer's fabliau-type tales, is more elaborate and uses a wider variety of types of comedy than other fabliaux. Knowing probably an analogue to *Heile of Bersele*, he keeps the symmetry but complicates it: the carpenter becomes an old husband, and he has two young *clerks* (which means the blacksmith necessary for the plot has to be brought in as an outsider to the main plot). Chaucer thus introduces themes of youth versus age and of masculine rivalry, linking his *Miller's* and *Reeve's Tales* back to the *Knight's Tale*. He further complicates the clear lines of a fabliau plot by halting the narrative for set-piece descriptions of the three young characters. One effect is to differentiate his two young lovers not by profession, as in the analogue, but by character: Nicholas clever, sexually attractive and wilfully successful; Absolon effeminate, sexually eager but nervous, and absurd.

He brings more precise class comedy into the stereotypical social comedy of the fabliau: his carpenter is a *riche gnof*, a prosperous oaf, and is both confident and stupid. That and his wife's over-emphatic jewellery and fashions – her low embroidered collar and barred belt (and perhaps the very fact that she wears fashion at all) – mark them as among the new rich artisans of the post-Plague decades, and they are seen, together with Absolon's over-energetic Oxford style of dancing, and the naive ready belief of Nicholas's neighbours in his predictions, with all the mockery of a London, court, eye.

Real-life antagonism between Town and Gown was often violent in Oxford and Cambridge, and Nicholas and John are, more generally, rival representatives of brain versus brawn. Nicholas boasts that an intellectual, a *clerk*, can outwit a manual worker, a *carpenter* (I, 3298–300). John delights in the chance to pity Nicholas for collapsing through too much brain-work, where an uneducated man would be safe (I, 3451–67). The narrator begins by designating the tale as one where 'a clerk hath set the wrightes cappe', and ends by again specifying the class insult: the 'swyvyng' of a 'carpenteris wyf' (I, 3143, 3850). (We notice how little this sympathy with clerks humiliating artisans fits the fictional narrator, a miller: it demonstrates how free of concern Chaucer can be on occasion for keeping complete consistency of character in the way a Victorian novelist strives to do.)

Nicholas rigs up a device as intricate as any carpentry in order to sleep with Alison. His intellectuality is directed to very bodily ends:

> As clerkes ben ful subtile and ful queynte;
>
> *complex*
>
> And prively he caughte hire by the queynte . . .
>
> (I, 3275–6)

The action is crude but the style of the couplet is subtle: 'queynte' at the period was a polite word, meaning something delicate or intricate, and *rime riche*, a rhyme on two senses of the same words was regarded as particularly elegant. The mixture of subtlety and crudeness all through the language of this tale suggests a conflation of intellect and body – the application of exquisite cleverness to lust – and of vulgarity and aesthetic delight, which represents a challenge to clear-cut moral polarities far more powerfully than a tale that was simply crude would do. Absolon, the victim of the arse-kissing, has a contrasting quality of being *squaymous* (I, 3337), and chary of approaching women except when they are safely barmaids, in church, or married and unavailable. If Nicholas is the adulterer and Absolon not, it is not because Absolon is purer; it is because Nicholas is cleverer at getting what he wants, and the tale celebrates that cleverness. If Alison 'hadde been a mous And he a cat . . .'. But Absolon is not a cat and Nicholas has already pounced. Absolon's ineffectual distance-wooing includes the language of the love lyric and even of the greatest mystical–erotic text in Judaeo-Christian tradition, the Song of Songs:

'What do ye, hony-comb, sweete Alisoun,
My faire bryd, my sweete cynnamome?
Awaketh, lemman myn, and speketh to me!'

(I, 3698–3700)[1]

Chaucer introduces a mock-heroic, or mock-romantic, verbal incongruity into this comedy of lower middle-class sexual adventures. As Donaldson (1970: 13–29) showed, he uses words associated with popular lyric and romance, slightly absurd and *déclassé* to sophisticated courtiers: 'hende', 'childe' in the sense of 'knight' or 'hero', 'lemman', 'derne love', 'gent and smal', 'gore', 'ore'. Terms appropriate to heroes ('child', I, 3325) and to heroines ('His rode was reed', 'blosme upon the rys', I, 3317, 3324) help to suggest Absolon's effeminacy. Bathos also helps: a heroine's eyes would be 'greye as glas': Absolon's are 'greye as goos' (I, 3317). Slang and colloquialisms ('gnof', 'viritoot', 'Jakke fool', 'Have do . . . com of', 'kiken') and taboo words ('towte', 'pisse', 'fart', 'ers', 'nether ye') mingle with learned vocabulary ('conclusiouns', 'interrogaciouns', 'astrelabie', 'augrim', 'astrology', which the carpenter stumbles over at I, 3457), and fashion terms ('voluper', 'suyte', 'a kirtel of lyght waget'). As often with Chaucer, the register appropriate to one area of life is used for another: Nicholas's 'conclusion', the scientific answer to his calculations, is to sleep with Alison (I, 3402); after smacking Alison's bottom and kissing her, his vigorous psaltery-playing is displaced and delayed sexual pleasure, and the carpenter's bed holds the ultimate 'revel and melodye' of the whole tale: their 'bisynesse of myrthe and of solas' there (I, 3652–4), contrasts with John's literal 'wery bisynesse' (I, 3643). Rhyme too brings together incompatible experiences (and body parts):

'This wol I yeve thee, if thou me kisse,'
This Nicholas was risen for to pisse . . .

(I, 3797–8)

'Spek, sweete bryd, I noot nat where thou art.'
This Nicholas anon leet fle a fart

(I, 3805–6)

The final chain of comic dénouements happens in the dark, as in the *Reeve's Tale*. Throughout the tale we readers enjoy the dramatic irony of knowing or guessing more than any of the characters. We are on the inside as well as the outside of bedrooms, at I, 3252–68, 3409–92, 3643–740, and 3787–81 – the last one is the revenge of the shut-out victim, and here we know the truth about what lies in wait outside the window, as Nicholas does not. Where we do not know exactly what is afoot, Chaucer whets our curiosity by other characters' questions: John at I, 3437, 3525; Gerveys at 3766–82. The carpenter bending down to peep in through the cat-flap in Nicholas's door to find out what is going on inside is the curious reader's *alter ego*. The only difference lies in our well-founded suspicions and his naivety. Chaucer makes his naivety unsympathetic by making it arrogant: the bustling arrogance of the practical man and his assistant, thundering up and down the stairs, going through the heavy complexity of getting the door up off its hinges – brawn quite misapplied in the attempt to catch up with the intellectual's inventions (I, 3431–86), while Nicholas, contriving entree into the Carpenter's bed and wife, resembles the cat. The carpenter's glee over scholars unable to see a pit in front of their feet prefigures his own fall into a trap created by a clerk (I, 3449–61). One of the pleasures of these fabliau-tales is to see one character carefully contriving something which, unbeknown to them, lands them into the contrivance laid by someone else. Chaucer uses soliloquy here (as in the *Reeve's Tale*, I, 4216–25, when we hear the wife think over to herself how she must avoid getting into the wrong bed). We see Absolon's sanguine enquiries and plan for taking advantage of the carpenter's absence (I, 3657–97). The text intellectualises the plots' comic ingredients of individual plans and fatally limited knowledge into the theme of *ymaginacioun* (in medieval theories of perception, the brain's faculty of image-making and visualisation), I, 3612: the tale is full of mental visions of the future, true and groundless. The motif of seeing, true and false, will be even more prominent in the *Reeve's Tale*. The brain, of course, is another kind of private chamber.

The three early set-piece descriptions of characters have several functions. Missing out John, they help to keep his point of view out of the reader's mind and sympathy (as do his age and 'jalousie', I, 3221–32, 3294–6). Nicholas is described in terms of four features which will make him the successful lover: cleverness, wilfulness, sweetness (kissability), and *myrie* melody. His private room has an impressive and expensive student-seducer's ambiance, with its pot-plants, learned tomes, equipment and neat details. His private room is part of the recurrent theme of 'privitee'. His 'prive' moments with Alison (I, 3271–302, 3651–7, 3721–806) contrast with Absolon's literally and metaphorically shut-out location. The window, through which Absolon tries to woo Alison and is repulsed, symbolises her sexuality and *hole* (I, 3732), dramatically refused to Absolon:

'Tehee!' quod she, and clapte the wyndow to.

(I, 3740)

Sexual symbolism runs through the narrative: the flood Nicholas predicts symbolises his own sexual performance; the phallic shape of the red-hot coulter symbolises Absolon's revenge for sexual shaming by Nicholas; Absolon's pre-kiss state is dominated by orality ('greyn and lyckorys . . .', 'trewe love . . . hony comb . . . sweete cynamome', 'tete').

'Hende' marked Nicholas as the hero and Alison's description starts with *Fair.* Her description combines natural details – with their implication that her sexuality is natural and blameless – aggressive similes ('as a bokeler', 'as a bolt', 'as any wezele', 'a wether', etc. – this is the heartless girl that said 'Tehee' as she clapped the window to), and a strong sense of her body inside her clothes: 'Upon hir lendes', 'likerous ye', 'by hir girdel', 'on hir legges hye'. It is a tactile, three-dimensional image ('al bifoore . . . eek bihynde . . . aboute . . . withinne and eek withoute', 'set ful hye', 'softer', 'wynsynge', etc.). The fashion points – barred belt, low collar, the purse 'perled with latoun', etc. – are combined with simple expressions of delight – 'Fair . . . ful moore blisful . . . gay... brighter . . . sweete', etc.). The apples, stored up, symbolise her still under-appreciated sexual sweetness. It is not surprising this description ends by focusing on what men might do with her. The snobbish element in the tale's social comedy surfaces here again: she is suitable for a lord to seduce or for a 'good yeman' (probably a prosperous artisan or employee) to marry. Alongside the saturation of the narrative with the archaic romantic language of traditional lyric and romance (a Mills and Boon or Harlequin Romance register), it uses terms which were clearly quite precisely placeable in class terms: 'wenche' had connotations of 'servant', 'country girl', and 'immoral woman'; the servant calls Nicholas 'Maister' as if he is a university scholar (I, 3337). Chaucer's reader needs always to attend to how *thou, thee, thy(n)* and *ye, yow, your* (when used to one person) imply either familiarity or respect. These characters, knowing each other well and not of *gentil* status, generally use the familiar *thou* forms. Robyn the servant addresses Nicholas with the respectful *ye* (I, 3437); Absolon's worship of Alison sometimes leads him to use *ye* (I, 3362, 3698–702), though hopes of imminent intimacy produce *thy(n)* at I, 3726. Nicholas moves straight into getting close to Alison (at I, 3277), verbally as well as physically; she attempts to keep him at a verbal and physical distance – 'Do wey youre handes, for youre curteisye!' – though in her flurry – 'I wol nat kisse thee' – she lapses into the familiar. He is probably slightly her social superior too, as well as so insistently intimate.

The tale presents the physical, workaday realisation of action: Alison washes her face after housework (I, 3310–11), and wears a 'barm-clooth'; for secrecy the carpenter has to make the ladders himself, rungs and stalks, and hang them in the 'balkes' (I, 3624–7); he shakes Nicholas 'myghtily' by the shoulders (I, 3475); snores because his head is awry (I, 3647). It is these details, as much as words like 'pisse' or 'towte', that challenge the world created by the contrasting subjects and styles of the *Knight's Tale*. After the *Knight's Tale*, the *Miller's Tale* introduces Chaucer's taste for linking tales by contrast and by fictional conflict between the pilgrims. Fabliau after romance, comedy after tragedy, bodily lust after philosophy, low styles after high, clerks and carpenters after princes: the tale turns upside down the literary experiences of the *Knight's Tale*, despite the plot-parallels of two young men after one girl. Patterson (1991: 244–79) argues that the *Knight's Tale* represents recognition of a crisis in the role of the aristocracy as governors of later fourteenth-century English society, and the Miller's insistence on taking over the story-telling symbolises a subversion of social hierarchy (the shadow of the 1381 Rising, political challenges to aristocratic power, and upward mobility in the lower and middle classes). The tale itself is a political 'quyting'. For Patterson, Chaucer reveals in these Fragment I tales problematic elements in knightly power and the chivalric myth that supports it, and at the same time a sense of alarm and distaste for the economic and political challenges from below. A related but different argument, that of Knapp 1990, is that the recurrence here and elsewhere in the *Tales* of subversive moves against authority, in many forms (including language and comedy), arises in part from the destabilising presence of Wycliffite discussion in the society of his day.

Yet it is important to note how Chaucer, in the *Miller's Prologue*, also in some ways distances himself from the disrespectful Miller who will not lower his hood to anyone: not only is he presented with the animal-like qualities traditionally attributed to peasants, but he is drunk; his reason is upside-down, like his overturning of social hierarchy (I, 3120–4), and that potentially defuses any serious challenge. Chaucer's pose of the narrator as mere recorder (I, 3167–86); suggests that decisions about the text lie in the readers' hands – including the decision about whether the *Miller's Tale* comes next at all, for the reader can *Turne over the leef* (I, 3177). Chaucer invokes the new optionality of the reader, as opposed to the traditional oral performance where the reciter (like the Host) decides the order of what is to be heard. Within the tale, as in the Reeve's, the working man is mocked by the clever *clerk* – and 'swyvyng' a man's wife mocks the man as well as enjoying the wife. The *Miller's* and *Reeve's Prologues* and *Tales* may show the world of the prosperous, confident craftsman, which potentially challenges the aristocratic assumptions about order celebrated in the *Knight's Tale*, but they also show this class as crude, stupid and baselessly confident, and they celebrate its defeat – within the fiction by young, socially unfixed students. The clerks in the tales 'disparage' the working men's womenfolk, but so at times do Chaucer's narratives – as we see in the remark about lords bedding Alison and the presentation in the *Reeve's Tale* of the Miller's women. Having used the Miller to undercut the vision of hierarchical authority after the *Knight's Tale*, a tale which itself contained evidence of the brutal cost of such authority, Chaucer also limits the degree of sympathy the text extends either to the obstreperous Miller or to John the 'riche gnof' and his charming 'wenche'. No single worldview is allowed to hold sway in the first sequence of tales. This first rebellion by the Miller against hierarchy, literary and social, is a highly original, thought-provoking device, and the way Chaucer links the tales in Fragment I shows him using the variety of social ranks that his fictional pilgrimage gave him to venture into relatively unchartered waters for exploring social, economic and political relations and conflicts of interest, through voices from different parts of the system and through a variety of genres and styles which themselves embodied class myths.

The *Miller's Tale*, presenting illicit sexual urges in terms of youth, natural imagery and 'melodie', hilarity and ingenuity, seems to use its art to challenge the moral rule that adultery must always be wrong. A network of religious references, however, makes sure we do not wholly forget the existence of a world of different priorities: references to Noah's Flood (which was a punishment for sin), Absalon (whose vanity led to his death), Herod, the Annunciation, and the Oxford friars in the chancel beginning to sing Lauds as Alison and Nicholas lie in bed. It is the world of medieval biblical plays as much as the Bible itself that enters the narrative from time to time. Historically, clerks often acted in mystery plays, as Absolon does. There is a reference to acting the role of Herod, a part full of bombast and juggling with knives, and Nicholas's use of Noah's Flood recalls the Noah plays in which Noah's wife is rebellious. In plays and apocryphal legends about the Conception and Nativity, Joseph was a carpenter, an old husband, subject to jealousy: in the *N-Town Plays* (1991), Play 12, 25–83, he refuses to believe Gabriel has brought the message of a divine birth, but says the so-called angel was a handsome boy, cuckolding the old husband. A potentially blasphemous Annunciation parallel runs through the tale, underlined by Absolon's misapplied Song of Songs, a text allegorically applied to the Virgin (lovers speak at a lattice window in Song of Songs 2: 9–17). Alison's radiant face, washed after house-work, too probably parodies the gilded faces or masks that represented the shining faces of those filled with divinity – among them Mary – in devotional texts, including plays (*N-Town Plays* (1991), Play 12, 15–16; on masks and gilding see Twycross 1990). The words of *Angelus ad Virginum* use the imagery of the angel coming to Mary's private room and soothing her fears, with a sacred use of quasi-sexual language – which this tale seems to re-embody, in both Absolon's and Nicholas's approaches to Alison (the *Decameron* 4.2 has a tale where an adulterous friar pretends to be the angel Gabriel).[2] Critics of the 'Exegetical' Princeton School saw the religious allusions as demonstrating the char-acters' absorbtion in lechery, pride and covetousness (D. W. Robertson 1962: 382–6). Medieval art, however, religious as well as secular, often took a more robust approach to religious parody, and to merging sexual and sacred images, than post-medieval centuries have done. While the religious references serve Chaucer's habitual method of never letting a single worldview dominate, they seem not to have the condemnatory effect they have in the *Merchant's Tale*, for the poetry endows lust with delight, natural energy and amusement here, and the worldliness is neither mercenary nor hypocritical.

The references to 'privitee' combine the sexual pun (a wife's private parts), elaborated in the imagery of the private chamber running through the text, with allusion to contemporary religious controversy:

because Wycliffite ideas encouraged lay people without clerical education to discuss and question religious traditions, some conservative churchmen tried to promulgate the belief that it was better to stay 'lewed' ('lay', 'uneducated'), trusting in simple faith, rather than delving into mysteries, 'Goddes pryvetee'. The Miller raises this controversy (I, 3164), and the carpenter's stupidity involves, as Fletcher (1991) shows, his smug adherence to this doctrine of pious ignorance and simplicity. Chaucer furthermore associates his religious naivety with an arrogance which also forms part of his class identity: 'What! Thynk on God, as we doon, men that swynke' (I, 3491). The picture of the working man in this tale is not a malign one, but it certainly has belittling elements. It has the potential to neutralise or at least render equivocal any political thrust in the Miller's rebellion. The other challenge of the tale is the question, however comically raised here, of how the unruly force of sex fits into moral systems. This is a question powerfully raised in much serious medieval secular literature, from Marie de France and Chrétien de Troyes onwards. The happiness with which Chaucer imbues illicit sex in this text poses a mystery, a delving into the 'pryvetee' of the design of Creation and morality, that is profound and will be raised much more starkly when Chaucer rejects his sinful tales in the *Retraction* that ends the *Canterbury Tales*.

5

The *Reeve's Tale*

The *Reeve's Prologue* shows Chaucer using the Link passages and his miscellany of pilgrims to throw the onus of interpretation implicitly onto the reader. Whereas everyone agreed the *Knight's Tale* was a noble tale, here 'Diverse folk diversely they seyde' (I, 3857): the fictional audience provides no guidance to the reader. The Reeve's response introduces a ploy Chaucer will use often, of a pilgrim interpreting a tale in a partial, bizarrely idiosyncratic way. From now on the fictional audience's comments, though significant in other ways, are not going to direct the reader to officially sanctioned interpretations. Their reactions are often provocative red herrings. Sometimes, as with the pilgrims' obedient unanimity after the *Knight's Tale* or their sober silence after the *Prioress's*, an absence of varied reactions after a tale containing painful tensions might itself underline the reader's sense that there are conflicts still to be explored.[1] The absence of pilgrim comment at the very end of the extant *Canterbury Tales*, however that came about, leaves us with a work built on irreconcilable juxtapositions, of which the addition of the *Parson's Tale* to the rest is the last and most provocative.

The Reeve's misinterpretation (that the *Miller's Tale* was an attack on carpenters) here introduces themes of anger and revenge which will dominate his tale. It establishes more overtly than the Miller's obstreperous desire to 'quyte' the Knight did, Chaucer's device of linking tales through the motif of male contest and rivalry (see Knapp 1990, an indispensable study of the role of contest in *Tales*). Parallels and contrasts also link the *Reeve's Tale* to the Miller's: both fabliaux about an illicit love-triangle, one set in Oxford, the other in Cambridge, both concerning two young clerks in sexual rivalry with each other and an older man. There is competition between the intellectuals and the manual worker, and satire against the prosperous tradesman. The *Reeve's Tale* has harsher social satire, in the descriptions of the Miller and his family, and harsher ecclesiastical satire: in place of the smug, bumbling simple faith of the carpenter, we have an outright case of financial abuse of Church office – a priest who has begotten an illegitimate daughter and is using Church property to endow his granddaughter to an advantageous marriage.

The *Reeve's Prologue* also presents a darker image of lust; instead of the *Miller's Tale*'s young lust, we have elderly lust visualising itself in misapplied natural analogies. They are unpleasant wintry analogies: the medlar, long a sexual symbol in medieval lyrics, is described in terms of its alternative name, the 'Open Arse' and the fact it is only edible when rotten; the leek, a winter storage vegetable, seems to be envisaged here upside-down, perhaps vitiating the Reeve's use of it to justify his unseasonal lust; the fire is a dying ember, and life's tun leaks away under Death's control. Kolve's illuminating analysis (1984: 217–33) shows how the negative imagery of the *Prologue* and its perversion of normally joyous imagery opposes both the 'pley' of the *Miller's Tale* and Christian meditations associating age and death with moral and spiritual rebirth. It is a vision of transience without any redeeming spiritual gleam. The Host's protest against the Reeve's 'sermonyng' attacks the inappropriate gloom, but directs the reader's attention also to its corrupt view of humanity's journey through life. A theme of false priesthood runs both through the *General Prologue* portrait, where the avaricious Reeve has acquired a quasi-ascetic air, and through the tale where the local priest betrays his office through personal avarice. A Reeve was a peasant official who operated as the bailiff of the lord who owned the estate; reeves, like haywards, ale-tasters and the jurors of the manorial court, were part of the village elite, administering and policing the community, serving the lord and yet building up local power and the beginnings of rural local government for their own class (see Dyer 1994: 1–12, on power groups and the potential for conflict within the medieval village). It is appropriate that Chaucer allots the Reeve a tale set in a village and concerning another kind of successful peasant, the rich miller.

The Tale

The *Reeve's Tale* resembles a thirteenth-century French fabliau *The Miller and the Two Clerks*, and the plot is found in the *Decameron* 9.6 and elsewhere.[2] Chaucer makes the clerks (merely anxious about money in the fabliau) students eager to revenge their college's losses, thus emphasising the themes of vengeance and competition between intellectual and tradesman.

On the face of it the tale is a nasty little piece: a tale of cheating met by cheating ('A gylour shal hymself bigyled be', I, 4321), where everyone is motivated by aggressive malice – including the author in the initial portrayal of his rural characters. The miller cheats his customers 'outrageously', when he gets the chance (I, 3998), and taunts the youths who try to stop him (I, 4110–26). He terrorises his local community, walking round armed to the teeth like a gangland boss. His wife is equally proud: a sin because pride is the primary sin, because she and her husband, a rich peasant, are presented as upstarts (claiming the title 'dame', yet because of her origins 'digne as water in a dich', I, 3964), but also because her hauteur is based on the fact that she is the illegitimate daughter of the priest (ironically 'noble kyn', I, 3942), and on people's heathly respect for her husband's vigilant aggression (I, 3942–68). In the fabliau the daughter is pretty but Chaucer gives her the brutish appearance he reserves for peasants with pretensions (not the modest Griselda). The simony of the priest grandfather, misappropriating Church property to help the family further up the ladder with a good dowery for her, adds religious sin to the social sins of being low-born but rich and pretentious and aggressive. Chaucer's satirical language (I, 3977–86) appropriates the holiest terms, 'hooly blood' and 'hooly chirches good' for the priest's irreligious aims, and overlaps also with the register of *gentillesse*, for this 'deynous' family has no lineage, no 'worthy blood of auncetrye' – as yet – to support its ambitions. This is a narrative where people drink, snore, fart, sneer, despise and cheat each other, and take revenge. The setting of most of it in a small dark beroom symbolises its pinched and limited moral horizons. The Cook aptly calls it 'a jape [trick] of malice in the derk'.

Yet the tale is funny and it attracts because of its energy and its economical suggestions of psychological and social verisimilitude (the young people sitting up finishing the beer, the sentimental parting at I, 4236–40), and Chaucer's virtuoso skill with speech and dialogue. This includes interior speech, and the reader is drawn in so much partly because Chaucer not only lets us know more then any characters do, but have insights into unseen thoughts: the miller laughing at the clerks' 'sleighte in . . . philosophye' (I, 4050) while planning his own sleights; John anxious for his masculine sexual reputation (I, 4200–12); the wife confident she knows what she is seeing (4290–306). In a tale where people triumph over each other, our superior knowledge gives us the pleasure of triumphing over them all. Chaucer's virtuosity with speech includes northern dialect for the clerks: *are, howgates, fonne, ille, lathe, fares* [for southern *fareth*] are examples, as is the *a* in words like *bathe*, *banes*, *raa*. Northern origin perhaps adds a slightly exotic or barbaric air to the students, though they are socially superior to the miller's family; perhaps it also had aggressive, tough associations – young Alan proves a match for the formidable miller The regionality certainly marks yet another division between the two groups of characters, and the wife's regionality (and class) are marked by her reference to the popular but, by the 1390s, unfashionable Norfolk pilgrimage shrine at Bromholm. It brings a further element of social variety into the *Canterbury Tales*.

It is hard to feel sympathy for the miller as depicted in the story, but it is important to note that he has been set up by the narrative: as proud, hostile to his community, and as deriving his social success from sin. The text dramatises the notion that the social ambitions of a man in his position, and any challenge they might pose within the system, are not based on sound grounds, and deserve to be trounced, and in this enactment, students – young, and socially and regionally unfixed – are the light cavalry of the conservative forces of the status quo.

Men and Women, Love and War

The plot is, of course, about rape: the students take nonconsensual sex from another man's women as vengeful exchange for the corn he has taken from them. Alan calls this legal 'esement': he will be 'releved' (I, 4169–87), both legal words though with possible sexual sub-senses; satisfaction can be sexual as well as financial. While in all versions of this plot the women are essentially counters, in this way, in an exchange between quarrelling men, the French fabliau shows the daughter a willing partner in her seduction, whereas Chaucer does not (though lingering over the last drop of ale with the students after the parents have gone up to bed hints at her interest). Sex seems to come to both wife and daughter as a complete surprise. The fact that the narrative claims they both enjoyed it is, of course, one of the oldest male excuses for rape. The text itself is taking a partisan, gendered, approach to what it is showing. The statement that the wife found more satisfaction than usual in John's sudden engagement with her is, in reality, physiologically unlikely, yet bears out the tale's general concentration on homosocial relations, for the wife's enjoyment is a further insult, by a young *clerk*, against her middle-aged, tradesman husband. And it is an insult the narrative makes against him, for our ears. John's soliloquy (I, 4201–10) makes explicit that his motives are, in part, to confirm his masculine identity in front of other youths. The bid for sex is an adventure, an *auntre* (I, 4205): they both perceive the danger to be the miller's vengeful violence, not the women's rejection. And it leads to the best fight description in Chaucer's work, far better than the rather desperate alliterative bluster, the generalities and tired images with which Chaucer represented action in the *Knight's Tale* on I, 2601–51. This description is precise about the exact physical location, in the bedroom or the body, of every throw, fall and blow, from the moment John rashly takes the miller 'by the nekke, and softe . . . spak' the fatal boast to him, I, 4261 (a confusion of sleeping companion which ironically symbolises the criss-crossed sexual and homosocial dynamics of this plot). It is effective partly because the space and number of combatants is restricted and every move is recorded, but also because it is the climax of a text in which the physical realisation and location of every twist in the tale has been made overt. Now we watch both strategy and error: the miller grabs Alan (by that rashly loquacious throat), Alan grabs back; the miller lands a telling blow, but trips on a stone. This well-matched male combat is in fact decided by a woman: a loose cannon in the fight scene, whose actions combine strategy and error, but still end up defeating her husband in the narrative's final insult against him, for he is hit by his own wife just as he was financially betrayed by his own daughter. The destructive division of the peasant family against itself, like the quarrelling of miller and Reeve in the Links and the even greater general unruliness depicted in the Cook's fragment, seems to show disorder as inherent in the lower orders of society.

Though the clerks' motive for revenge is financial, Chaucer adds the description of the peasants' snoring and farting, which makes their own animality seem a justification of their downfall. People generally are compared to farm animals in this tale: the fighting men go up and down like 'two pigges in a poke' (I, 4278), whereas Palamon and Arcite are compared to the exotic and heraldic tiger and lion (I, 1656–7, 2625, 2629–30). Like the *Miller's Tale*, and unlike the *Knight's Tale*, this is a workaday world where everything has a specific, limited reality: sacks are loaded and unloaded from a pony, flour is 'sakked and ybounde', extra guests means sending a daughter into the village to buy ale and bread, a horse has to be approached gently and stripped of its bridle, before being let loose. These practical details go far beyond what a fabliau plot requires, and they have complex effects: pleasure in the imaginative construction of a fictional world is one; they also constitute part of the implicit challenge these fabliau-tales make to the transcendence of economic realities in the Knight's romance; and generally, despite the effect of the peasants' snoring on the clerks, they enact a celebration of the ordinary, the physical and the bodily as sources of anarchy, energy and fulfilled desire. The drunkennes makes everyone not quite themselves or in control of where things are (I, 4150–5), so does the darkness and later the sexual exhaustion. As Kolve shows (1984: 233–56), the traditional symbolism of the horse without a rider as sensuality uncontrolled by reason, functions as the tale's emblem for the release of humanity's lower instincts portrayed in it. The tale is a counterpart to the *Knight's Tale*'s vision of the whole of the microcosm and macrocosm under the governance of reason. Theseus controls both warfare and love; in the miller's bedroom both are chaotically let loose. Whether this release is celebrated or deprecated in the tale or the *Canterbury Tales* at large, is a question on which readers and critics have diverse opinions.[3]

6

The *Cook's Tale*

The *General Prologue* Cook is introduced in the context of the Guildsmen and their social aspirations. Their silver knives, their wives' dreams of grandeur, their hopes of sitting up high on the dais in the guildhall council, like their wives' hopes of walking ahead in the procession, all mark their upward ambitions. They represent the wealthy burgesses, who dominated town and city offices and from whose members were elected the town councils, which had a certain amount of civic autonomy (on towns, see Keen 1990: 77–107). Chaucer's portrait stresses the stately rituals of this developing urban elite (liveries, fraternities, sitting in the guildhall on the dais, vigils and processions) and the verbal exaggeration suggests emulation of *gentils*: 'solempne and greet fraternitee', 'wisdom', 'madame', 'roialliche', though the basis of their claims to wisdom and dignity is their incomes, and their rising status is as new as their expensive accessories. The *Cook's Tale* is also concerned with urban order and with a challenge from below to established authority, but it is the challenge from below the ranks of the guildsmen and their like: the threat to public order and morality from tradesmen's unruly apprentices.

Town councils ruled and policed almost every aspect of commercial and civic life: businesses, tolls and rents, weights and measures, markets, pricing, hygiene, apprenticeships, the upkeep and good order of streets, bridges, town walls and ditches – everything from dog-control to bells to announce the closing of the town gates at the end of the day. Towns were not democracies; the ruling oligarchy in many ways repressed enterprise from below, using restrictive laws to govern trading, prices and employment in its own interest. Yet the guildhall's authority was necessary: medieval towns needed controls to reduce dangers like epidemics and fire, organise clean water and waste disposal (cities had butchers' shops, cooks' shops, vegetable-sellers, horses and other animals, domestic and public latrines), and monitor trading standards.

Chaucer's satire against the Cook combines gourmet cuisine and disgusting food-hygiene – flies, stale and twice-cooked food and dubious stuffing (I, 4346–52); both themes combine in the couplet about *blankmanger*, an elegant white dish of finely chopped chicken or other meat in a sauce with breadcrumbs, and a *mormal*, a scabby ulcer (I, 386–7). Is Chaucer suggesting they looked alike? The similar dish *mortreux* perhaps sounded and looked like a *mormal*. Complicated dishes were high fashion; Richard II liked *recherché* styles of cooking (his chef's recipe-book survives, the *Form of Cury*, 'Art of Cuisine': on medieval cookery, see Hieatt and Butler 1976). Chaucer's references to 'poudre-marchant tart and galyngale', 'mortreux' and 'blankmanger' characterise his Cook as producing that type of fashionable, over-elaborate delicacy. The *Pardoner's Tale* also satirises the absurdity and moral excess of fashionable cookery. The style and content of food was, like clothing style and material, a class marker: excess in either, or the presumptuous crossing of the class boundaries, could be matters for socio-ethical alarm. The Wife of Bath's and the Prioress's portraits employ the hierarchical status of fine white and barley bread as readily understood symbols. The *Nun's Priest's Tale* widow's self-produced peasant diet and Griselda's vegan frugality both win approval. *Piers Plowman*, A VI, 309, contains a vision of how Christian society should be organised and how the classes should relate harmoniously together, and it satirises workers' dissatisfaction with the traditional rural diet and their demand for sophisticated dishes and hot breakfasts. The disgusting elements associated with the Cook symbolically represent satire on social pretensions and ultimately unease about how towns and commerce alter relationships of production and (here literal) consumption.

The Cook is quarrelsome, enjoying the Reeve's malice (I, 4325–43), sparring with Harry Bailey, making the Manciple wary of antagonising him (IX, 76–80). His drunkenness (IX, 5–101), shows the purveyor of gluttony hoist with his own petard, harmed by his own commodity. Wrath is personified as a cook in *Piers Plowman*, V, 155–65. Chaucer's linking of the Cook to anger and drunken lack of control may symbolise aspects of city life. Different guilds clashed in town politics; perhaps Chaucer displaces and coalesces wider urban rivalries onto a lower level with this contentious Cook and his tale of *riot*. Everything about him connotes discord, including the discordant mingling of elegance and disgust in the images of his food, perhaps symbolising an ethical preference for an imagined non-commercial society, structured on generosity, service, and old settled authority based directly on the land (on the image of the town in the *Canon's Yeoman's Tale*, see p. 204).

The *Cook's Tale*

This tale, long neglected, began to interest critics more when political and New Historicist criticism became dominant in the 1980s and 1990s. The main thesis of New Historicist criticism is that the relation of literature to history is not that of autonomous texts with a socio-historical *background* (as New Critical and 'old historicist' approaches assumed): rather texts are themselves socio-historical statements, and can be both instruments of control by culturally dominant groups and influences on cultural change. The *Cook's Tale* depicts lower-class society in the streets and workshop-households of contemporary London, and it depicts them from a point of view that distrusts this as a social enclave breeding unregulated, anti-social and rebellious attitudes. These milieux are the seedbed of political unrest as well as of the lower levels of commerce, where businesses are less regulated and shade off into crime, and Chaucer often presents commerce as discord, in contrast to the idealised communal relationships of older models of Christian society. Before there were any police, disorder posed special dangers for everyone, rich and poor. A 'meynee', band of retainers of rioters, whether revellers or rebels, was a threat to the peace and security of any household (the alternative sense of 'meynee').

After two fabliau-style tales of youth in conflict with age, one urban and one rural, with students as protagonists, this tale moves to London and its obstreperous young protagonist is an apprentice. Attractive, successful with girls, a good dancer and musician, handsome, with a smart hair-style, he combines characteristics of Nicholas and Absolon, without Nicholas's intellectuality, Absolon's weakness, or their financial honesty. As the opening description proceeds, the point of view from which it is written shifts and narrows, from one expressing a positive picture: 'propre', 'so wel and jolily', 'as . . . hony sweete', 'wel', to one that is disapproving and suspicious. In I, 4386–9, 'fairer' and 'free' (generous) initially seem to look back to the preceding, positive description, but turn out to be linked to gambling and to secret payments, which from I, 4390 onwards becomes an outright revelation of theft. The viewpoint the text inscribes after I, 4390 is not confined to an individualised character, but the opinions would tally with those of any 'maister' of apprentices like this, and Chaucer begins with 'oure citee', verbally connecting the tale's opening to the Cook in the Link. The text conveys a more generalised sense of social *fear*: street gangs of youths, rushing freely around the City, day and night, resistent to the control represented by masters' anger or short prison spells in Newgate.

The specific misdemeanours that are relevant to a master's anxiety are leaving the shop unattended and robbing the till, but those wider anxieties emerging in the text include potential political anxieties: its repeated terms 'revel', 'revelour', 'riot', 'riotous', combine meanings of carnival (Middle English *riot* meaning 'dissipation' and 'violent revelry') and rebellion (*revel*, from Latin *rebellare*, meant 'be riotously festive'). Chroniclers denigrated the 1381 rebels by identifying them with animalistic mindless rampage and revelry (Strohm 1992: 34–6). A mix of antagonism and carnival ('game and pley', 'lough . . . cheere', I, 4355–7, 4363) is figured in the *Cook's Prologue*, and Knight (1986: 75) sees the sudden bluntness of I, 4421–2 as a revolt against verbal decorum. Mobile groups of young people with no responsibilities to tie their behaviour down are ingredients for social unrest and the individual apprentice's misdeeds are always linked by the text to assembly: to groups and to gangs of like-minded youths in the city streets (I, 4375–80, 4384, 4415); and the master's worry that Perkyn will lead others astray (I, 4406–7), and Perkyn's role as ring-leader of his own *meynee* (I, 4381). Wallace (1997: 168) suggests the second line's reference to the victuallers could have reminded contemporaries of the antagonism between London's all-powerful victuallers' guild and the non-victuallers, excluded from city power, and the affrays and disputes between their adherents frequently recorded in guildhall reports. The text links 'thefte' with 'riot' – a roistering lifestyle needs to be funded – and 'revel' with loss of 'trouthe': 'loyalty' and 'honesty'. When the scene moves to the shop run by Perkyn's friend, a young man on his own level (I, 4419), this lower-class enterprise is visualised as fraudulent and immoral: a front for prostitution.

Chaucer's Cook illustrates how characterisation is only an intermittent concern of medieval narrative; personality traits often serve thematic functions and character-consistency may be sacrificed, in unnovelistic fashion, to other ends. The narrative voice of the tale is disapproving of the evils associated with tavern drinking, whereas the Cook in the *Manciple's Prologue* is himself paralytically drunk. His association with quarrels contributes to the motif of male conflict that links many of the tales together. The Cook's conflict with Host and Manciple may symbolise professional and commercial tensions in the City. It involves two employed professionals, the Manciple and Cook, neither working independently but employed by higher-status urban groups, an Inn of Court and the guildsmen's 'solempne and a greet fraternitee' (I, 361–87). And those parish fraternity members themselves all want to move up to the next step in the hierarchy and join an even higher-status group: to be burgesses in the guildhall council, even aldermen (I, 369–72). The Manciple's and Cook's type of employment is a reminder of the role and variety of such institutions in late medieval town culture, power and economies. Their tales both focus on employer–employee problems. *The Cook's Tale* is, additionally, signalled as a tale about the urban lower class: the text announces it as the 'tale of . . . a povre man', and identifies as a specifically lower-class vice the tendency of '*Revel*' to lead to dishonesty (I, 4396–8); while the phrase 'oure citee' occurs twice (I, 4343, 4365), and the Cook's London identity is stressed: he is the Cook *of Londoun* (I, 4325), his ale is 'London ale' (I, 382).

The Cook raises the question of how far Chaucer alludes to real people in his *General Prologue* portraits. There was a cook called Roger of Ware and an inn-keeper called Harry Bailey (see Cooper 1996: 60). The question for the critic is not only whether such direct allusions might be there, but what the occasional use of, and possibility of, allusions indicate about how Chaucer conceives his figures, and how realist the style(s) are he employs for them. If the text contains 'faction', what part is it playing in the *fiction*? Targeting living people would mean the Cook's diseased shin and drunkenness are personal attacks, but the main counter-argument against reading the portraits as records of historical individuals is the fact that the details serve other, dramatic or ideological purposes: Harry Bailey's unremitting bossiness throughout the *Tales* is a function of Chaucer's construction of him as one of the displaced centres of authorship and literary organisation in the work; the Knight, even if his lists of battles closely resemble Henry of Lancaster's or Sir John Hawkwood's, is still overwhelmingly an ideological portrait. The literary significance of a passage is not the same as the historicity of any of its details. Being ideological does not mean that all the details are imaginary; it is about how they are deployed. Chaucer's use of historically specific allusions – whether to the siege of Alexandria, the Roncevall hospital, or conceivably Roger of Ware – does not correspond to modern expectations of a neat division between the 'historical' and the 'literary'. They are perhaps best explored as part of his wider technique of mingling general and specific styles of information in the portraits.

7

The *Man of Law's Tale*

A Hagiographic Romance

Like the *Clerk's*, *Second Nun's* and *Physician's Tales*, this is a tale about a woman greatly oppressed whose story demonstrates the triumph of virtue over worldly adversity and oppression. It presents the world as a place of insecurity and mutability, but the heroine has an inner stability born from spiritual strength and her lack of concern for either earthly joy or earthly sorrow. The *Man of Law's Tale* is full of movement: its heroine Custance (a form of the name Constance) gets buffeted around the world, in boats and by circumstances she cannot control, her security constantly snatched away by malign forces. This only underlines the characteristic symbolised by her name, for she herself is completely unmoved and constant because her essential being is safely in another realm: she rests calmly in God's eternal changelessness. She begins and ends her journeys and vicissitudes in the same place, safe with her father in Rome. This frame of security to a narrative of insecurity is only one of several ways in which Custance's experiences are enclosed by textual elements which are at odds with them (see pp. 78–83 below, and David 1976: 118–34).

The plot is filled with implausible coincidences; any periods of happiness and safety the innocent heroine has are temporary and soon destroyed by fresh blows of adversity. This story presents the world humans inhabit as a habitually hostile and untrustworthy place. It resembles in this sense a Hardy novel but, unlike Hardy, Chaucer posits a loving and reliable deity whose power, though beyond this world, keeps the heroine ultimately safe within the untrustworthy world, and, unlike the Victorian novelist, he offers no sense either of inner personality or of a life experience and identity formed in relationship to landscape and community.

The tale of Custance incorporates several motifs found elsewhere in medieval romances; these include a falsely accused wife, a Christian marrying a Saracen, a woman who is punished by being set adrift in a rudderless boat, and the motif of the unsteered boat itself, which in some romances may be magically guided. The plot is similarly a type common in many romances (an example is the fourteenth-century *Ipomedon*): a loosely strung-together sequence of exciting perils, journeys and triumphs spread over years, in which a high-born hero or heroine leaves home and safety, travels widely and ends up back in security and honour, with a reunited family. The tale's basic plot belongs to a group of romances and folktales concerned with a queen falsely accused of a crime; in some versions the tale includes father–daughter incest. Scholars label this the 'calumniated wife' plot. Though there are many analogues, Chaucer drew specifically on Nicholas Trevet's Anglo-Norman tale of Constance (*c.*1300) and was also probably influenced by a version of the plot in Boccaccio's *Decameron* V.2 (*c.*1330) and John Gower's tale of Constance in his *Confessio Amantis* II, lines 587–1598 (*c.*1390); see Bryan and Dempster (1941: 165–81), Ellis (1986: 119–38), Cooper (1996: 127–8).[1]

Hagiography was an immensely popular medieval genre, long neglected by modern criticism, whose interest and cultural and literary importance are now being belatedly recognised. The saint's life offers a literary form in which woman characters, while remaining meek, chaste and virtuous, could be heroic protagonists of sensational adventures, dangers and victories, though the potential for erotic excitement in the depiction of tortured bodies is clearly in some cases an element in the attractions of the genre (on female saints' lives, see Wogan-Brown and Burgess 1996). Saints' lives and romances, both wide categories containing many types of narratives, are often more similar than modern readers might expect. Manuscripts which contain collections of narratives often include romances together with religious works, among them saints' lives. Saints fearlessly defy their enemies, show dauntless endurance and courage, often in martyrdom, and work miracles. Conversely it is not uncommon for romances to have a highly moral, religious or even sombrely penitential important.[2] Though hagiography and romance share many characteristics as genres, tensions and contradictions are discernible within Chaucer's handling of his own merger here of a hagiographic pattern – characterised by a meek hero or heroine where it is God who does all the action really – with a typical romance pattern – where tough and resourceful protagonists survive sensational dangers and triumph over foes through their own supreme capabilities and sometimes with the aid of magic.

In creating this effect of a double genre for the tale, Chaucer makes

Custance a figure of exaggerated power and exaggerated weakness. In its outline of events and sometimes also in the depiction of her actions (for instance, emboldening Hermengild to acknowledge her faith), Custance's story celebrates invincible strength, resourcefulness and repeated victories over all challenges. Yet the mode in which it is told makes it also a canvas depicting an over-ruled and abject female victim, destined to unending insecurity, whose every experience is presented as pity-inducing, who is serially menaced by foes who are virtually demonic and by friends who are seemingly always prevented from valuing or safeguarding her sufficiently. Custance is not a saint: her story is a sort of secular saint's life, and, because she is a secular woman in a patriarchal society, political issues relevant to her female identity in the world – her position as a marriageable daughter, wife and royal person – become as much part of the tale's exploration of the interwoven themes of power and subjugation as do the specifically Christian aspects of power and subjugation which belong to hagiographical and ascetic writing. The rhetorical voice of the narrator, regularly interrupting the narration to comment on its events, is often discordant with the tenor and values of the story: it is strongly anti-feminist, for example, in II, 358–71. The markedly polyphonic and dialectic nature of the text is experienced by the reader both in the texture of writing within the tale itself and also in the relationships between the central narrative and the various passages that frame it: the Host's and Man of Law's speeches on time, Chaucer's writings, and poverty.

The ending of the tale illustrates something of the kind of variation to be found between different extant manuscripts of the *Canterbury Tales*: three manuscripts follow it with a Link passage where the Host invites the poor parish priest to tell the next tale, as another learned man, but another pilgrim suddenly intervenes to protest that the Parson, being a Lollard, will give them a sermon and spread religious disagreement among them, and offers to tell a 'mery' story, without any philosophy, Latin and complex legal terms, that will wake everyone up. Different manuscripts present this obstreperous pilgrim, orthodox in religion but philistinely keen on entertainment rather than moral seriousness in literary tastes, as, variously, the Shipman, the Wife of Bath, or the Squire. It looks possible therefore that Chaucer, at an early stage of planning the *Tales*, toyed with the idea of following the *Man of Law's Tale* with what is now the *Shipman's Tale*, which at some point may have been attributed to the Wife. In many manuscripts the *Squire's Tale* follows the *Man of Law's* (though usually without this epilogue); in others, including the Ellesmere Manuscript, which is usually believed to represent an order for the tales that goes back to Chaucer, the *Wife of Bath's Tale* follows but without this epilogue or, indeed, any other Link passage: we cannot assume the *Wife's* tale was meant to follow the *Man of Law's Tale*, even though that is the situation in modern editions of Chaucer. This epilogue (authenticity unproven) shows both the device of using Harry Bailey as the fictional source of the plan for the tale's order, and the device of using the independent-minded pilgrims to bring about apparently random and unhierarchical sequences of tales. As with the Link passage after the *Knight's Tale*, it shows Bailey trying to continue the story-telling in serious, respectable vein but forced by intervention from a pilgrim to accept a frivolous comedy: the device such Link passages use, of passing fictional responsibility from Bailey's direction to a rebellious member of the audience, could be, on the moral level, Chaucer's method of evading responsibility for the presence of the more disreputable secular fictions in his collection, as well as an exercise in an aesthetic of randomness. 'Blameth nat me', said the narrator who represents the author, in the *Knight–Miller* Link.

The Introduction to the *Man of Law's Tale*: Time, Money and the Author

The Introduction is intriguingly varied, voicing several themes that seem initially quite unrelated to the tale. First comes a lengthy rhetorical allusion by the Host to the fact that it is 10 a.m., followed by a moralistic speech on the virtues of not spending time idly, and the theme of time passing, exemplified by the Host through decidedly worldly and unelevated instances of loss of money and the loss of a peasant girl's maidenhead. He then appeals to the Man of Law who declares he has no tales, since they have all been told by Chaucer. This is an instance of metafiction: the text, referring to its author's texts, briefly makes the readers aware they are in fiction not reality. He lists subjects Chaucer has written about, all concerning lovers and noble and tragic women (Ceyx and Alcyone from his *Book of the Duchess*, and a set of heroines who killed themselves, similar to, though not identical with, those found in his incomplete *Legend of Good Women*).[3] Throughout the *Tales* Chaucer uses stories and links, as we have seen, to explore the figure and function of the writer: this passage signals this theme. Here, with the startling reference to the real-life Chaucer and his oeuvre by a fictional character, as if this character has not been invented by Chaucer and as if the first-person narrator does not appear to represent Chaucer, the particular aspect of authorship that is foregrounded is the issue of the distinction between an author and the narrative voice that presents fiction.

Next the Man of Law prefaces his tale with an invocation to Poverty. At first sight a topic unrelated to that of the writer's art, this can be seen as an indirect reference to the economic realities of authorship: obliquely this passage represents the author's need to be paid. If this is in effect that fairly traditional medieval motif, the author's begging poem to patrons, that prior separation of the speaker from Chaucer the famous writer is a tactful move. Poverty here is presented as a situation to be shunned, which may be appropriate for a begging petition to patrons but is a strange prologue to an unworldly tale in which a rich queen is reduced to destitution and does not care. The pervasive impression of incongruity between these introductory speeches and the ensuing narrative contributes to a disparity perceptible at times throughout the text between Custance's story and the points of view from which it is presented, which will be examined later. Yet these themes of the Introduction are not purposely miscellaneous: we can discern in them motifs and references, albeit in disconcertingly alien mode, which parallel central elements in the tale. The Host's reference to passing time could on the one hand be seen simply as one of Chaucer's practical devices which bring a forward momentum into the Links – the kind of effect we see later when the canon and his yeoman gallop up, or when the *Manciple's Prologue* announces there are only two miles to Canterbury, and the Link after the *Manciple's Tale* says the sun is sinking. It also, however, foreshadows wittily a central theme of the tale: within the fictional everyday scene of the pilgrims on their pilgrimage, it prepares us for the idea of transience which is the counterpart in the tale to Custance's spiritual stability. In contrast to the *Parson's Tale*, which links the whole Canterbury pilgrimage to the soul's spiritual journey, the *Man of Law's Tale* will visualize the soul's state as stillness and the world as constant journeying. The highly secular Host on his sociable worldly pilgrimage presents awareness of transience in a style which is highly incongruent with the lofty mode of the tale: he relates waste of time to financial loss and a peasant's (to him) comic lament for virginity. By the time we come to the *Parson's Tale* Link, where there is a similar rhetorical allusion to time (X, 1–21), the whole warning is transformed into an image of human death, the need to prepare 'fructuously' for Judgement (X, 67–74), and life as a pilgrimage to God (X, 75–80).

The Man of Law's observations about poverty could, somewhat

similarly, be seen as both congruent with the tale's theme of earthly adversity and loss, while voicing through the fictional rich lawyer a completely contrasting tone and a cynical and this-worldly approach to them. The periphery to this tale is thus sharply dialogic, as are the peripheries to the Clerk's and Wife of Bath's tales (see pp. 90 and 122). It provocatively reverses the ethos of the tale it frames, expressing an irreconcilable materialistic viewpoint in the fictional narrator's voice.

A warning against wasting time, though here couched in secular mode, was frequently associated by medieval writers with literary activity. It was commonplace especially of monastic writers in their prologues, to justify putting pen to paper with the plea of eschewing idleness (see the *Second Nun's Prologue* and pp. 195–6). Because they were often dependent on payments from patrons, poverty is another theme sometimes voiced in medieval authors' prologues and epilogues, and especially in 'begging poems' (some of Chaucer's lyrics operate as begging poems, notably the *Complaint of Chaucer to his Purse*). We could see both the passage on wasting time and the passage on money as representations, in disguised form, of convential peripheral themes often presented together with medieval literary compositions: the justification for authorship as a rejection of idleness and the plea for renumeration by the author to a patron. The lament against poverty here may function either as a covert 'begging poem' or more generally as an allusion to the figure and traditional social and economic position of the author, a witty inclusion of one of the classic modes of medieval authors' self-presentation: it is unlikely to be by chance that it follows a rollcall of Chaucer's own works in the same area as this tale. The subject of poverty as an evil to be avoided may also be wittily appropriate to this fictional narrator, a lawyer – since, as is well known, lawyers never open their mouths except with hope of payment.

The tale itself is introduced as if it too is merchandise: the narrator has received it from a merchant. Story-telling is a debt, he jokes in II, 41. He is just now short of a story (II, 127–33; the wording makes it sound as if words are a commodity or ready cash – which is what his professional rhetoric is to a lawyer). This commercial symbolism resurfaces when the fame of Custance is said to have been brought to Syria by international merchants (II, 134–54). This way of depicting the relationship of the teller to his narrative, appropriate as it is to the notorious mercenariness of lawyers and at odds in its worldly materialism with the main import of Custance's story, nevertheless corresponds disconcertingly to the way marriage is also presented in the tale as a transaction between men, with woman as the commodity. Commerce is a very important theme in Chaucer's thinking and writing and it takes many forms. Women, like literature, can be commodities. Custance is shipped out to Syria together with a certain quantity of gold, in exchange for an agreement on the Muslim side to convert to Christianity.

The apparently disconnected sequence of themes in the introduction is thus united above all by the idea of literature: the list of Chaucer's works is the key element. It reminds us of *literariness*: both the tale the Man of Law are literary constructs. It sets the tale of Custance as one of many such tales of unhappy women in which Chaucer seems to have specialised, inside and beyond the *Canterbury Tales*, and also sets the *Tales* in the context of other story collections, the *Legend of Good Women* and those by Ovid and Gower: a reminder that the whole *Canterbury Tales* itself belongs to a particular literary genre, that of the story-collection. Most dramatically of all, it breaks the illusion of fiction momentarily, pointing beyond the illusion of the pilgrims on the Canterbury road, to Chaucer the author, the external creator of it all. The fictional Man of Law is placed during this passage as if he is among the inscribed audience, the readers of Chaucer's books in the real world, It places Chaucer modestly but boldly as an English vernacular writer in a poetic heritage from Ovid to a fellow vernacular contemporary, Gower. The most dramatic of all Chaucer's disruptions of the world of art to point outwards to greater realities will come at the end, when the Parson refuses to tell fiction and directs his listeners, fictional and actual, towards the next world and the business of saving their souls.

The *Man of Law's Tale*

Central to the tale is its spatial symbolism: a woman propelled round the world against her will, twice in a rudderless boat (symbolising her absence of individual will), yet always maintaining her perfect calm, a kind of stillness, because of her trust in God's providence and mercy. The opening comment that travelling merchants brought the tale to England adds a prefatory image of movement. It is not surprising that Chaucer saw this as an appropriate plot onto which to graft echoes of a famous thirteenth-century moral treatise, the *De miseria conditionis humanae*, 'On the Misery of the Human Condition', a classic expression of the medieval concept of 'Contempt for this World'. The unwished for and unfair voyages, oppressions and reversals Custance endures aptly epitomise the misery of the human condition as set forth in that work. Chaucer also incorporates echoes of *Melibee*, another work he translated, which advocates patience in adversity (see p. 176).

To the Custance story as found in other versions, Chaucer adds many rhetorical statements, exclamations and appeals in the narrator's voice, which generalise the plot's events as manifestations of universal, recurrent truths: II, 190–203 on the stars ruling our lives; I, 288–94 where sorrow at Custance's departure is compared to famous classical lamentations over national disasters; II, 295–315, apostrophes (rhetorical addresses) to the First Moving of the 'Crueel firmament', the cosmic mutability that causes all movement; to the unfavourable astronomical influences and the emperor's failure to avoid astrologically unfortunate days; II, 358–71, apostrophe to the pagan sultaness as vice itself; II, 421–7 on the 'sodeyn wo' which changes all worldly joy and effort into bitterness. These rhetorical comments on events, marked as formal and external in style, also at times strike a gratuitously discordant note in content: obvious ones are the complaint against the 'imprudent Emperour', Custance's father (II, 309), and the remarks about sex (II, 708–14). Dinshaw (1989: 88–112) sees this uneasy detachment of the narrator from the narrative as Chaucer's awareness that in some folklore versions this plot contained father–daughter incest, whereas his own narrative stresses father–daughter love but as the benign face of patriarchal social control over women, moving them around as counters in homosocial exchanges and alliances. The narrator's stance of detachment, the tale's rigid division of good and evil, and the extreme control which events and others' wills exercise over the heroine, would all in such a reading express a denial not just of the incest motif but of the tensions and suppression within patriarchal order. Chaucer brings in the incest motif but outside the tale itself, in the *Prologue* (II, 77–89), where the sexual crime is sharply rejected: 'Of swiche cursed stories I sey fy!' The themes of rich traders and perverted father's love in the *Prologue* seem thus to represent aspects of the social control of women which are potentially present in the paternal power that rules Custance but which the narrative denies.

Custance's trials are halted at line 691 with her happy marriage to King Alla, but then the whole cycle begins again: she is again falsely attacked and once again set adrift. If the reader, faced with this repetition of plot motifs already encountered once, thinks 'here we go again', that exactly fits the moral theme, for its message is that life is always changing and happiness inevitably temporary and unstable in this world. It is essentially a Boethian fable: the true nature of the world is mutability and the only reliable happiness lies in trust in the immaterial things

of the spirit, which are not subject to change or unmerited reversals.
Although eventually Custance ends restored to happiness and safety
with her father and her husband, the narrative insists on reminding us of
this fact in the very stanza that records her 'happy ending' on reminding
us of this fact, once again taking the sea as an image of human life:

> This kyng Alla, when he his tyme say,
> With his Custance, his hooly wyf so sweete,
> To Engelond been they come the righte way,
> Wher as they lyve in joye and in quiete.
> But litel while it lasteth, I yow heete,   *warn*
> Joye of this world, for tyme wol nat abyde;
> Fro day to nyght it changeth as the tyde.
>
>   (II, 1128–34)

It continues, with overt verbal repetition:

> That litel while in joye or in plesance
> Lasteth th eblisse of Alla with Custance.
>
>   (II, 1140–1)

It tells us that 'Deeth, that taketh of heigh and logh his rente . . . Out
of this world this kyng Alla he hente' (II, 1142, 1144; notice the narrator's image of money even for death). Custance returns to live in virtue
with her father in Rome. Then with further repetition the narrative says
they live together 'Til deeth departeth them'.

So the motif of the happy ending, the traditional satisfying literary
closure, is itself turned by Chaucer into another cycle of instability. The
true happy contrast to Custance's miseries in the text is not this narrative conclusion – for that turns out only to teach the lesson that every
conclusion is temporary – but the strength of Custance's trust in God's
mercy, shown throughout her troubles. The final lines sum up these two
types of happy solution and put them into their relative importance:

> Now Jhesu Christ, that of his myght may sende
> Joye after wo, governe us in his grace,
> And Kepe us alle that been in this place! Amen.

It is Christ who can provide joy after woe, unlike anything in this
world. The really vital thing is to ask to be governed and trust to be
kept in his grace. The uniting of the two ideas of being governed and

receiving grace is striking: we expect grace to collocate with words like mercy, so that divine grace is a free gift. Here the wording suggests humanity has something to do: submission to being 'governed' and acceptance of what is 'sent' are presented as, if not theological prerequisites, at least accompaniments to the reception of grace. This theme of subjugation has run through all the tale.

Whatever the original effect of the Host's words about the passage of time in the Introduction, we see the narrative of the *Tale* bring together the idea of time passing on the Canterbury road and the theme of earthly mutability, when the narrator comments (II, 1114–20) that he must curtail describing the characters' joy when Custance meets her father, because the pilgrims' day is waning: he must hurry on with his tale. In these final stanzas we are reminded that the movement of the narrative, progressing towards its end, keeps pace with Custance's concluding journeys as they move towards her death, and also that the day of the pilgrim-audience, fictionally external to the tale, is fading. The narrator picks up again this integration of self-reflexive remarks about the progress of his narrative with the tale's theme of mutability in II, 1124–34, when he says he let the material concerning Maurice 'passen by', and continue with the topic of Custance. And as the much-travelled heroine finally approaches Rome again for the last act of her circular earthly journey, from her father and back again to him, he interposes into that narrative a fitting reference to his own finalising efforts, as story-conductor and story-articulator:

> And dame Custance, finally to seye,
> Toward the tourn of Rome goth hir weye.
> . . .
>
> In vertu and in hooly almus-dede
> They lyven alle, and nevere asonder wende;
> Til deeth departeth hem, this lyf they lede.
> And fareth now weel! my tale is at an ende.

(II, 1147–8, 1156–9)

One of the central themes of the tale (a Boethian message) is that God fulfils his will through, and not merely despite, the flux and movement of all things subject to Fortune:

> God liste to shewe his wonderful myracle
> In hire, for we sholde sen his myghty werkis;
> Christ, which that is to every harm triacle,   *medicine*

By certeine meenes ofte, as knowen clerkis,
Dooth thyng for certein ende that ful derk is
To mannes wit, that for oure ignorance
Ne konne noght knowe his prudent purveiance.

(II, 477–83)

This passage expresses confidence that, though only 'clerkis' (Scholars)
can make sense of its mysteries, the world of apparently unreasonable
adversity is under the control of a loving God's providence. The passage
can be contrasted with Dorigen's speech questioning this very proposition in the *Franklin's Tale*, II, 865–93.

Custance is a helpless pawn under multiple domination: subject to
not only the stars' but her parents' will, Christ's commands, and also to
the general law of the 'thraldom' and punishment of women under
men. She says to her father, as she sets off:

'Allas, unto the Barbre nacioun
I moste anoon, syn that it is youre wille;
But Crist, that starf for our redempcioun   *died*
So yeve me grace his heestes to fulfille!   *commands*
I, wrecche womman, no fors though I spille!   *even if I perish*
Wommen are born to thraldom and penance,
And to been under mannes governance.'

(II, 281–7)

Woman's congenital states is slavery and punishment, for Eve's crime. The
annexation here of the theme of women's sexual subjugation, to a wider
range of domination, is repeated again at II, 708—14, when a whole
stanza is devoted to pointing out that even the holiest of wives must accept
sex: 'Thye moste take in pacience at nyght / Swiche manere necessaries . .
.'. Sex becomes a metonymic sign of other ways in which female free will
and subjectivity is curbed and expropriated. This identification of the
female self subjugated to others' will is paradoxically close to the qualiti-
ties that makes Custance a perfect ruler, ideal queen of all Europe:

'In hire is heigh beautee, withoute pride,
Yowthe, withoute grenehede or flye;   *immaturity*
To alle hire werkes vertu is hire gyde;
Humblesse hath slayn in hire al tirannye.
She is mirour of alle curteisye'

(II, 162–6)

Medieval treatises about kingship were much concerned with the difference between a true king (generous, responsible, unselfish and accepting subjection to the law) and a tyrant. Though it may not immediately seem so, there is a line of thought which links Chaucer's frequent references both to tyranny and patience under adversity: as Burnley shows (1979: 11–19), the role of a ruler (and Custance is constantly a queen, moving among people of authority) was usually analysed is essentially psychological terms in the medieval period. A king or queen with personal desires under control would not be a tyrant. When the narrative gets to Alla and Donegild these themes of kingship and meekness surface again: Alla is a king who acts with compassion but his mother Donegild is 'ful of tirannye' (II, 696). There is an element in this of the Mirror for Princes tradition: literature that teaches rulers how to act. At one point the narrator addresses, as his inscribed readership, queens, duchesses and ladies, pointing out that Custance provides an instance of how 'blood roial' may find itself without friends at a time of need (Anne of Bohemia was a foreign emperor's daughter, with a special devotion to St Anne, mentioned in II, 641).

Though Custance's trust in a father-like deity is in one sense justified by the way she is repeatedly saved by the plot, and her happy ending is to return to her father – back to her source and begetter, it was her father, and patriarchal assumptions about the right of men to barter women as pawns in exchanges between them, that set her off on her trials. The narrator's rhetorical interjections make wandering Custance a figure representing both women's 'thraldom' under the will of fathers, families and national policies ('O Emperoures yonge doghter', II, 447) and, more generally, hapless and ignorant humanity swept hither and thither by Fortune, like the globe itself 'hurled' by the 'firste moevyng! Cureel firmament' (II, 274–301, 446–8). God is there but distant, above change: 'He that is lord of Fortune' (II, 448), just as the father, 'Emperour of Rome', remains on the frame of the story, sending his daughter out and receiving her back. Custance, as representative of the power of Rome, bringing religious conquest to Syria, converting the pagan Northumbrians, is also the 'doghter of hooly chirche' (II, 674). Daughterhood becomes in this narrative a symbol of one of Chaucer's favourite concepts: 'pacience' – obedience in the face of whatever is sent, in trust that beyond the immediate travail there is a divine father and home. Evil is defined as, and displaced onto, the Other: primarily Satan, enemy of God and the Church. The human villains are instruments of this essence of evil, Satan, and each embodies a psychological Other to masculine control: a lecher consumed with desire for a woman, and two older women: the 'feendlych' and 'mannysh' tyrant, the Queen Mother Donegild, and the Sultaness, who adds to the sins of being female and powerful that of being Muslim.[4] As in the antisemitic *Prioress's Tale*, evil is externalised and territorialised both psychologically and politically, whereas the protagonist is an oppressed representative of complete innocence.

Why does Chaucer assign a lawyer to this tale? It is impossible to hold that the main purpose of the tale is to tell us more about the personality or professional life-experience of the Sergeant of Law described in the *General Prologue*. This not a tale about lawyers, a legal case ancient or modern (the Physician's tale of the false judge Appius would do better for that), or London legal life, nor about some weighty issue of justice. The direct links between teller and tale are few and on the surface. Initially Host and Man of Law exchange aptly legal-sounding banter in II, 33–45, but having neatly made thus direct reference back to the teller's profession, Chaucer has no intention of creating a straightforwardly 'lawyer's tale'. Two stylistic features remind us of the narrator's fictional profession: wording which stresses the notion of 'law', especially as a way of describing Christianity and Islam as two opposed laws, for example II, 220–4; and the narrator's rhetorical and emotionally persuasive comments and appeals to an audience. And we have noticed the potential for anti-lawyer satire in the narrator's prologue concerned with money.

At the deeper level, however, this tale of the subjugation of human beings, significantly here a woman, to a relentlessly oppressive order of things gains from its attribution to a leading Man of Law. When we juxtapose the subject-matter of the tale with the concept of a male judge, we can perceive the external duress, the lack of self-determination or security which rule all Custance's experience both as an inescapable law of life, as Boethius would have us believe, and as patriarchal oppression.

Adding law and a lawyer to this tale places it in both a benign and a malign light: tragedy and human helplessness seem part of natural law and divine order, on one hand, and on the other the imposition of order, as it affects women in patriarchal society, is revealed as brutal and exploitative. Like the *Knight's Tale* it celebrates order, power and control and it presents them as necessary principles in human life, but dialectically it also reveals the destructive pain of such hierarchical suppression. As the Knight represents those who dominate and regulate regions of England, in economy and administration, so the London Sergeant is a regulator of order in the legal world, and the two men are associated with similar tales. In both stories individuals must abandon freedom, free will and desire; the female must be subjugated: women's marriage serves the will of others; and amid a bleak world security resides only with the father–ruler–deity: in the *Knight's Tale* this is Theseus–Saturn–the First Mover and in the *Man of Law's Tale* it is God and Custance's father.

8

The *Wife of Bath's Prologue and Tale*

The problem with the Wife of Bath – for the critic – is that she seems so real: more than any other character in English literature she tempts us into talking about what *she* says or does, rather than what Chaucer is doing in his presentation of her. The *Wife of Bath's Prologue*, far from being the spontaneous outpouring of an individual reporting her highly individual life and outlook – or the fictional equivalent of that – is a tissue of literary allusions, and much of it would have sounded like that to a contemporary audience. So the first question for the critic is how Chaucer creates so strong an impression that we are hearing a real person speaking out of a real life. The second question is whether Chaucer's creation is feminist or anti-feminist in its effect: the text may seem a defence of women's rights, especially to modern readers, but the Wife embodies most of the faults for which medieval anti-feminist authors condemned women. This double text (*Prologue* and *Tale*) also raises sharply the by-now familiar question for the reader of the *Canterbury Tales* of how the teller relates to the tale.

Because of the text's fame in English literature, we approach it with preconceptions and an image of what sort of figure the Wife is. Kittredge's theory of it as the first salvo in the Marriage Debate has been widely influential, characterising the Wife's tale as a text constructed to be the programmatic opposite of the *Clerk's Tale*: representing wifely dominance, or *maistrie*, just as the Clerk's is the counter-representation of wifely obedience (see pp. 120–1). Yet we shall see the Wife's and Clerk's tales in agreement on many issues: not only on their shared theme of virtue as true nobility, but even on the topic of submissiveness, for the conclusion of the Wife's story teaches voluntary submissiveness as an answer to many problems, social as well as marital. Hansen (1992: 26–57) warns of ways in which the text's renewed fame in the history of modern feminism has sometimes led to pre-suppositions about the Wife as entirely triumphant and powerful, especially in her use of language to turn the tables on male authority; this sort of over-sanguine feminist perception neglects the complexity with which the text presents the feminist task of speaking against misogyny. Her speech is always framed within, and framed to respond to, masculine authority, and her male author counters the potential of this figure to speak – subversively or directly – for women, by anti-feminist or conservative controls in the text.

There is not the consistency we would expect from a text expressing the point of view of a fully characterised personality. The popular image of the Wife of Bath in modern culture sees in her a celebration of uncomplicated lust, and her language in the *Prologue* is certainly bawdy, yet the first part of her *Prologue* is intellectual and theological in content, and distinctly academic in mode, as she analyses the meaning of a number of biblical passages long disputed by scholarly interpreters, and conducts a debate about them in what is essentially the university lecture-style of her era, citing authorities *pro* and *contra* an argument and analysing the strength of the cases.[1] On her lustfulness the *Prologue* has inconsistent statements: III, 203 says she had no interest in sex, and III, 408–17 says she consented to it with her first three husbands only to get money out of them; in III, 508 she praises her fifth husband's ways in bed; in III, 485 she assures us she never committed adultery, but III, 622–6 boasts that her indiscriminate promiscuity knew no bounds.[2] What Chaucer is giving us here are a number of different medieval anti-feminist stereotypes of women, attributed to this speaker who is a representative Wife: they are not attempts to paint the sexual personality of a coherently conceived individual character. There is also inconsistency between the Wife as presented in the *Prologue* as greedy for money, spending her time at a funeral looking out for a new husband, and the *Wife of Bath's Tale*, which preaches that poverty is to be desirable because it brings a person closer to God (III, 1201–2).

The text does not always say what its reputation, or our literary preconceptions, or first impressions, lead us to expect it to say, and Chaucer also often designs it to say more than one thing at once. The opening couplet,

'Experience, though noon auctoritee
Were in this world, is right ynogh for me . . .'

is the Wife's famous declaration of the validity of experience against the bookish *auctoritee* which formed so much of the basis of knowledge in a pre-scientific, pre-experimental age. *Auctoritee* meant both authority and the authority of books, of ancient authors. Against this, the couplet champions the life-experience on which women traditionally base their opinions, against the authority of the official, male-dominated, world of learning. Yet the sentence goes on:

> '. . . is right ynogh for me
> To speke of wo that is in mariage'.
>
> (III, 2–3)

Is the real meaning of these three lines then something far more pessimistic and anti-feminist? Is the *Prologue* going to be a demonstration of how miserable marriage is? For whom? The socially oppressed wife? The Wife's wife-oppressed husbands? Or for all parties in human marriage? This third line draws on a branch of misogyny – misogamy, 'hatred of marriage' – which condemned marriage (and saw marriage as the special province of women).

Lines 1–3 are, in fact, as they evolve – and in spoken performance we absorb poetry in time, serially – saying several different things. They do indeed defend *experience* boldly against *auctoritee*, wisdom from life against knowledge from books, female consciousness against male hegemony; but they also introduce the idea of the traditional misogynist assertion that marriage proves to be 'wo' for men, and it is women like the Wife who know just how to make it so. These lines say something in little about how this text is both imaginatively pro-women and cynically anti-women. They also illustrate how Chaucer's writing is frequently polyphonic – many-voiced – not just because the *Canterbury Tales* contains so many fictional voices, but because in one sentence several registers and worldviews may be there to be heard.[3]

The *Prologue*

The *Prologue* is in three parts: a discussion of marriage and virginity, a description of the Wife's methods of dealing with her first three husbands, and narratives of her relationship to her fourth and fifth. The last ends with the famous battle of the book: Alison becomes so outraged by her clerk-husband's readings from an anti-feminist book of examples of wicked wives from history and legend, she takes physical revenge, tearing the book and hitting him. This clash of mind and body takes us back to the opening lines, with the conflict between the masculine world of books and *auctoritee* and the female *experience* which it often denigrates. It also focuses on the misogynists' stereotype of women as aggressive and incapable of reasoning. The Wife's physical reaction to the anti-feminist book exemplifies precisely the faults anti-feminists claimed women had, yet at the same time it dramatises women's dilemma in such a society: masculine control of culture and of the cultural image of women leaves women no place to reply within it. This final episode epitomises a contradiction at the heart of the whole text. What seem from the culture's masculinist point of view faults in the Wife which prove the inferiority of women, can also reveal the deficiencies and contradictions in that masculinist discourse.

The Wife's discussion of marriage, widowhood and virginity (III, 1–162), draws on classic early Christian texts about the superiority of celibacy to marriage. St Jerome's *Against Jovinian* (AD 393) was a pro-celibacy tract which formed part of a debate in the early Church about the relative power of priests and laity. In the fourth-century Church, celibacy was becoming the distinctive mark of the priesthood, and Jerome was replying to the views of Jovinian who had defended the status of lay-members by arguing that marriage did not make them spiritually or morally lower than celibates. Jerome's own arguments, though ascetic and often anti-feminist, contain praise of many chaste wives and widows, but he included within his book quotations from Theophrastus', *Golden Book of Marriage*, which is flamboyantly anti-feminist and anti-marriage (see Blamires 1992: 63–77). The *Wife of Bath's Prologue* discusses some of Jerome's points:

> Jovinian had argued that St Paul had sanctioned marriage: 'It is better to marry than burn' (1 Corinthians 7:9).

> Jerome countered that this was only where the alternative would be fornication; it was like saying that wheat flour is better than coarse barley bread, but barley bread can be eaten 'if it will save a starving person from having to eat cow dung'.

> Jovinian had argued that, since Abraham and Isaac had several wives, it must be acceptable for widows to remarry.

> Jerome replied that when, in John 4:17, Jesus told the Samaritan with five husbands that her fifth man was not her husband, he meant remarriages were not real marriages. The Wife alludes to these arguments in III, 14–29, 55–61, and 142–6 (adding to the barley bread

dispute the gospel-based point that Jesus used barley bread to feed the five thousand). Other arguments derived from *Against Jovinian* include those about the reasons for genitals, the comparison of marriage to lowly dishes of wood and clay, and the need for virgins to be born of married parents.

St Paul furnished some of the other material:

'It is good for a man not to touch a woman.'
1 Corinthians 7:1 (III, 87)

'Wives, submit to your husbands. . . . Husbands love your wives'
Colossians 3:18–19 (III, 160–2)

Another Pauline precept, 'the marriage debt', gave rise to the comic equation between money and sex Chaucer exploits with the Wife in Bath and the unfaithful wife of the *Shipman's Tale*: Paul's concept of the duty, for both partners, of not withholding sex from a spouse, 1 Corinthians 7:4. This marriage 'duty', *debitum* in Latin, was translated as 'debt'. The Wife appropriates the idea to justify her manipulation of sex for money (III, 411), and her bullying – her husband becomes her 'dettour and . . . thral' (III, 155).

Her whole *Prologue* contravenes 1 Timothy 2:12–15, 'I suffer not a woman to teach, nor to usurp authority over a man' (also 'Let your women keep silent in churches: for it is not permitted to them to speak', 1 Corinthians 14:34). Medieval women were forbidden to preach or to be university students. Women were believed to be less rational than men, to be more sensual, earthly, and material: Aristotle had believed the father supplies the 'form' which makes the offspring a rational human being, but the mother only supplies the matter (see Blamires 1992: 38–49). The Wife speaks, and speaks at length (as the Friar, a man and a professional preacher, complains, III, 829–55); she conducts an argument, citing and dissecting biblical authorities as efficiently as a university debater. The intelligence with which she wields arguments counters the anti-feminist tradition that women were stupid. Yet Chaucer also credits her with some grossly sensual statements (III, 37–8, 151–2); his debating woman may be intimidating but her principles are (to a misogynist) reassuringly low.

The Wife cleverly uses traditional arguments in new combinations and against each other: Paul's 'debt' theory is deployed against Jerome's arguments about genitals in III, 129–32. Her summaries of arguments often expose the weakness of interpretations she attacks, for instance on the Samaritan's fifth husband (III, 15–25). Against that tortuous style of interpretation, typical of an 'exegetical' approach to the Bible, which was already falling out of favour in Chaucer's day, the term 'Jhesus, God and man' (III, 15) raises a very pointed counter-argument, one far closer to the Bible's actual text, that the Incarnation implies respect for the human body. There may be a parallel here to Wycliffite demands for plainer biblical teaching to replace the super-structure of elaborate interpretation which centuries of clerical exege-sis had laid over the Christian message.[4] When the Wife quotes Jesus's command about poverty (III, 105–11), this direct gospel quotation is perhaps used to hit at the contemporary Church's reluctance to acknowledge that its wealth was contrary to gospel values; she uses the celibates' contention that virginity represents 'perfeccion' (III, 105) to imply that clerics trying to live perfectly should also practise poverty and give money to the poor.

The fourth-century debate about whether widows should remarry was hardly a topical issue, but we begin to see why Chaucer might have made it a topic for his Wife of Bath. It had been part of a wider conflict over power in the early Church, which the clerical party had won. As non-celibate, lay, and female, Chaucer's Wife represents groups excluded from highest status in the Christian Church in its traditional structure. Wycliffites were advocating more status for the laity, reduc-tion in the Church's economic power, and the abolition of clerical celibacy. There is potentially a protest against priestly dominance of the contemporary Church hidden in the Wife's rumbustious debates about virginity (i.e. the priests) and the married state (i.e. laypeople). Chaucer shows the Pardoner, Friar and Summoner, representatives of the most criticised elements in the Church, all trying to interrupt this speaking laywoman. There were many other reasons to depict women and *clerkes* as enemies: celibate clerics had produced much of the corpus of anti-feminist and anti-marriage literature; women were barred from the *clerkes'* preserves of priesthood, education, Latin literacy, intellectual debate and preaching. What better voice than a woman's, then, to voice Wycliffite opposition to the power of the priests? It is appropriate in view of women's legitimate grievances against an intellectual tradition that belittled them, and it could also be safely dismissed as simply an illustration of archetypal female aggressiveness and sensuality. The *Prologue* is, certainly, primarily about conflict between men and women, but like most of Chaucer's explorations of the relationships between the sexes, and the power structures of marriage, it sees these as reflections of a wider social context.

Given that the material in the first section is academic and the structure of the arguments is complex; how does Chaucer make it sound so
fresh, personal and alive? The answer lies in his skill with speech: it is
personalised by the frequency of *I*, *me*, *my*; and the illusion of immedi-
acy, of speech taking place in a three-dimensional reality – a woman
talking to listeners who are around her – is created by frequent use of
we, *oure*, *ye*, *yow*, and even more powerfully by forms which imply the
presence of interlocutors, in particular the use of question and
commands: 'Herkne eek', 'lo . . . I pray yow', 'telleth me . . .', 'Telle me
also', 'to what conclusion . . .?', 'Why sholde men . . .?', 'I pray yow,
telleth me. / Or where commanded he virginitee?', spoken discourse
markers of the type of 'Lo', 'eek', 'I woot', 'I trowe' and frequent use of
'But' to mark a new topic. She is a one-woman debate, answering
objections, hearing opponents' points, urging her interlocutors to take
her point: 'But that I axe, why . . .?', 'I graunte it wel . . .', 'For wel ye
knowe . . .', 'sey ye no?'

The second section uses such devices too, and extends that sense of
a drama acted out with unseen interlocutors by introducing into
speeches by the Wife her responses to what her husbands are supposed
to have said: 'Thou seyst . . .', 'Thou seyst . . .', 'Thou seyst . . .', 'Thou
seyedst this . . .', 'Thou liknest...', 'Thou liknest', (III, 248–376). This
verbal strategy does not just add realism, bringing the Wife and her
husbands' quarrels (and her victories) to life: it also brings anti-feminist
arguments into the text, allegedly voiced by the husbands:

> Thou seist that oxen, asses, hors, and houndes
> They been assayed . . .   *tested*
> But folk of wyves maken noon assay
>
> (III, 285–90)

This, like much in the Wife's replies to her husbands, comes from
Theophrastus (extract in Blamires 1992: 70–1). Her actions too are
derived from anti-feminist texts: Theophrastus said wives grumble at
husbands at night, within the bed-curtains, the so-called 'curtain
lectures': the Wife's complaints in III, 236–41 are from this passage
(Blamires 1992: 70). The Wife's behaviour at the funeral, looking out
for her next husband (III, 587–99), is from the anti-feminist *Mirror of
Marriage* by Chaucer's French contemporary Eustache Deschamps
(Bryan and Dempster 1941: 220). It also appears in the *Lamentations of
Mathéolus* (*c*.1371; sometimes called the *Evil of Marriage*), a misogynist
satire featuring the miseries of a man who marries a wily widow

(Blamires 1992: 177–97). Anti-feminist themes were passed on from one era to another; there is often no single source for Chaucer's details, like women's taste for gadding about (III, 553–9). The thirteenth-century Bartholomaeus Anglicus says a bad wife 'cries and quarrels, is drunk, lecherous, changeable, contrary, costly, inquisitive, envious, lazy, wearisome, wandering, bitter, suspicious, and hateful'.[5] It sums up much of Chaucer's Wife of Bath. In many respects, the details that compose the *General Prologue* are chosen to convey themes, not verisimilitude, for instance the reference to the age of twelve, the legal age of marriage for girls, probably underlines the Wife's representative status as a generic wife. Yet Chaucer's handling, not only in such virtuoso technical skills as his representation of speech, but also in the text's capacity to imply subtle psychological links and complexities, means that to analyse the poem primarily as a patchwork of inherited conventions misses as many of its meanings as a wholly character-based approach does. The twelve-year-old bride may have a representative function, yet it meshes in with the Wife's dismissal of her old husbands as 'bacon', whose failure to give her 'delit' justifies taking their money; the exploited tend to become exploiters. The *Wife's*, *Merchant's* and *Shipman's Tales* show this, within marriages, without approval but also without surprise.

A masculine fear fostered by male-dominated society is the difficulty of ascertaining a wife's real love, and anti-feminist literature exploited this in its pictures of wives using sex only for gain, or lacking grief at the funeral. The second section shows the Wife exploiting her three old husbands for money. Her definition of a good husband is a rich and old one.

During marriage a medieval woman was dependent on her husband, losing almost all legal and financial rights – and the Wife's sexual manipulation of her husbands for clothes and money reflects that – but widows gained legal autonomy and usually inherited one-third of the property. Once the old husbands have made over their 'lond and hir tresoor' to the young Alison (III, 204), she takes no pains to please them any more. Chaucer makes his *General Prologue* Wife a widow and a businesswoman, and the *Prologue* shows a mercantile approach to marriage as her trade:

> Wynne whoso may, for al is for to selle . . .
> For wynnyng wolde I al his lust endure
>
> (III, 414, 416)

A source for the mercenary Wife is La Vieille, the old woman, in the *Romance of the Rose*, who advises women on how to fleece men, since

'All men betray and deceive women . . . Therefore we should deceive them in return' (Blamires 1992:161), and behind La Vieille lies Ovid's Dipsas, an old prostitute (*Amores*, 1.8 in Blamires 1992: 21–3). The *Prologue* is in a satirical tradition where vices are described in self-revealing speeches by figures who embody them; so is the *Pardoner's Prologue* (see p. 150). Chaucer, however, develops the device of putting anti-feminist material into the mouth of a woman in such a way that it can also attack anti-feminism: he depicts his Wife of Bath often in argument both with men and men's misogyny.

The ambiguous structure of the *Prologue* seems at first the cruellest of tricks against women: to stage an attack on women's detractors and then to reveal its spokeswoman as one who exemplifies all their charges against women. And historical information seems at first only to deepen the negativity of the portrayal, revealing that the characteristics which modern feminism applauds – such as boldness, the capacity to argue, articulacy, sexual honesty, the desire for freedom and autonomy – were regarded as faults in an age which required the ideal woman to be restrained, passive, quiet, uninclined to sex, confined to the house, and obedient. The problems post-Victorian feminism faced differ from those medieval defenders of women faced; the medieval stereotype was that women were more prone to sin than man, and inherently lustful, deceitful and untrustworthy. Many qualities that make the Wife like a confident, outspoken modern feminist actually imprison her in the medieval definition of a bad woman, and Chaucer darkens the picture with the mercenary, deceitful and gross elements. Yet all is not pessimistic. The modern first impression, that she represents a positive defence of women, does have support in the text: first, the fact that Chaucer makes her a protester and not just a Dipsas-type *exposé* of female tricks; secondly, the fact that none of the husbands (in as far as they are presented at all) evokes sympathy; thirdly, the attractions of her energy, wit, cleverness and candour, which are, as we have seen, presented through spoken-discourse devices that create a sense of being drawn into the views of the speaker. Chaucer's stylistic skill in presenting direct speech itself strengthens the female case for recognition: the obstreperous voice is undeniably, palpably *there*, the style claims – demanding to be heard. Most of all, the double bind in which Chaucer places his representative Wife – damned (by oppression) if she does not complain, damned (as a bad woman) if she does – is not just his invention as author; it corresponds exactly to the double bind in which real wives were caught in such a society, which demanded that they submit in order to be acceptable, and cut them off from education and economic power.

Chaucer makes the Wife, in her own way, voice this crucial problem: the problem that the only language in which women can speak, the inherited cultural language of gender identities and sexual relationships, is itself male-created. Men, often celibate *clerks*, have written the agenda: the literary tradition is masculinist:

> By God, if wommen hadde writen stories,
> As clerkes han withinne hire oratories,
> They wolde han writen of men moore wikkednesse
> Than al the mark of Adam may redresse.
>
> (III, 693–6)

This passage seems to show Chaucer's awareness, at least, of the problem Hansen explores (see pp. 89–90), that woman's protest and challenge to male culture is undercut because men have written the language of that culture which characterises female independence as 'wikkednesse'.

The fight over Jankyn's book illustrates this: we as readers experience the endless tirade of clerical misogyny – as it has gone on through endless centuries – including the jibe about female anger (the book is another device for getting anti-feminist attacks on women into the text). The wife has no resources but anger and violence against it.[6] If the ambiguity of Chaucer's presentation of her, here and in general, is not just a cruel anti-feminist joke, then the acuity with which Chaucer's text shows how difficult it is to protest against misogyny without infringing its stereotype of the good woman, does something all fiction has the power to do: it shows up the tensions and denials within an ideology. The explicit conclusion he suddenly gives to the Wife of Bath's narrative of her married *wo* with Jankyn offers, however, a different and very unrevolutionary social paradigm: a voluntary submissiveness on her part that brings resolution of conflict. And that will prove also to be the concluding message of the *Wife of Bath's Tale*.

If we ask what aspect of authorship the *Prologue* represents, at first sight it is the author as autobiographer. But autobiography as a genre and a concept – a text which is interesting primarily simply as an account of another human being's experience of life – was not really known in medieval society.[7] Moreover the Wife is fiction, and she is a woman. The *Prologue* is an extended exercise in the author's role as ventriloquist, acting the role of his characters. Both the subjects Chaucer uses for his extended first-person texts in the *Tales*, the Pardoner and the Wife, have attributes that make that element of theatricality, and that distinct gap of veracity between the author and the words the character speaks, particularly clear: the Pardoner is a professional liar, and the Wife of Bath is a woman whereas Chaucer is a man. The extent to which first-person writing is a mask is particularly clear with these two subjects. (Perhaps it also indicates Chaucer's consciousness of the special challenge of a masculine author writing in a woman's voice that for both the Prioress and the Second Nun he moves into a very formal mode, prayer, as their Prologues. It may indicate his equivalent to Jane Austen's recognition that she could not write dialogue for men when there were not women present.) On the theatricality of the Wife of Bath, see Rogerson (1998).

The *Wife of Bath's Tale*

The *Wife of Bath's Tale* is about transformation. An old hag becomes, through magic, young and beautiful; a nasty arrogant youth is turned, through a lecture by the hag, into a husband who takes others' wishes more into account. The tale's own message (its lecture) for social transformation is that the rich should act with virtue, not arrogance, and the poor should see their state as a blessed opportunity for spiritual well-being. More than in any other tale, Chaucer here presents relations between the sexes as a mirror of social and political relationships. It starts with a rape, which is called an 'oppressioun' (III, 889); it ends with a resolution of conflict through the voluntary abnegation of rights. Like the Wife, the hag, having won a degree of 'maistrie', willingly becomes obedient to her husband (III, 1255–6).[8]

It was a stroke of genius by Chaucer to make the *Wife of Bath's Tale* so unexpectedly unlike the *Prologue*. It is a tale, like the *Pardoner's Tale*, with a sense of mystery and the supernatural at its centre, and also philosophical dignity. Like the Wife's *Prologue* it is about sex and inequalities of power, but in a different mode. Despite its anti-knightly message, the tale is in a knightly genre; it is a short Arthurian romance. The heroine is, like the Green Knight in *Sir Gawain and the Green Knight*, what folklorists call a 'shape-shifter', a human who can change form. Two romances, *Sir Gawain and the Loathly Lady* and *Sir Gawain and Dame Ragnell*, and Gower in *Confessio Amantis*, tell a version of the story (Bryan and Dempster 1941: 223–68).

King Arthur's name and the words 'greet honour' in the first two lines establish expectations of a Golden Age of knighthood, but the knight we meet abuses his power to rob a maiden of her virginity 'by verray force' (III, 882–8). Already the Wife has introduced the theme of the replacement of beautiful antique myth with exploitative modern reality by her comic picture of predatory friars taking the place of the Elf Queen and her fairies (see the illuminating, and very different, readings of this passage by Finke and Fradenburg, both in Beidler 1996: 171–88, 205–20). King Arthur's grant to his wife of the right to sentence the rapist prefigures the power the tale will later give to its female protagonist. Yet the queenly power is only power temporarily ceded by the King, and throughout the tale power or rights given to women are kept within a structure of masculine dominance. Thus the hag uses her cleverness and magic to educate and comfort the youth in the exercise of his own power; she thinks it worth marrying him and gives up to him the 'maistrie' won from him by her superior wisdom. 'Maistrie' turns in the final twist of the inherited plot to be her ability to turn herself into the kind of woman who most conforms to male desires. The grounds she gives for valuing old, ugly women are male-pleasing ones: they will not cuckold their husbands. The surprises in the tale, the moments when it seems to depart from established power assumptions, all turn out to be muted, at least in terms of social and gender politics; they teach obedience and *pacience* (III, 1198), in worldly matters, and submission to God. The balance is redressed, it is true, back towards assertiveness, but in unsubtle terms and, as in the *Clerk's Tale*, outside the tale itself, by a swing into a quite different mode – the Wife's aggressive and mercenary final prayer–curse against husbands who will not submit. In 1380, a woman called Cecily Champain agreed to drop a charge of rape against Chaucer in the Court of Chancery (see Pearsall 1992: 135–8); the background is unknown and therefore it is not clear what bearing it might have on the treatment of rape in this tale.

The tale is interrupted, III, 925–82, with an anti-feminist passage and an embedded story about Midas's wife. Chaucer seems to take special pains to bring a reminder of the voice of the pilgrim-narrator, the Wife from the *Prologue*, into the tale, and this passage in content and style (*we*, *oure*, *us*) does that. At several points a first-person speaking voice introduces a new section, as in III, 914 and 983. It is, however, a carefully limited touch: there is none of the *Prologue*'s bawdy, its first-person anecdotes or aggressive appeals to the audience; the old woman cites *auctoritees* respectfully rather than challenging them, she advocates docility rather than self-advancement, and her attitude to men is maternally nurturing rather than adversarial or exploitative.

Misogynist assumptions in the plot go unquestioned: first, there is the whole idea that 'what women want' is so difficult to answer; next, the answer itself – that they want domination; and finally, the instant acquiescence of every woman to this answer. These unquestioned assumptions are akin to the way the *Prologue* used a woman to voice anti-woman clichés, but without any irony here. The old woman is, nevertheless, the most powerful figure in the plot: in her magic, her power of coercing the knight to marry her, her possession of the knowledge to answer the knight's question, her apparent double-life as the Elf Queen, and perhaps most of all in the calm and amused contempt with which Chaucer depicts her observing her spoilt husband's sulky writhings and temper-tantrum – another passage of realist writing residing in Chaucer's special skills with representing speech, response, and the gestures that accompany speech.

Chaucer used a bourgeois woman in the *Prologue* to challenge theories that underwrote the priests' special status; in the tale he uses a low-born woman to challenge the theories that supported the special status of the *gentil* class. The idea that virtue, rather than ancestry, was true *gentillesse* was often stated by fourteenth-century writers, notably by Dante in his *Convivio* (*c*. 1307; see Burnley 1979: 151–70). As in the *Franklin's Tale*, Chaucer combines a vision of marital power-conflicts solved through voluntary forbearance by those to whom rights have been given, with an exploration of social ranks; like the *Franklin's Tale*, this tale questions whether the *gentil* have, inherently, qualities that non-*gentils* cannot possess. Here, however, the exploration is wider, considering the respect due to the old and the ugly, as well as the issue of *gentillesse*. The central arguments against conservative positions are religious ones, and that is what gives the attack on the 'lineage' theory of *gentillesse* its boldness:

> 'But, for ye speken of swich gentillesse   *because*
> As is descended out of old richesse,
> That therfore sholden ye ben gentil men.
> Swich arrogance is nat worth an hen.'
>
> (III, 1109–12)

Christ is called the source of all claims to gentility (III, 1117), both as the leader of Christians, and the source of virtues, which are the criteria for *gentillesse*, but also because all are equal in Christ. The hag denies the label *gentil* to aristocrats who do evil, and celebrates the rise of humbly-born Tullius Hostilius into the nobility. Yet her lecture is not urging democracy: the section on *gentillesse* (III, 1109–76), centres most of all on the plea to the ruling class to behave well, and the section on poverty (III, 1177–1206) is a plea for the lower classes to be contented. The recipe for social wellbeing is not social or economic change, but individual moral reform: if high and low behaved well there would, after all, be no need for social conflict, for the poor, far from *challenging* the 'possessioun' of the rich could recognise their own advantage in being in a position where no robber challenges what they possess (III, 1187–1200): the political doctrine is bland but the language has a potentially sharp application to real-life challenges from the poor against the power of the rich. There is behind these two conservative social lessons a spiritual conviction, one we have seen already in the *Man of Law's Tale*, that true reality lies in the relationship of the soul to heaven. That is why true poverty, 'verray poverte', can sing 'properly', legitimately: for true poverty is an emptying of the soul of attachment to this world. There is a shift here from concern with issues of power and conflict within human society, between sexes and between ranks, to a sense that all reality lies in heaven, a message that will be expressed dramatically in the last pages of the *Canterbury Tales*.

For the moment, though, interpersonal conflict, in the form we have become familiar with in the fictional pilgrim group, enters as the tale finishes. The Link revives at first the conflict between the Wife and the ecclesiastical males (it would have been interesting to have the Prioress's and nuns' reactions). The Friar praises her grasp of scholastic, university-type disputation (III, 1270–4), warns her off this male preserve (III, 1275–8), and then alludes to her implied promiscuity (III, 1279–85), by suggesting she might like to tell a tale about summoners. A Link quarrel between a male and female pilgrim thus serves the purpose of bringing back homosocial conflict, and that is the springboard for the next two tales, the *Friar's* and *Summoner's*. In as far as the *Wife of Bath's Prologue and Tale* function, as Kittredge visualised, as a challenge that calls for a reply in the form of the *Clerk's Tale*, that connection is not made in the Headlink to the *Clerk's Tale* (which begins a new fragment); but it is made retrospectively in the Clerk's words after his tale (IV, 1171–2), and his Envoy: a song in honour, it seems, of the Wife and her 'secte' (a word with sexual and Wycliffite connotations) of 'archewyves', urging them on to yet further use of their tongues in the cause of female boldness, government, protest, disrespect, pleasure, extravagance, flirtation and creation of male *wo in mariage*. With friends like this, what woman needs enemies?

9

The *Friar's* and the *Summoner's Tales*

Realism and Moral Satire

These tales are fabliaux about the punishment of cheats, 'beguilers beguiled' in the Reeve's phrase (I, 4321). They are paired by the frame-story fiction of their tellers' quarrel and also by deeper points of relationship and interaction between the tales themselves. In the two Links and the *Friar's Tale* conclusion the spiteful fury of the two pilgrims is caught with much naturalism and Chaucer injects more sniping from the Summoner into early stages of the *Friar's Tale* (III, 1332–5), using this device to launch a satirical jibe against friars: they are not, he says, subject to summoners' jurisdiction, but that is because they sink into the same low category as prostitutes (a foretaste of the *Summoner's Tale's* view of friars as parasitic opportunists). Despite this vivid, amusing dramatisation of combativeness in the periphery to the tales, the tales themselves are not expressions of personality or character: the *Friar's Tale* is not, as a text, an evocation of this Friar's hatred of this Summoner, nor does the *Summoner's Tale* voice this Summoner's hatred towards this Friar. Instead they are primarily examples of the established literary tradition of anticlerical satire (a common element in the fabliau tradition, as the *Shipman's Tale* illustrates). The *Friar's Tale* is a development in fabliau style of an exemplum – a story told to illustrate a lesson by preachers (see Benson and Andersson 1971: 362–5). The *Summoner's Tale* resembles a French fabliau (Benson and Andersson 1971: 344–59) but has other elements, all without any conceivable relation to the two pilgrims' quarrel, like its powerful drama of class relations and its virtuoso network of references to topical intellectual theories – a tale about a fart becomes an excursus into theology, mathematics, logic and epistemology.

The tales do, however, neatly link the punishments they depict to the two professions and draw on contemporary satires against summoners and friars. A summoner's job was to summon defendants to answer charges in ecclesiastical courts, which dealt with marital disputes, wills, simony (the abuse of ecclesiastical office to make money), non-payment of tithes, and sexual misdemeanours, and the *Friar's Tale* shows the bullying, the perversion of justice and the extortion rackets (see p. 107) which satires and historical records depict some summoners and archdeacons committing (see Hahn and Kaeuper 1983). Appropriately its summoner-protagonist is judged and hauled off for punishment – not in an earthly court but by the Devil. The villain of the *Summoner's Tale* similarly recalls anti-fraternal ('anti-friar') satires (see Mann 1973: 37–54) in cadging money to fund luxurious lifestyles and expensive building projects – quite contrary to the intention of the friars' founders that they should live in humble poverty. And his punishment is a donation that is insulting, humbling and worthless: a fart. It also symbolises judgement on his own empty rhetoric; these two tales point to gaps between surface and reality, and the Devil in the first tale arbitrates (as the morally insensitive summoner cannot) between what is truly meant and what is not.

The establishment of the full doctrine of purgatory, from the thirteenth century on, encouraged people to pay contributions to chantries and religious orders for Masses and other meritorious practices to try to preserve themselves and their loved ones from long punishments in the after-life. The theme of infernal punishment is found in both tales and also in the mini-tale in the *Summoner's Prologue*. The insecurity of earthly life, the surrounding presence of another world, and the imminence of Judgement are delicately symbolised in the *Friar's Tale* by the Devil's references to another country (III, 1397–1402) and the passing of the day (III, 1476–86), a metaphor from the Parable of the Vineyard, a parable about the Last Judgement (Matt. 20:1–16), culminating in echoes of the evening service of Compline and its warnings against temptation in III, 1654–7.

We shall look in vain for coherent characterisation underpinning all the actions of the narrative: for example, as D. W. Robertson (1962: 267) observes:

> Psychologically speaking, we might expect the summoner to be quite alarmed by the discovery that his newly sworn brother is a fiend, but morally he is quite at home with him.

Chaucer readily ignores psychological verisimilitude to use actions to express a moral, satirical or symbolic meaning. These tales well illustrate how Chaucer's realistic writing is employed more in intermittent devices in the texture of narrative, especially speech and gesture, than in the structure and motivation of the plot; though we can certainly find realistically plausible actions and illuminating revelations of motive, equal to the greatest of novels, to use the plot to create the illusion of consistent personality is not Chaucer's priority, as it would be for George Eliot or Trollope.

There is brilliant social realism in details of gesture and speech which depict the two villains' manner and methods. And the *Summoner*'s *Tale's* lord and lady and their squire (III, 2162–2293), provide a lengthy scene of country-gentry household conversation looking forward to Jane Austen: the lady's contentedly and consolingly unreflective snobbishness is that of a Lady Middleton or Lady Bertram; her husband's momentary amazement at the cleverness of his peasant is a little more ruffled, but only because he finds the challenge to his own settled, proprietorial view of the world around him all the more unthinkable ('How could this *peasant* think up such a thing? *My own* serf! Answering my own confessor like that! There must be the Devil at work in such behaviour! But come and have your dinner; forget the crude fellow!', is the essence of his musing in III, 2218–42). There is aptness in the markedly class-conscious reaction, since the decisiveness of the peasant's revenge against years of exploitation, the intelligence of his crude revenge, is something to give privileged authority pause for thought. Chaucer also catches in tones of voice the close working relationship and affection – almost human-to-human – between the carter and his horses in the *Friar's Tale*: his frustrated anger with them when the hay-loaded cart gets stuck in deep mud and the rush of relief, praise and blessing when they heave it free.

> 'Heyt! Now,' quod he, 'ther Jhesu Crist yow blesse . . .   *Hey-up!*
> That was wel twight, myn owene lyard boy.   *pulled, grey*
> I pray God save thee, and Seinte Loy!'
>
> (III, 1561–4)

The Devil, observing this, is more generous to temporary human frailty (as God himself is believed to be) than the ruthless human Summoner, and Chaucer's skill with spoken English, capturing the temporary quality in the carter's anger, thus serves the purposes of moral satire as well as verisimilitude.

Though Chaucer catches naturalistically in speech both accurate features of spoken English and suggestions of mood and character, there are moments even in this most naturalistic area of his writing where speech clearly has purposes other than characterisation: the Friar's prayer, III, 1654–93, in its general function expresses his enmity towards the Summoner, but its details are fervently religious and pastoral, in a way the worldly Friar of the *General Prologue* and Links could never plausibly be imagined to be: it is a genuine prayer for the text's audience, real as well as fictional, breaking through the fiction of the quarrelling pilgrims here. The reference to Saint Simon in Thomas's riposte to the Friar (III, 2094–8) comes similarly from beyond the character: it reminds the reader of simony, the Friar's sin.

Peasants and False Ecclesiastics

Chaucer's picture of peasants in these two tales is empathetic, unpatronising, and respectful: for their sound moral judgement, sense of fair play and disgust with rogues, in contrast with his presentation of the arrogant clerical predators and even his bemused country gentry. Of course, those two well-established evils, avarice and clerics behaving badly, provided comfortably traditional and stereotypical scapegoats for social problems, but none the less these two tales celebrate, if only in fantasy-dénouements, the forceful overthrow by the victimised of their oppressors. Peasants triumph over their betters ('nyce, proude cherl' – 'foolish arrogant peasant' – splutters the lord, 'I curse his cheek!' (III, 2227), but he is impressed and disturbed by Thomas's cleverness and insubordination); similarly a fart is promoted into figuring as a theological and mathematical conundrum: arse presumes to become *arsmetrike*. In the power reversals in both tales, lower-class laypeople's aggression against rapacious clerics is attributed to the help of a benign devil. If these tales indicate, however indirectly, an aspect of Chaucer's response to subversive tendencies against feudal and ecclesiastical establishments, it is not one of simple conservative opposition to the benign devil of social change.

In other fabliau tales all the characters are flawed; here the beguilers are attempting to beguile innocent decent people. The *Friar's Tale* Mabely is defenceless, 'povre and oold', though undeceived and forthright. The *Summoner's Tale* Thomas, however, is a wealthy peasant with a 'meynee' and money enough ('Ful many a pound', III 1951) to expend on donations: his wife is worth cultivating and accepts the Friar's greeting, 'Dame . . . youre servant', complacently and with flirtatious disloyalty (III, 1805–31). Chaucer's depiction of the peasant's righteous anger at the friar (and it is a principled and dignified religious indignation, III, 2094–8, as well as contempt for financial chicanery), and of Thomas's wittily articulated punishment, is entirely sympathetic. The hypocrisy and unChristian ruthlessness of the two villains is expressed as much by their contemptuous style of address to the peasants (employing either calculating persiflage or slang insults) as by their actions. As Cooper (1986: 174–5) shows, class relations and the ebb and flow of courtesy and contempt are subtly conveyed here by the variation between *thou/thee* and singular *ye/yow* in both tales. (In late Middle English *thou/thee* expressed affection or contempt, *ye/you*, when singular, respect or formality.)

Chaucer shows the clerical villains' aggressive jealousy of anyone else threatening their privileges and opportunities for profit. The Friar lashes out against summoners and at the Wife of Bath for presuming, as a woman, to preach (friars were notoriously reputed to use their preaching skills to make money); the Summoner denigrates parish priests – a display of unbrotherly wrangling amongst 'ecclesiastes', thieves falling out and warning competitors off their patch.

The *Friar's Tale*

The *Friar's Tale* Summoner is an Archdeacon's henchman (Archdeacons were responsible for moral disciplinary matters in a diocese); he makes money from false summonses and bribes, using pimps and prostitutes to report likely easy victims. The tale uses the widespread folktale motif of the fatal promise; usually the victim rashly agrees to give something, which proves to be someone he loves; but here he signs himself away by his greedy readiness to enter a contract with the fiend devil that they will share anything consigned to him. The agent of the summoner's fall is his projected victim. We see his ruthless terrorising of Mabely, designed to bleed her of all her possessions, and her initial scared, respectful responses. The exchange gradually goads her into an outraged curse:

> 'Thou lixt!' quod she, 'by my savacioun . . .
> Unto the devel blak and rough of hewe
> Yeve I thy body . . . !'
>
> (III, 1618, 1622–3)

The fiend recognises truth in this and takes off his prey, the summoner, to dwell in hell where he will 'knowe of oure privetee / Moore than a maister of dyvynytee'. This suggests a location for sinners (often shown in iconography of hell) in Satan's private parts, which prefigures the mini-tale in the *Summoner's Prologue*.

Chaucer employs dramatic irony for moral satire: as we watch the summoner fail to see what we see, his own devilish nature and affinity with the fiend are demonstrated and, as often with Chaucer, wickedness proves also to be stupidity. At the fiend's first appearance various clues suggest to the reader that here is something sinister: he seems to be on the edge of darkness, glimpsed riding 'under a forest syde', between dark wilderness and beaten track, with sinister-hued black-fringed hat and green garb – a colour associated with fairies and the supernatural, as in *Sir Gawain and the Green Knight*, and with dangerous greenwood robbers like Robin Hood. These are mixed signals: there is something jolly as well as sinister about the fiend – compared with the human rogue – which matches his revelation of the theological truth that the Devil actually serves God's will. Like Robin the fiend has bow and arrows: what 'preye' is he out to poach? Like the Knight's Yeoman, however, another strand in his alarming multiple persona is that of an estate servant (III, 1389–1446): both collect rents due to a 'lord'. Sinners are the Devil's due, but gradually we interpret this ambiguously described master as God, the fiend's true overlord. The fiend lives in the north, often associated with Hell—not just because of southern prejudice but because Isaiah 14:13 says Lucifer dwells there.

The summoner's inability to spot the clues symbolises moral blindness, and the most telling satire in Chaucer's narrative, a symbolic indictment of the summoner's evil nature, is the conversation where he delightedly hails his new companion as a soul-mate: here is someone exactly like himself! Constant use of 'brother' underlines this: the summoner defines himself as devil-like. 'Purchasyng', 'rente' (III, 1449–51), and 'wynnynge', 'profit' (III, 1425–33, 1478, 1570) used for 'damnation' verbally identify the summoner's money-making with the Devil's.

The summoner's speech about his lack of conscience and penitence (III, 1434–44) is not naturalistic psychology: as if in a morality play, or the confessions of personified Vices in *Piers Plowman* Passus V, a Sin reveals its nature. Similarly his subsequent questions to his companion are devices to render assimilable what is actually a theological exposition voiced by the fiend. It teaches that God permits temptation, but assures humans that the temptation will never go beyond their strength to resist – if they will – and that 'Crist wol be youre champion and knyght' (III, 1662). God and Christ are overlord and heavenly chivalric champion, the Devil ultimately their servant, humanity safe as long as it is vigilant against temptation and expresses penitence. The *Friar's Tale* becomes towards its end a serious and theologically purposeful religious tale. Unlike the conclusion to the Pardoner's performance, there is no sign that this should be read as the fictional character's exploitation of preaching skills. The worthless Friar of the *General Prologue* and the ill-natured Friar of the *Friar's Prologue*, whom the Host considers a disgrace to his profession (III, 1286–7), seem virtually forgotten. Chaucer's return to a mode of frame-story verisimilitude, with the Summoner, at line 1665, standing up on his stirrups for rage, comes as quite a shock.

The *Summoner's Tale*

The dénouements of Chaucer's fabliaux often enact insults between men in contest with each other: Alison and Nicholas in the *Miller's Tale* are essentially saying 'Kiss my arse' to Absolon; the *Friar's Tale* tells the Summoner 'You're a devil' and 'Go to hell'; the *Summoner's Tale* is telling the Friar he is worth a fart. In the satirical cartoons sometimes found in the margins of medieval manuscripts both farting and bared bottoms feature as insults. The *Summoner's Tale* and the miniature anti-friar story told in its Prologue are scatological. Scatology is usually a simple, low kind of humour but it can also be used with more complex cultural and psychological meanings. It is a devastating deflater of dignity and can be sharply powerful used against failing or hypocritical clerics (as here) since it challenges their particular duty to cultivate spirituality and purity. As an area of life where euphemisms and *doubles entendres* proliferate it can create subtle verbal wit, parody and bathos: the *Miller's Tale* rhyme *kisse/pisse* illustrates such bathos (I, 3797–8); and rhyming *fart* with the Courtly Love line 'Spek, sweete bryd, I noot nat where thou art' (III, 3805–6) creates parody. Psychologically, scatological images can also express dark fears and guilts, as in their projection onto Jews in the *Prioress's Tale*. Here, we have two tales, the *Friar's* and the *Summoner's Prologue* story, concerned with hell and Satan. The bodily disgust and obscenity in the vision of friars dwelling under Satan's tail clearly draw on psychological horror which parallels, and had entered into, traditional doctrines of hell. This tale is a parody of a pious fable told to promulgate the idea that the Cistercian monks were especially dear to Mary; they cannot be seen in heaven because she keeps them protectively under her cloak. Chaucer's parody hits the pretensions of the friar: he jumps to the smug conclusion that friars are so virtuous they have no place in hell, only to find them in its most shameful centre, Satan's arse. This prepares the reader for the savagely satirised hypocrisy of the friar in the later tale and the Fall by which he is reduced to his true moral worth – a fart. These anti-friar stories use scatological physical insults, the Devil's arse and the fart into the Friar's hand, both to denigrate friars and to symbolise contempt for their worldliness and lack of genuine spirituality: as images of the vanity of materialism they resemble the rubbish in the *Canon's Yeoman's Tale* (p. 209).

Anti-friar satire was common, motivated by general concern to castigate clerical abuses and backsliding and by particular grievances against friars. They had been founded by St Francis as a religious movement dedicated to apostle-like poverty, and the growth of institutional wealth had by the later fourteenth century aroused criticism. Parish priests disliked the fact that friars were mobile preachers, coming into a parish to collect donations and offering parishioners what their own priest often saw as irresponsibly easy absolution for sins. The passage at III, 1709–1822, depicts abuses to which friars were popularly believed to be prone: competing with the parish priest, *'possessioners'* (III, 1720–3), for donations; frightening people into giving money for expensive sets of thirty masses, 'trentals' (III, 1724–32), to protect their souls from long periods in purgatory; collecting, almost commandeering, food aggressively and declining to pray for the givers; preaching in fancy styles to gain money rather than to expound 'hooly writ' (III, 1789–96); flattering and seducing women (III, 1797–1811). Like the equally mobile monk in the *Shipman's Tale* this friar makes himself at home visiting generous friends (his gesture in ousting the peasant's cat from its seat epitomises his invasive self-interest), and courts a wife into disloyal confidences about her husband, getting between husband and wife for his own profit.

As in the *Miller's Tale*, the really powerful comedy comes not just from the release of taboo subjects into the text nor from clever trickery in the plot, but from verbal, syntactic and metrical manipulation of these ingredients within the style, in particular Chaucer's command of speech to create personality, mood and class, and through them to convey exploitation, moral blindness and, in opposition to these, indignation, disgust and revenge. Chaucer, here and elsewhere, uses the dramatic irony common to fabliaux to demonstrate the type of imperceptive stupidity that is bred by habitual self-centredness, and celebrate its downfall. Though the physical gestures, when they come, are isolated into sharp and symbolic focus – the brushing away of the cat, the friar's hand groping under the sick man's buttocks – the tale consists almost entirely of speech. The friar is a wind-bag. Like the Pardoner, Canon and Yeoman, he exploits words to make money. Chaucer paints theatrically, in words, the man's monstrous falseness and materialism, with his French phrases, his cant about friars' poor and simple lifestyle (juxtaposed with his list of the kind of menu of delicacies he might like to eat), and his overbearing refusal to let anybody else talk:

'O Thomas, *je vous dy*, Thomas! Thomas!'

'. . .Taak heede what I seye!'

'But herkne now, Thomas, what I shal seyn.'

(III, 1832, 1901, 1918)

His unctuous repetition of the victim's name, the perversion of biblical references to promote donations, the torrent of eager self-centred arguments, build up suspense and irritation in the reader, tempered deliciously by our awareness (through several references to it) of Thomas's growing 'ire'. Thomas has to endure, as one-man congregation, the sort of rhetorical sermon in pursuit of money for which friars were notorious. When the long-expected punishment comes, as with the insult at the climax of the *Miller's Tale*, Chaucer slows down: we watch the hand of the Friar, greedy and unperceptive, searching around below and even between Thomas's buttocks; he spins out the suspense from the first reference to 'hand' (III, 2131), until we get finally to the 'fart', (III, 2149). As with the *Miller's Tale*'s delaying of the dénouement insults ('hir naked ers', 'he smoot', I, 3734, 3810), furious sudden movement by the victim follows, reduced – with the cluster of animal metaphors in III, 2150–61 – to bestial humiliation. He cries out against his punishment by the man he formerly flattered, as a 'cherl's' blasphemy against his 'hooly convent'. Class conflict is only just below the surface right through this tale, and just as the Miller's and Reeve's tales pitted the wits of students against artisans, so the lord muses how a churl could have the 'imaginacioun' (which meant both 'inventiveness' and 'plot') to devise such an insult for a friar (III, 2210–42). Having failed to make money from the rich peasant householder Thomas, the friar abuses him and flees to the soothing safety of the lord of the manor and his lady. Knight (1986: 107) sees in this flight Chaucer's characteristic retreat into conservative, feudal safety after exposing the individualist commercialism of the friar's style of avarice. Chaucer certainly lets the narrative pause while the Friar recovers his composure and the gentry soothe his (and their own) alarm at clever insubordination by reasserting over and over again the peasant status of the 'cherl'. Like his other fraudsters, Chaucer's friar represents not just unholy worldliness and deceit but also a social cause for fear: the danger of a clever, mobile and highly commercial money-maker to the settled community of parson, farmer and squire.

The tale, like others, is about the true and deceptive use of speech as well as contempt for materialism. It touches on the issue of how words, physical signs, relate to meaning. The lord talks of Thomas's expressive fart as speech, and as clever speech: 'subtiltee / And heigh wit made hym speken as he spak' (III, 2290–91). O'Brien (1997: 19) shows that Chaucer plays on the fact that speech is, in one sense, only expended air (the medieval philosopher Abelard distinguished words as meanings from words as mere air, in his influential work *Sic et Non*). The churl's bodily expelling of air conveyed truth more accurately than the friar's empty rhetoric. Chaucer draws attention to this double nature of speech when he has the friar quote the first line of Psalm 45, whose Latin '*Cor meum eructavit*' can be translated both as 'My heart has uttered [a good word]' and as 'My heart has belched', underlining this through the friar's contemptuous belching sound 'Lo, "buf!" they seye' (III, 1934). A series of scatological *doubles entendres* demonstrate how a single word can refer both to bodily private parts and to more elevated concepts: 'fundement' (foundations of a building, or arse), 'pryvetee' (God's secret truths, or the genital area), 'ars-metrike' (arithmetic, or arse metrication: the division of a fart). The tale moves towards an ending where the extremely bodily – fart, cart-wheel spokes and the reverberation of air – and the extremely intellectual – arithmetic, logic and epistemology – provide parallels to each other in a surrealistic dance.

The fantastical final joke, that a bequest of a fart should be divided between twelve friars by each holding his nose to the divisions of a cart-wheel and breathing in a stupendous fart from Thomas, is a virtuoso intellectual conundrum as well as an obscene anti-friar joke. Cooper (1996: 177) summarises the argument that it may be a religious parody, of the descent of the Holy Spirit (the supreme Breath) to the twelve disciples. O'Brien (1997) shows that the whole text alludes to contemporary scientific ideas about whether anything in the universe except God was indivisible, and to a new interest in experiment, like the Squire's suggestion of the wheel, rather than relying on abstract arguments from logic, as earlier medieval 'scholastic' problem-solving methods did.

The tale can also be read as part of the *Canterbury Tales'* multi-faceted exploration of aspects of authorship. The mystery of language and speech, that signs which include noises created by expelling air from the body can convey ideas, is at the centre of the writer's profession: in that sense the highly intellectualised fart is a pretty good symbol of what a writer does. It may be a wry comment on the author's role, particularly under its aspect of satirist, just as the Pardoner's patter, the poverty-shunning Lawyer's rhetoric, and the dilemma of the Manciple's caged crow are apposite of other uses of authorship. The tale is an extravaganza mingling bodily and metaphysical humour, a fusion of fabliau and the tradition of anti-friar satire, but wrapped up in it are deeper reactions to contemporary change: what looks like a welcome for new experiential approaches to knowledge, and a distrust of free-wheeling individualistic enterprise compared with settled traditional rural society. Yet Chaucer's ending is also a vindication of two irreverent jokers, the squire and the peasant, and their plan to give the friars a fart. And if we take the tale too seriously, this ending presses us to remember that, above all, what the story is about is a wind-bag and a fart.

10

The *Clerk's Tale*

Judged by the criteria of realist fiction, the *Clerk's Tale* is psychologically implausible and morally unacceptable, but it is a fable about heroic martyrdom and endurance, and about different kinds of power. It is also one of Chaucer's studies of *pathos*: of poignant innocent suffering and 'pite', appreciated for its own sake (Gray 1979). Like the *Nun's Priest's Tale*, it provides also an example of a characteristically medieval way of reading, for both tales end with their narrator's invitation to the audience to interpret the tale allegorically. Issues of interpretation, authorial intentionality, and the symbolic potentialities of narrative are always central to the work of the writer, but both these tales create a particularly strong impression at their close that the text is open to a multiplicity of readings. Chaucer had probed the question of interpretation in several of his writings, including the Prologue to the *Legend of Good Women*. Wycliffite criticism of the often far-fetched allegorical exegesis of the Scriptures that the medieval Church had traditionally promulgated, and contemporary debate over how far the Bible could and should be read literally, and what kind of 'glossing' (interpretation) was legitimate, made the whole question of textual meaning and multiple interpretation one of great current interest.[1]

Griselda's story, like the *Man of Law's Tale*, resembles a secular saint's life. It has the same emphasis on victimisation and the same demonstration of spiritual and moral strength. At times the language reminds us of the life of Christ (see Cooper 1996: 190–1; also Ellis 1986: 61). God came down to earth into a humble setting, like Griselda's:

> . . . hye God somtyme senden kan
> His grace into a litel oxes stalle.
>
> (IV, 206–7)

The religious parallels relate also to the theme of *gentillesse*, 'nobility', explored in this tale as in the Wife of Bath's: there we were told the truly *gentil* man is the virtuous man and Christ is the source of true *gentillesse*, rather than a person's ancestors (IV, 1113–24). In this tale the marquis Walter, though high-born, lacks qualities essential in a ruler, selfishly failing in his responsibilities to protect his subjects by refusing for so long to marry and produce an heir (IV, 78–140), and showing caprice and oppression in his treatment of his wife. Conversely the peasant Griselda possesses two types of true nobility: first, her moral virtue – evident already while she lived in a hovel – but secondly, the ability she reveals, once elevated to a palace, to fulfil the duties of a noble as well or better than those born to it (IV, 393–441). She shows wisdom, goodness, eloquence, dignity, discretion, and attention to the 'commune profit', bringing social concord and equitable judgements: peace and justice, two essential qualities of good rule. She exemplifies *pacience*, a virtue Chaucer often presents as the wisest response, morally and philosophically, to adversity (on the background to these ideas and Chaucer's treatment of them, see Burnley 1979, 64–81).

Behind the plot of a husband's testing of his wife lies a folktale pattern, that of a mortal married to a supernatural spouse, who imposes tests on the mortal (the legend of Cupid and Psyche is an example). This underlying folklore stratum may explain, historically, some of the harshness and brutality in Walter's behaviour. Chaucer's narrative veers between different explanations for it. Those expressed within the tale generally treat it as evil, a 'wikke usage': first he describes it as baffling and a wickedly misplaced exercise of ingenuity, 'subtil wit' that 'yvele . . . sit' (IV, 459–61), creating 'angwyssh and . . . drede'; later he presents it as a needless whim illustrating the excesses to which bullying husbands are prone 'Whan that they fynde a pacient creature' (IV, 618–23); and as a type of obsession (IV, 701–7). Through dramatic irony the text also lets us know that Walter's real feelings are that he is pleased, not angry, with Griselda (IV, 512), and that, Prospero-like, he has staged everything so that those she thought were lost are alive and have come to no harm. Knowing her pains are temporary, the reader is manoeuvred thus by the text into less outrage than her plight merits. This, however, does little for the image of Walter, except in so far as the text can cast him in the role of restorer of everyone's happiness as well as depriver of it.

A different type of interpretation, offered after the story is told, does rehabilitate Walter: it is the Clerk's proposal for allegorical interpretation. Walter, according to this reading, symbolises God, who lovingly tests humans' obedience and trust through the adversities they meet in this life (IV, 1149–62). There are not exact point-by-point correspondences between this Christian message and the story: Walter's bullying of Griselda is not, like God's, a 'governaunce' that is designed for the recipient's good (IV, 1161), or to exercise our moral strength or teach us constancy. Chaucer has shown it as illogical, purposeless, unjustifiable and born out of some personal weaknesses in the human husband. (Medieval allegorical interpretations of the Bible, however, often fail to fit well with the details and morality of the literal story in much the same way: contemporary readers might not have found the parallel unacceptable.) The strongest reason for respecting the allegory, at least as one possible reading, is that the narrative itself focuses more on Griselda's moral fortitude than on Walter's motives. And her reactions are a triumph: as the hurdles are set higher and higher, one after the other, she clears each one; her ever-victorious stoicism gives us a success story to enjoy and celebrate. As in *Sir Gawain and the Green Knight*, where the Green Knight subjects Gawain to all sorts of disguised tests and trickery, but is accorded the right to pronounce judgement on the hero's slightest fault, the narrative concentrates on the moral status of the people who are tested, and how they acquit themselves, not on the moral status of the tester. Like the *Man of Law's Tale*, the *Clerk's Tale* is another triumph by a weak, powerless person over oppression, through a mixture of endurance (a form of earthly bravery) and lack of attachment to worldly joys (a form of spiritual independence).

Chaucer underlines this triumphal element in the figure of Griselda by making her voice her own endurance, often in firmly patterned rhetoric:

> 'Ye been oure lord; dooth with youre owene thyng   *do*
> Right as yow list; axeth no reed at me.   *advice*
> For as I lefte at hoom al my clothyng,
> Whan I first cam to yow, right so,' quod she,
> 'Lefte I my wyl and al my libertee . . .
>
>   (IV, 652–6)

The power here lies partly in her imperatives: 'dooth', 'axeth'; and the control which is created through verbal patterns, including: repetition, 'Right as yow list . . .', 'right so', 'al my clothyng . . . al my libertee'; alliteration, Right/reed, Lefte/libertee; antithesis, oure/youre; yow/me, and chiasmus, I lefte... Lefte I. The phrase 'oure lord' prepares us to hear echoes of biblical resignation to divine dispensation here: Mary's 'Be it unto me according to thy word', Luke 1:38, and 1 Timothy 6:7, 'For we brought nothing into this world and it is certain we can carry nothing out'. The text reiterates Griselda's gladness, benignness, busyness and calmness. As she states, 'Al youre plesance ferme and stable I holde' (IV, 663), words expressing an immoveable strength, like that of Custance: it is derived from these women's spiritual independence from the transient world. References at key moments in her vicissitudes to clothing and stripping her symbolise her indifference to mutability: changes in Fortune seem mere external trappings to such a soul. Tension between two kinds of power, one moral and internal, the other political and external, is thus built into the text's language.

While inscribing Griselda thus, verbally, as a victor, Chaucer surrounds her trials with highly emotional evocations of pity. These two effects do not fuse but remain distinct reactions to the terrible events: the pity is ours, the strength hers. The expression of pain and anger is shifted onto the spectators:

> The folk hire folwe, wepynge in hir weye,
> And Fortune ay they cursen as they goon;
> But she fro wepyng kepte hire eyen dreye . . .
>
> (IV, 897–9)

It is only when her heroism has brought the reward of happiness that Chaucer permits emotion to engulf her, repeating in six lines: 'aswowne', 'falleth', 'pitous joye', 'swownyge', 'in hire armes', 'pitously wepynge', 'embraceth', 'tendrely kissynge', 'teeres' (IV 1079–1085); see Ferster 1985: 95–121, and Johnson 1994: 204–5, on the presentation of Griselda's identity and physical body.

It is a bizarre plot, offensive to morality and sensitivity, whether medieval or modern, and Chaucer's treatment of it is primarily as a drama of themes rather than psychological plausibility. The twin themes of love and testing, central to the parallel between Walter and God, are introduced early with the description of Walter as:

> Biloved and drad, thurgh favour of Fortune,
> Bothe of his lordes and of his commune.
>
> (IV, 68–70)

'Favour of Fortune' prefigures the theme of transience; 'lordes and . . . commune' prefigures that of social power-relations. Obedience and power are signalled together early on in the wordplay of the plea to the marquis to marry:

'Boweth youre nekke under that blisful yok
Of soveraynetee, noght of servyse,
Which that men clepe spousaille or wedlok'

(IV, 113–15)[2]

Once again, 1 Timothy 6 seems relevant: teaching service 'under the yoke' and godly contentment. The *Clerk's Prologue* had introduced the theme of obedience to authority: the Clerk says he is under Harry Bailey's governance and will do him 'obeisance' (IV, 23–4). As often, a Chaucerian narrator's demeanour in the Link passage mirrors central thematic patterns in the tale.[3]

Another topic the *Prologue* introduces is Italy and the great flowering of vernacular literature there during the fourteenth century. Chaucer did more than any English writer before him to bring the wider range of European literature and culture, including the new classicism of the Italian Renaissance, to England and to establish a flexible, elegant English style of writing, operating in continental and classical traditions as confidently and creatively as within native traditions – an English literature that could rival those of contemporary Italy and France, as well as ancient Rome. His *House of Fame* and *Legend of Good Women* show the inspiration of Dante (1265–1321); Boccaccio's *Il Teseida* and *Il Filostrato* are sources for the *Knight's Tale* and *Troilus and Criseyde* respectively. Chaucer refers to Petrarch's crowning as Poet Laureate in 1341 (IV, 31), a ceremony which, by reviving an ancient Roman honour to poets, declared a confidence that European literature could now equal that of classical Rome. Though his writings rarely exhibit the overt grandeur of Dante and Petrarch, and his self-image never takes itself as seriously, there seems no doubt he was aware that he was himself forging a literary language and vernacular tradition of new dignity: the decision to make the *Canterbury Tales* such a conspectus of English society and of literary genres in both a European and a classical literary context, suggests an ambition of speaking for a nation taking its place in the great tradition.

Boccaccio's version of the Griselda story concludes his *Decameron*. All his tales on Day Ten tell of 'those who have performed liberal or munificent deeds' (see p. 137). As if recognising the tale's moral discordancies, however, Boccaccio prefaced it with the narrator's observation that the marquis behaves with 'senseless brutality' rather than generosity. It is uncertain whether Chaucer knew the *Decameron* version, but he knew a letter by Petrarch, *c.*1373, praising it and containing his own version (on sources, see Bryan and Dempster 1941: 288–331).

Comparison with his predecessors reveals the original emphases in Chaucer's handling of the story. Boccaccio describes Griselda's beauty as Walter's reason for marrying her. Petrarch creates a picture of her industrious, frugal life and virtue as well as beauty. But Chaucer adds the idea of her voluntary embrace of an ascetic, hardworking lifestyle: his Griselda, desiring to please virtue, positively avoids 'ese' (IV, 217); never wants to stop working (IV, 224); makes her bed hard (IV, 228). Both Petrarch and Chaucer stress her obedient respect for her father, prefiguring the main theme of her married life, and preparing us for the allegorical interpretation that makes her a model for the Christian soul's obedience to God. Chaucer, however, juxtaposes with that reading the completely incompatible reading, IV, 1163–1212, that urges wives to reject meekness entirely. And, of course, Chaucer's tale is embedded in the ongoing diversity of the *Canterbury Tales*, with different and incompatible worldviews challenging its extreme endorsement of female passivity and obedience to authority. Boccaccio presents the story as a tale of amazement: he foregrounds the unexpected nature of Walter's actions, Griselda's exceptional responses, the twists of Fortune in her life, and the onlookers' wonder, while framing the tale with comments that acknowledge the moral and emotional problems inherent in it. The main virtue his Griselda evinces is stoicism, refusing to complain or show how much she is hurt. Petrarch elaborates more the moral implications of each event, reassuring the reader, for example, that the servant who removes the daughter is a trustworthy man, conveying the baby with great care to the aunt, who will rear her with a mother's love. Chaucer, with his concern for pathos, depicts the man as frightening: 'Suspecious was the diffame of this man, / Suspect his face, suspect his word also . . .' (IV, 540–1); 'The ugly ['of frightening appearance'] sergeant' at IV, 673.

Petrarch describes the setting, but Chaucer makes it symbolic of psychological and hot and cold passions (IV, 57–9). His narrative itself offers a cold/hot dichotomy between its elegant and chaste representations of stoic and religious themes and its moments of intensely painful pity. The effects of the hagiographic triumphalism of the writing and the Clerk's concluding allegorical interpretation are to negate the *pitous* evocation of human pain.[4] Chaucer seems to seek a contrast of values, to appeal separately to intellect and feelings in the reader: to construct a narrative enigma.[5] In the *Physician's Tale* a similar dichotomy is accompanied by a clash of cultures, Roman and Christian (see p. 146).

The *Clerk's Tale* is set in Lombardy where the notoriously tyrannical Visconti family ruled. Petrarch, having earlier condemned their tyranny, took service with the regime (Wallace 1997: 262–77). Chaucer was sent on a diplomatic mission to the Visconti regime in 1378. He includes the murder of the tyrant Bernabò Visconti, 'scourge of Lumbardye', in the *Monk's Tale*. For Chaucer, Lombardy is the setting for marital tyranny. Is it also a tyranny of traditional, male ways of viewing intepretation as well as women? A text and its interpretation were sometimes figured as a veiled woman, to be uncovered by the interpreter, and Dinshaw (1989: 132–55) associates Walter's oppression of Griselda with the all-male sequence of authors re-interpreting the tale. Just as Griselda is dressed and undressed, her own will and subjectivity negated, so the *translatio*, the 'transmission' of her story, Dinshaw argues, fails to encompass a feminine viewpoint on male oppression: 'In the *Clerk's Tale*, *translatio* is represented as an act performed on the female body, but woman's experience does not enter into the conceptualization of the act . . . the model [of interpreted text as an unveiled woman] is based on man's experience' (p. 147).

The tale presents tyranny in gender terms, but social power relationships and differences are recurrent themes in a more general sense too: Griselda and Walter represent opposite ends of the social spectrum, as the narrative, and both characters' speeches, continue to remind us, but her personal elevation – proving such a successful political experiment, and beneficial for the common good – is not accompanied by any respect towards the common people in general. Their opinion is represented as unreliable in a stanza of political warning unique to Chaucer:

> 'O stormy people! Unsad and evere untrewe!   *unsound, faithless*
> Ay indiscreet and chaungynge as a fane! . . .   *weather vane*
> Youre doom is fals, youre constance yvele preeveth;   *opinion*
> A ful greet fool is he that on yow leeveth.'   *believes*
>   (IV, 995–1001)

At the beginning, though he yielded to their plea, Walter insisted they must accept his manner of implementing it without grumbling or opposition (IV, 170). The last two stanzas of *Prima Pars* are a ballet of dominance and submission: the lord giving directives and his subjects kneeling and scurrying away obediently, without discussion, to carry out his orders with 'diligence'. The tale's happy ending is also in terms of dynastic autonomy: a reassurance that the Walter dynasty continues, with an heir who rules in 'reste and pees'. The 'glad . . . humble . . . bisy . . . servyse' Griselda constantly manifests is a fourteenth-century ruler's vision of the best kind of guarantee of 'reste and pees' in a society, as well as a hagiographic victory of unworldliness which can create peace for a victim in the midst of adversity.

The distrust of the common people shown in IV, 995–1001 contrasts with the ending of the *Physician's Tale* where their shrewd judgement and willingness to take mass political action are what saves Appius and restores justice. One reason for the difference may be that the *Clerk's Tale* is, on one level, a political myth about a theory Chaucer often offers as the optimal solution to social conflict. This solution is that all classes should accept their situation, the rulers should act for the common good and the subjects should give their submission voluntarily. This willing subjection, a self-subjection, whether in marriage or politics, is an ideal often sketched: the wife at the close of the *Wife of Bath's Tale* gives up the right of autonomy she has just been given; all three men in the *Franklin's Tale* decline the rights to which they are entitled. Griselda's self-subjection elicits, finally, from her ruler the kindness that ensures a future of 'concorde', 'reste', and 'heigh prosperitee'.

The people's instability also contributes to the theme of this world's mutability, while Griselda's low status is sanctified and spiritualised through her lack of interest in worldly power or autonomy. Christian forbearance and patient poverty, rather than revolution, are the medieval answer to injustice, Diamond points out (1977: 73–5). Through all vicissitudes, Griselda, like Custance, has stability because – though she can love – she does not seek to own or control anything. Diamond sees Chaucer as aware of the injustice of the marital power-relations in the tale but unable to relate this to the political power-relations, and producing the plethora of reactions at the tale's end because of his 'inability to confront the sexual dilemma woven into the very fabric of the tale' (p. 75).

The polysemantic nature of the tale's ending encapsulates its many possibilities of meaning – as an exposé of male authority, as emblem of triumphant patience, divine testing, even as a challenge to readerly interpretation. See Johnson (1994: 195–220) on 'shifting evaluations' of the Griselda story, within and outside the tale, medieval and later, and the gender issues they raise. Knapp (1990: 129–40) suggests the tale, though fitting the modest, plain-living *General Prologue* Oxford clerk who directs his knowledge towards 'moral vertu', also fits contemporary late fourteenth-century academic concern, Wycliffite and more generally philosophical, over questions of human authority, as well as the controversies over Bible-based preaching and biblical translation. Proponents of a plainer gospel theology, permitting more direct access to knowledge of God's will by laity, however lowly, met the opposition of Church authority. Is this a context for the tale's double attitude to lordship and the exemplary virtue of passivity?

Despite the tensions and dichotomies it contains, there is minimal sense of conflict overtly in the narrative. Its use of stanzas, arranging narrative into even units, contributes to a sense of containment and consistency, and its division, like the *Knight's Tale*, into parts gives the text overall an air of controlled design and elegance. It has been a tale of extreme subjugation of women: not just in the excesses of the husband's domination but in the extremes of the wife's submission; after a tale of such chaste and formal speech, a tale where the main character conforms her opinions exactly to those of her master, the mixture of reactions that surge into the *Canterbury Tales* narrative at its close bring back all the colloquialism, the polyphony and the contention that had been exiled from the performance. First comes a denial that the tale is a lesson for wives; then the allegorical interpretation, applying a religious message equally to men and women; then, switching into farce, a plea not for 'vertuous suffraunce' but for belligerence from the 'archewyves'. The Clerk's song contrasts both in stanza-form and in its stylistic exuberance and anarchic vision with the rhyme royal and controlled range of the *Clerk's Tale*. The song offers, of course, a masculine view of what a feminist alternative to Griselda's obedience might be. There follows, if it is genuine, the Host's insistence on taking it as if it were, indeed, a lesson for wives, and finally the start of the *Merchant's Prologue*, which refers back to Griselda's patience to make a link by contrast with the tale he promises to tell. The Merchant has misread the *Clerk's Tale*, or read oversimply and personally; Chaucer depicts him as relating both it and his own tale to his personal depression. He is very much like a Kittredgean reader, seeing the narratives as speaking of a personal state. That self-identification with literature is another aspect of the many-sided exploration of authorship, meaning and reading that seems to run through the Links and tales.

11

The *Merchant's Tale*

Like the *Miller's Tale*, this is another fabliau about an old husband and an unfaithful young wife. The inequality of the marriage is emphasised by Chaucer's allocation of allegorical names to the ill-matched partners: January and May. The names draw attention to considerations not just of age but of Nature: the mismatch of ages is a human social and economic arrangement which goes against Nature. And in medieval thought Nature was the direct representative and executive of God's will in the world.

The *Merchant's Tale* is also about sin and the Fall of Man. The main action takes place in a walled garden with a tree, a husband and wife, and in the tree a deceiver (May's lover Damian). Verbal reminiscences of the Garden of Eden story throughout the tale underline this episode's visual symbolism: January talks of Adam and Eve's creation, (IV, 1324–9); a wife is compared to Eden, the earthly paradise: the 'paradys terrestre' (IV, 1332), 'his paradys' (IV, 1822); Fortune is a 'scorpion . . . deceyvable' (IV, 2058).[1] The word *fruyt* occurs several times, with worldly or ambiguously immoral senses: it has a financial sense in January's: 'Thanne is a wyf the fruyt of his tresor' (IV, 1270); it refers to pears, drawing on a traditional *double entendre* between them and sex, when May says that she will die if she cannot slake her appetite for 'fruyt' by climbing into the tree (IV, 2335–7); and *fruyt* is January's metaphor for an heir at IV, 1462. The garden theme is reinforced by the subplot which introduces Pluto and Prosepine, whose story was told in Claudian's *Rape of Prosepine*, well-known in the Middle Ages, which contained a description of the setting for Prosepine's rape which was a classic source for later, medieval, descriptions of gardens; IV, 2030–33 mentions the *Romance of the Rose*: another classic literary garden, not Eden but the worldly, courtly, Garden of Delight.

Alongside allusions to fruit, gardens, paradise and heaven there are unambiguously darker references to 'purgatorie', and 'helle' (IV, 1467, 1964), and when the metaphor of the tree and branches appears in IV,

1640–2, it is used ominously for the traditional allegorical depiction of sin as a tree with seven branches: the Seven Deadly Sins. Pluto, too, is the classical God of Hades. While this is a tale about 'felicitee', pleasure, it is also undeniably about sin.

The resemblance of the *Merchant's Tale* garden to the Garden of Eden does not mean the tale depicts January's Fall from virtue to sin – January never was virtuous, even at the start of the tale. What the tale shows rather is people in a fallen state. That makes the moral structure of the narrative more interesting: the Fall it reveals is not one action in the plot (not, for example, specifically May's adultery) but something for the reader to discover beneath the misleading gloss the *mores* of the world, represented by January, lay over the actions of the story. It is also accurate theologically. From St Augustine (AD 354–430) on, the Church taught that ever since Adam brought Original Sin into the world, humans had reproduced the Fall in their own daily lives: disobeying the illumination God sends through reason and conscience and succumbing to their lower powers of sensuality ('appetyt') and passion. Augustine described this as a reversal of the hierarchical natural order: sin involves overturning reason, which should rule human conduct. Adam's decision to be guided by his wife (who in marriage should be obediently subject to her husband) in rebellion against God's command, corresponds to the symbolic rebellion which occurs when a person acquiesces in the impulses of sensuality.[2] The *Parson's Tale* repeats common medieval teaching in saying that in the Garden of Eden story Adam symbolises ('sheweth') reason, overcome by the flesh, symbolised by Eve (X, 260, 330).

It is January's blind, muddled thinking at the beginning of the tale which already manifests the pattern of the Fall. January is so sunk in materialism, selfishness and sensuality that these blur and obscure his attitude to marriage. He sees it as supplying a convenient source of sexual pleasure and an heir for his money and land: something he can buy, without concern for the feelings of his partner. Symbolically this clouding of his reason by sin makes him blind, mentally blind, long before literal blindness hits him. His sinful disregard for the true purposes of marriage within God's design makes his marriage an act against Nature; the age difference between him and May is only one element in the unnatural and ungodly arrangement. Medieval churchmen had a variety of views on marriage and sex – some thinkers laid much greater stress on love and mutuality while a stricter, more extreme and traditional view, represented in the *Parson's Tale* (X, 940), taught that marital sexual relations are only justified for three reasons: procreation, to pay the marriage 'debt', and to

avoid lechery, which means that 'to assemble only for amorous love' is a
mortal sin. The most serious faults for a married woman are adultery and
disobedience. Throughout the Middle Ages, financial and family considerations played generally a more important, and certainly a more overt
and acknowledged, role than they do in modern assumptions about
marriage. Ecclesiastical law, however, required from the twelfth century
the consent of both parties, as the essential condition for a true and legally
binding marriage, and this marked a new recognition of the claims of
affection and personal preference.

January's marriage offends against all medieval standards in its lechery, but the disgust the tale evinces for his lack of tenderness and sensitivity, and his failure to view his wife as different from other possessions
he has bought, seem to belong to the more modern camp. Certainly its
presentation is more condemnatory than that of his wife's adultery and
disobedience. The fact that the core genre of this tale is clearly fabliau,
not a marriage treatise, presupposes a comic, lenient, handling of the
latter, but given the stern satire against the husband here and the sense
in which the tale constitutes quite a sombre debate on marriage, the
lack of explicit or implicit condemnation of May is striking.

The Discussion of Marriage (IV, 1245–1576)

Like the *Franklin's Tale* but at much greater length, a discussion of
marriage prefaces the actual story in this tale (which, also like the
Franklin's Tale, acknowledges that women naturally desire liberty and,
like the *Manciple's Tale*, shows wives will take liberty if marriage is a
prison to them). The writing of this first half is full of non-sequiturs
and strange juxtapositions. The obvious effect of its combination of
cynical and idealistic worldviews, and of incongruous stylistic registers,
is to show how January's attitude to sex is at odds with the order of
Nature and divine will. For example, his statement:

> To take a wyf it is a glorious thyng,
> And namely whan a man is oold and hoor   *especially*
> (IV, 1268–9)

goes against medieval belief that each age of a person's life, paralleling
each season of the year, had its appropriate character and duties. Love
and begetting children were fitting for men in youth and middle years,
but old people should turn away from sensual life to concentrate on

spiritual preparation for death and God's Judgement. January's unseasonal elderly lusts are, like the Reeve's, not just disgusting but ungodly. In IV, 1400–14, his speech includes reference to his age and impending death, but concludes that marriage with a young bride is the appropriate response to his situation. January's morally topsy-turvy reasoning similarly declares his white hairs are not incompatible with fatherhood: they are like the blossoms that precede fruiting (IV, 1461–8).

Chaucer also attributes to January foolishly optimistic visions of what a wife can do for him, which every reader can see fly in the face of experience of the real difficulties and responsibilities of married life: 'wedlok is so esy and so clene', he declares (IV, 1264). And on the harmony of married life:

How myghte a man han any adversitee	*could*
That hath a wyf? . . .	
She seith nat ones 'nay', whan he seith 'ye.'	*once*
'Do this,' seith he; 'Al redy, sire,' seith she.	
	(IV, 1338–9, 1344–5)

Bachelors can never have certain happiness, whereas married men are assured of bliss:

For who kan be so buxom as a wyf?	*obedient*
Who is so trewe, and eek so ententyf?	*attentive*
To kepe hym, syk and hool, as is his make?	*mate*
	(IV, 1287–9)

The question format in itself incites the reader to sceptical response. The combination of true and false, moral and immoral statements in this first section also ensures that correct Christian theories of what marriage ought to be are present in the text. For example, lines 1287–9 above, echo a bride's wedding vows, to be faithful, obey, and love her husband in sickness and in health. Other statements with powerful theological weight behind them include:

Mariage is a ful greet sacrement.	
	(IV, 1319)

That wyf is mannes helpe and his confort.	
	(IV, 1331)

The latter recalls God's purpose in making Eve: to be a help to Adam, Genesis 2:20, 24. These textual reminders of more holy standards provide a yardstick by which January's attitudes and the selfish sordid nature of the marriage are judged.

Stylistically this first section can be disconcerting to modern readers, since it glides more readily than a novel typically would between three different structures: narration, January's first-person speech, and Free Indirect Discourse (narrative coloured by the speech or thoughts of a character). Such a technique is more successful and natural in oral performance than we, used to reading visually and silently from a page, may recognise. Here it also has a moral significance, matching January's mind, where the dividing lines between subjective fantasies and objective realities are not at all clear. From IV, 1475, Chaucer moves to a more polarised format by dividing the debate between three speakers: January, Justinus and Placebo. The latter are personifications symbolising approaches to the issues. Justinus represents a just, objective assessment (something January would never come to), while Placebo, meaning 'I shall please' in Latin, reflects back to January what he wants to hear. Flatterers were called 'placebos', and a placebo is also a false remedy, a pill with no medical ingredients: Placebo's responses are pleasing but do not aid January in the least. He resembles at times the false, flattering counsellors about whom the *Canterbury Tales* warns rulers at several points, including the *Manciple's Tale*, *Melibee* (VII, 1170–80), and the *Nun's Priest's Tale* (IV, 1491–1505). He says he is a 'court-man' and never disputes his lord's opinions, but reflects them (1484–1518). Like the image of the mirror (IV, 1582), this echoes an idea found also in the *Miller's Tale* (I, 3611–13), that people can harm themselves by attending too much to subjective fantasies. Being self-centred, January sees his wish-fulfilment, 'Heigh fantasye', more than he sees external reality.

Justinus' moral, sensible and religious arguments do dispute and counter January's. Sometimes he sets January's foolish fantasies against a pessimism about women and marriage which draws on anti-feminist tradition (IV, 1519–65); sometimes reminds him of religious priorities, (IV, 1674–85). These two approaches combine in the serious joke that a wife may prove to be not heaven but purgatory (IV, 1670–3): in purgatory worldly sins were cleansed away so that the soul could enter heaven.

May's Marriage

January treats conjugal pleasure as a commodity he can buy; his mercantile and blindly subjective approach is summed up in the image of a mirror in a market-place (IV, 1580–7). The text has already compared a wife with the acquisition of other possessions:

As londes, rentes, pasture, or commune	*grazing rights*
Or moebles . . .	*furniture*
	(IV, 1313–4)

Chaucer juxtaposes description of the marriage contract, whereby May is *feffed in his lond* (IV, 1698), with the religious service which also makes secure what Justinus calls January's *right* (IV, 1662). In the next passage the priest

| . . . made al siker ynogh with hoolynesse. | *secure* |
| | (IV, 1708) |

Whose point of view is expressed in that last line? Is it the priest's: either naive or worldly? Or is it January's: expressing his blind confidence that a married man cannot commit sin with his wife? Or is it the narrator ridiculing January's smug assurance that law and religion sanction him – presumably using *siker* with savage irony? Aers (1986: 72–3) argues that Chaucer here exposes the Church's role in 'the perpetuation of a marital institution based on economic power and male enthralment of females' (p. 72). The complexity arises because the narrative voice captures incompatible attitudes in these words (*siker* and *hoolynesse* do not relate quite so easily in the context of this marriage, and both words are being used in questionable senses), and the lines could be spoken both by someone within the hypocrisy it points to and by someone outside it. There is no single answer to the question of who speaks here. This absence of fixed narrative stance may relate to Chaucer's revelation in this tale of a range of attitudes to gender relations: the many tones and assumptions we hear, even within one sentence; and the text's readiness to enter constantly into a predatory male's mindset, but with horror, may reflect the complexities for a male author of an undertaking an enlightened examination of multiple perceptions of marriage within a male-dominated society. This is another sense in which it is a tale about points of view:

Ful many a man weneth to seen a thyng,
And it is al another than it semeth.

(IV, 2408–9)

We have seen January's predatory approach to women already as early
as IV, 1249–50: he has been a bachelor for sixty years:

> And folwed ay his bodily delyt
> *On* wommen, ther as was his appetyt.

(IV, 1250; my italics)

Here the horror is in the preposition. Now, dreaming of his wedding-
night –

> . . . in his herte he gan hire to manace   *menace*
> That he that nyght in armes wolde hire streyne   *press*

(IV, 1752–3)

– it is in the register of the verbs *manace, streyne*. Their sexual union (IV,
1821–54) is described in terms of uncomfortable actions he does to
her: 'lulleth, kisseth . . . ful ofte, rubbeth hire aboute hir tendre face',
'trespace', 'laboureth'. He acts upon her, speaks at her, chatters, jokes,
sings in bed next to her – all actions that might normally involve
communication and mutuality – and we never hear of any response.
The physical details of his body, bristles, slack throat, scrawny neck, are
disgusting in their total effect not simply because he is old and badly
shaven but because physical desire is not being reciprocated here.
Paradoxically the absence of May from the description creates the
context that turns the experiences it describes into truly obscene
immorality: paradoxically the viewpoint is hers.

The *cliket* gate, whose key January has, but May gives to Damian,
symbolises entry to her body – a garden of delight – and also January's
attitude of ownership of her – a private treasure-box. Holding on to
her, he manifests both possessiveness and blindness. Objects, images
and actions in the text tend to be sexualised or commercialised or both:
the key passing from one man to another; fire in the bed-straw (IV,
1783); a man's 'owene knyf' (IV, 1840); the purse containing the love-
letter May puts in her bosem (IV, 1937–44); the 'warm wax' men can
plie with their hands (IV, 1430–1 and 2117–21). Bathos is used, both
to satirise elderly lust (the cough that wakes January leads to a demand
for sex, IV, 1956–61) and to rein in the moderate amount of sympathy
the narrative allows us to feel for young love (May puts the love-letter
down the privy, IV, 1950–4).

The plot uses a traditional fabliau and folklore plot (see Benson and
Andersson 1971: 203–73). Several versions of the story incorporate a

sequence where two supernatural beings have power both to restore sight and to sit positioned above the human world with superior knowledge of what is going on. They have the same viewpoint as dramatic irony gives the reader (who may not sympathise with January). Yet, at first sight, they also represent a morally normative role when, with stern concern for morality, they restore January's sight. But that they also allow May to escape punishment is a surprising addition to the tale's treatment of marriage. Below the comic level of the anti-feminist joke about women's tricks involved in this escape by May from punishment, this is also the culmination of the unusual line the tale takes on marriage and lust, allowing May's response to emotional brutality more rights in the artistic balance of the tale than the low moral level of her reaction justifies. Chaucer here, as perhaps with the *Wife of Bath's Prologue*, shows degrading treatment producing a reaction which is just as devoid of conscience, but apparently justified. With the Wife's exploitative attitude to her first three husbands we were not shown what caused it: any sense that society is to blame is implicit. Here, however, oppression of and assault on May is recorded in detail.

The text's most striking element is its *tone*, not just sentences but even single lines shift dizzyingly between registers with smooth skill:

> And folwed ay his bodily delyt
> On wommen, ther as was his appetyt,
> As doon thise fooles that been seculeer.
> And whan that he was passed sixty yeer,
> Were it for hoolynesse or for dotage
> I kan nat seye, but swich greet corage
> Hadde this knyght to been a wedded man
> That day and nyght he dooth al that he kan
> T'espien where he myghte wedded be,
> Preyinge oure Lord to graunten him that he
> Mighte ones knowe of thilke blisful lyf . . .

(IV, 1249–59)

Shock here is contained in the incompatibility of pairing 'hoolynesse' and 'dotage', and in the two senses of 'corage' (amorous desire and soldierly bravery), in the unexpected 'on wommen', and the long-delayed 'T'espien', and the syntax that makes a wife sound like a place (where . . .), 1257; but even more disconcerting is the shifting view-point – the contempt in the third line and the wistful tone of the last two lines. Whose voice speaks this? From what basis does it condemn

'seculeer' fools? Is the belief in God's gift of bliss the narrator's or only
the knight's fantasy cynically observed? The narrative says here 'I kan
nat seye', and in a general sense that stands for the absence of a single,
identifiable, narrative voice in these lines. When lines from the Song of
Songs, famous as love poetry and as mystic allegory, are called 'lewed'
(VII, 2149), again: whose attitude is this? Is the lament to Fortune for
making January 'deceyved' (IV, 2057–68) sincere or mock-heroic
contempt for one so self-deceived?[3] This is the tale that best fits the
Exegetical School of criticism. The opposing tenets, concupiscence and
charity, which the School proposes all medieval literature teaches, are
clearly poles on which the portrait of January is built. The *Parson's Tale*
sums up the polarities clearly:

> And this concupiscence, whan it is wrongfully disposed. . . in man,
> it maketh hym coveite, by coveitise of flessh, flesshly synne, by sighte
> of his eyen as to erthely thynges.   (X, 335)

Yet the nature of January's sinfulness, as Chaucer's poetry presents it,
goes beyond these polarities, centred as they are on attitudes to God
and this world; his sin lies in how he treats others, in his insensitivity
and exploitiveness as much as in his disregard for God. January sins as
a husband as well as a soul. To strict exegetical criticism, January's lusts
and Nicholas's would be the same, but it seems to Chaucer they are not,
since Chaucer does not attribute to Nicholas the lack of concern for
mutuality which clearly makes his portrait of January's lechery damning. Similarly, though Aurelius in the *Franklin's Tale* is associated with
a garden, Chaucer takes no pains to render his desires an affront to religion by invoking the setting's biblical associations, or by any other
methods. Strict medieval Christian teaching would see procreation as a
virtuous justification for sex, but January's vision of May as 'fruyt of his
tresor', source of an heir, is satirised, by 'tresor', as valuing money more
than the individual. What Chaucer stresses through his verbal handling
of January is not simply that he follows ever his 'bodily delyt' and
'appetyt', but that he follows them 'on women'. As with the treatment
of the sin of avarice elsewhere in the *Canterbury Tales*, the evil of
exploiting others as objects, commodities or dupes, arouses as much
moral horror as the spiritual personal evil of being absorbed in money.

  This tale depicts sexual oppression of a woman within marriage,
because of partriarchal power, the economic dominance of men, and –
Aers would argue – the connivance of Church and culture which facilitate such oppression through such requirements as the obedience of

wives. Yet it is an *exposé* of the horrors of male sexual oppression written by a man, which uses biblical images (the garden especially) against this, and Chaucer focuses not just on January's lechery but on May's situation: her negation – by the system and the advantages January takes from it, as rich man and husband.

> God woot what that May thoughte in hir herte,

Chaucer comments (IV, 1851). He does not tell us, but the question makes this negative in the text its most original element, morally, in his description of the marriage. The extraordinary virtuosity of the 'mixed style' of the *Merchant's Tale* speaks of the incompatibility of the different viewpoints that confront a male author contemplating contemporary marriage practice, biblical and clerical teaching, masculine desire and power, and trying to take in the situation of women at the same time. Its core is a simple fabliau plot about seeing and not-seeing, but the style suggests there is almost too much, in this subject, to see, and little possibility of arriving at a single, monologic lesson or conclusion.

12

The *Squire's* and the *Franklin's Tales*

The *Squire's Tale* begins with an exotic visitor riding into the hall where King Cambyuskan of Tartary sits in state. Many romances begin in this way, with a stranger bursting into a hall where a king holds court, including Chrétien de Troyes' *Lancelot* (*c*.1170), and *Sir Gawain and the Green Knight* (*c*.1390). The *Squire's Tale* is a text which is self-conscious about its own nature as a narrative. Chaucer alludes to Gawain and Lancelot (at V, 95, 287), paragons of *curteisie* from romance, a reference which verbally underlines the theme of the cultural ideal of *gentillesse*, and also enhances the sense of his tale's lineage in old romance and its representative role in the *Canterbury Tales'* anthology of genres as an example of romance as vehicle for the knightly myth. The preliminary motif of the stranger bringing a challenge, a message or – as here – a gift is a narratological device heralding the start of the adventure, for the story itself arrives with the visitor. Similarly, these gifts speak, indirectly and mysteriously at this stage, of the narrative which is to unfold: the brass steed that will fly anywhere, the mirror which warns of danger, the sword that can disable or heal, and the ring which reveals what birds say – these all arouse suspense, and yet we also anticipate that each will form part of the tale to come. They are a half-veiled table of contents for the forthcoming narrative.

Romances set in Asia, and tales with mechanical and magical marvels and devices, were popular. Long romances with interwoven subplots were also common, and the leisurely style with which the presents are described, and the introduction of a new story with the falcon's lament, may, Cooper suggests (1996,1996: 217–23), indicate Chaucer intended an 'interlaced' romance of this kind. Self-conscious recognition of the text's structure appears at V, 401–8, with a comment on narrative construction: the 'knotte why that every tale is toold' (V, 401) is a rhetorical concept – the design of the parts of a narrative to lead to a point. Many of the *Canterbury Tales* seem, as we have seen, to represent different aspects of authorship and the *Squire's Tale* appears to focus attention on the narrative itself as a design or a mechanical contraption. There are further comments on the conduct of the narrative, for example at V, 651–70. The tale shows general interest in the mechanics of how things work: the people, wondering at the magic ring, remind themselves that scientific explanations have made plain the operation of many phenomena that first appeared merely wonders – a good analogy for romance, a machine for generating wonder, or, indeed, for any fiction. Cambyuskan asks to have the working of the horse explained, the knobs and 'al the gyn' (V, 310–39), like any man with a new machine, and the text gives us too the detailed pleasure of the narrative system. Scientific explanation of another kind appears in V, 346–75: the process of digestion and the effects of alcohol on the human system.

This particular machine, the narrative, however, goes nowhere. Does the summary of the rest of its plot in V, 654–70, just before the text breaks off, mean that Chaucer never intended to finish it?[1] It is hard to suppose the courteous Franklin interrupts the Squire: that would be *ungentil*. Yet it is possible Chaucer meant us to imagine this, and what more *gentil*, if a tale potentially enormous and belonging to a lengthy type of romance, has to be cut short, than an interruption full of praise for its quality rather than its length? What we have, bears out the Franklin's praise: *gentillesse*, virtue, feeling, and eloquence are its hallmarks. *Gentillesse* is demonstrated in the virtues of sincerity, fidelity, and intensity that characterise the falcon's love, and in the *pite* of Canacee's response to her: she voices a central tenet of Chaucer's:

> '. . . pitee renneth soone in gentil herte'
>
> (V, 479)

(see Gray 1979, and Burnley 1979: 116, 126–70, on the importance of the theme of *pite* in Chaucer). The dashing tercelet, however, expert in the arts of love – fine speeches, an air of abasement to his lady, kneeling, weeping, lamenting – represents empty *gentillesse*, very reminiscent of hypocritical knights who betray faithful women in Chaucer's *Anelida* and the *Legend of Good Women*.[2] Chaucer left those two studies of abandoned women and male deceivers unfinished too: perhaps he found the theme one it was impossible to leave alone but too much an emotional and moral *impasse* ever to bring to artistic closure. If this story is deliberately left unfinished, then the 'wordes of the frankelyn to the squier' and the *Franklin's Prologue* are integral parts of a continuing text.[3] If we take them as a sequence, this tale and the *Franklin's Prologue* and *Tale* develop together themes of *gentillesse* and virtue. The Franklin, having paid the Squire many compliments, pays him a further one in disclaiming for himself the eloquence the young man demonstrated V, 716–18 (he associates rhetorical High Style directly with rank, *gentil* versus *burel*, making explicit the links implicit in the *Knight's Tale*). The Franklin praises the Squire for showing promise, considering his youth: he talks of his great future in eloquence, foresees *continuaunce* of his gifts. This would fit well with the hypothesis that Chaucer intended that the continuance of his tale should for now be left to the imagination, and a more fatherly figure should take the reins into his own hands. The *Squire's Tale* is as *gentil*, as promising, and as unfinished, as the Squire himself is. Since Chaucer provides no fictional statement that the Franklin interrupts, but just lets the text of the *Squire's Tale* stop and the Franklin's words take over (V, 672–3), do we have a moment here which breaks the fictional illusion for a moment, rather as the *Parson's Tale* does, with its anti-fiction manifesto and its non-fictional conclusion, the *Retraction*? The simple, safe explanation is that Chaucer intended to come back and finish the *Squire's Tale*, but it is possible he was content to break it off and do so in this metafictional manner, with the material text momentarily taking the place of the fictional narrative. At all accounts, it is clear Chaucer was prepared to use non-completion as an aesthetic device: within the fiction the *Monk's Tale* and *Thopas* are broken off; perhaps neither the *Cook's* nor the *Squire's Tale* were meant to be finished.

The *Franklin's Prologue*

Critical discussion of the Franklin and his *Prologue* has been dominated by controversy over whether franklins were *nouveau riche* landowners in the period or an established category of country squires (see discussion on p. 38), and whether this particular one is presented as *arriviste* (Knight 1986: 117–24), a blunt man (Pearsall 1985: 148–50), or a fine old English gentleman (Pearcy 1973–4). Whereas that last definition fits the *General Prologue* portrait well, these passages linking the *Squire's* and *Franklin's Tale* actually operate in a fusion of all three: the Franklin expresses, with the appreciation of a gentleman, admiration for the truly *gentil* qualities of the *Squire's*

Tale; he also speaks bluntly of money and n'er-do-well sons, and declares himself *burel*. Yet he also combines together *gentil* and *burel* responses in a socially anxious and self-conscious fashion: in considering gentility (like land) in relation to money, and as something he is most anxious for his son to *lerne*, by suspecting the Host is *desdeyning* him (V, 683, 694, 700), by apologising for the way he talks (a characteristically English anxiety of the socially ambitious even then?), and above all by being able to define *gentil* qualities so distinctly, he speaks for, and as one of, those who were conscious of having achieved social ascent. Chaucer himself became a Justice of the Peace and entered the fringes of the *gentil* class as an esquire – became Franklin-like in some respects – a reward for ability as an upwardly mobile civil servant (if he acquired gentility, his too was learned). The Franklin, like the Manciple, may dramatise perhaps an aspect, a sociological aspect, of Chaucer himself, but what he certainly is in this Link is an appropriate voice, a social boundary-crossing voice, to take us over from the *Squire's Tale*'s definitions of *gentillesse* (decorative, cultural and emotional) to the *Franklin's Tale*'s encounter between inherited and meritocratic *gentillesse*.

The *Franklin's Tale*

Like the *Wife of Bath's* and *Clerk's Tales*, the *Franklin's Tale* is concerned with definitions of nobility; all three tales present virtue (specifically generosity towards others) as central to the true concept of *gentillesse*, a proposition that was virtually a literary cliché by Chaucer's time (see p. 101). It is also offered as a power which can elide distinctions between social ranks and resolve potential power conflicts within marriage and society. In this tale the theme of true *gentillesse* is presented without a religious dimension. Instead, the proposition about nobility and generosity is set in relation to money and to the figure of the professional, a magician, who works for a fee. The other two tales remain within the literary equivalents of feudal, dynastic realms: an Arthurian setting for one and the all-powerful rule of a Lombardy marquis in the other. The *Franklin's Tale*'s locations, however, shift between the castle of Pedmark, in feudal Brittany, and Orléans, a university town: between a world whose inhabitants inherit their wealth – Aurelius is waiting to come into his inheritance – and a world whose inhabitants can drive a 'bargayn' (V, 1230), negotiate a 'tretee' over the 'sommme', price (V, 1219–20; it is noticeable how

Aurelius returns negotiation to knightly terminology: 'lord', 'we been knyt', 'trewly', 'trouthe', V, 1227–31).

The tale's plot resembles two narratives by Boccaccio: one in *Il Filocolo* and one in the *Decameron*, told on Day Ten, when the theme is those who have performed generous acts (see p. 118).

> A wife, tired of an importunate suitor, sets him an impossible task, to make a garden bloom in January. When, with a magician's help, he succeeds, her husband tells her to keep her promise. The reasons vary: because the suitor has earned it (*Filocolo*); because her motives were pure and one should keep promises, and the husband fears what the suitor and magician might do (*Decameron*). The suitor is so impressed by the husband's generosity he declines the offer, and the magician refuses his fee: how could he lack the courtesy (*Filocolo*) or generosity (*Decameron*) the other two have shown?
>
> (Bryan and Dempster 1941: 377–83)

To the *Filocolo* tale's concluding question, which of the three men was most generous, the judgement is that it was the husband, because what he was willing to sacrifice, his honour, is more valuable than love or money; the *Decameron* narrator judges the lover is more generous than the lady, but the audience discusses the claims of the lover, husband and magician without coming to agreement.

Boccaccio depicts fictional listeners discussing the issues in his tales with a formally stated theme (generosity here) in mind, perhaps an inspiration for Chaucer's more informal pilgrim discussions. The Franklin's concluding question, 'Which was the mooste fre?' (V, 1622), implies that this tale's over-riding theme is 'fredom', but it offers a multiplicity of issues for discussion. *Free* itself had three main senses: 'generous', 'noble', and 'without restraint' (the main modern meaning): three ideas all explored in the text.

Like the *Wife of Bath's Tale*, the plot hinges on transformation. Its two dénouements are both transformations: the magician's removal of the rocks, which resolves Aurelius's seemingly insoluble problem of how to sleep with Dorigen, and the magician's act of generosity, which releases Aurelius from his debt. That second dénouement is the last of a concatenation of generous reversals of natural expectations, preceded by Arveragus's reformulation of a husband's rights and a wife's honour, in which he gives up his exclusive rights to her body; and by Aurelius's abnegation of rights so dearly won by performance of a promised feat. It is about transformations by magic and by the magic of human self-sacrifice.

Dilemmas of Love and Honour

Kittredge (1915: 185–211) believed the tale solved the dilemma of the Marriage Debate, showing how perfect love could replace striving for *maistrie*; his reading may have been over-optimistic on that score, for today the tale seems to be a problem-posing tale rather than an answer. Yet the story does begin with an ideal of friendly equality between a man and woman who love each other: such an ideal *is* voiced in the passage on marriage (V, 745–98), however much what is said there is also full of ambiguities and contradictions, which we shall examine later. And the plot ends with another ideal, one already proposed in the *Wife's* and *Clerk's Tales*: that conflicts of interest in society or between individuals can be solved by acts of individual voluntary selflessness. Both these ideals are problematic, of course, especially in a society where hierarchies in marriage and relationships between different ranks are fairly fixed. After the opening discussion of power in marriage, the story seems to have come to a premature storybook happy ending: a blissfully happy marriage. And it is premature, for all marriages sail on seas with black rocks. The *Franklin's Tale*, for all its fairytale air, is in part a tale about what happens after the happy ending of marriage.

At its centre is the image of the black rocks, which seem to threaten the safety of Dorigen's husband and destroy her peace of mind. Fortune's residence is on rocks amid pounding seas in the *Romance of the Rose*, lines 5891–6562, a passage which discusses both the random adversities of life and the need for nobles to have courtesy and prowess. These rocks are made, in Dorigen's speech, an occasion to question the whole purpose of God, not in the smaller structure of marriage but in the whole design of human life (V, 865–93). How could a good creator, she asks, who – we are told – loves humanity, create a world with such dangers in it? She calls them 'feendely': her question is about not just physical dangers and adversities, but also the existence of sin in the world. In the *Man of Law's Tale*, it was God's hand that solved Custance's problems. If there is an answer within the tale to the question Dorigen raises so boldly here, perhaps it is human generosity of spirit. The *Knight's Tale* asked similar questions and the answers were more philosophic, but bleak: endurance, trust in an ultimate design, and trust in change and time's passing. The *Franklin's Tale* perhaps stands between that Stoic answer and the fully religious answers of the Second Nun and the Parson, that this transitory life is nothing, except a place for moral choice and the making of a soul for eternal life.

In practice, in the tale it is not so much sin or rocks as love which threatens Dorigen's security, the unfortunate love which Aurelius conceives for her. As with the *Squire's Tale* falcon, love brings pain. Chaucer never builds up in the style of the writing any sense of this passion as sin; it is presented simply as a fact and a problem. Aurelius is virtuous (V, 926–59); he suffers terribly and sincerely. Chaucer eschews using the garden setting (V, 902–17) to suggest Eden or sin (as the *Merchant's Tale* does). A tragedy of virtue is created. Dorigen's fatal promise was motivated by her love for her husband. Chaucer presents us with a series of conundrums about morality and ethical decision-making, rather than any strongly felt sense of evil. One conundrum is that it is not through evil but through love and devotion that the moral problem arises; another is that Dorigen's promise raises the question of what kind of action is most truly honourable. For a woman to have sex with someone other than her husband is a loss of honour – in medieval society loss of honour for him as well as for her; but to break a promise is also dishonour. Chaucer's tale faces us with the fact that there may be co-existing but conflicting moral imperatives.

Aurelius expresses his love in song, and emotional situations are presented quasi-operatically in this tale. At intervals the narrative halts while aria-like speeches or mood-expressing background descriptions fill our attention. Aurelius's highly rhetorical prayers to Phoebus and Diana are arias of this kind; so are Dorigen's speeches to God and Fortune, each expressing despair about whether any loving power exists to avert danger to marriage, and whether there is any honourable alternative for a raped woman than death. Her address to God (V, 865–93) gives dignity to her subsequent rash promise by its religious and philosophical profundity and the intensity of emotion it suggests on her part. The speech about women who have committed suicide establishes her as an honourable woman. In its very length and its classical elaboration of her theme, it marks the gravity of her state of mind before the story requires that that state of mind is over-ruled by her husband's ruling. From the point of view of realistic narrative, it is absurd: it is too long and she does not act upon it, but this is not simply a text of mimetically plausible speech, action or motivation; it is fable or fairytale raising questions for discussion about human relationships. The elements of psychological verisimilitude and naturalistically observed speech it possesses are only intermittent. In the tradition of oral reception of texts, to which Chaucer's composition, despite its written state, still to some extent belongs, a speech's length and homogeneity strengthen its emotional power. The reply her husband gives answers both kinds of despair, that she must either die or lose honour, by offering love, a new concept of the husband's role, and a wider concept of female honour.

Their dialogue (V, 1457–92) catches her despair in its distracted repetitions, ' "Thus have I seyd,' quod she, "thus have I sworn" – / And toold hym . . .'. Arveragus's *freendly* calm is the reader's first surprise: before anything else, he reassures her of love, reduces the magnitude of the problem. He releases her from the narrow concept of a woman's honour as consisting solely of her sexual chastity. He does her the honour of commanding her to act as an honourable man would do: to keep her word (see Mann 1991: 111–20). Such fidelity to a promise is also traditionally central to feudal, knightly, identity. Chaucer presents him as emotionally wracked by the dilemma of different kinds of love – sexual possession versus selflessness – and different kinds of honour – chastity or fidelity. To the modern reader this does not make his behaviour wholly honourable. His command to her to accept rape raises further issues; this woman's moral identity and will are still being defined by a man. Possibly, medieval readers too could have seen that Dorigen is being sacrificed: the question of whether the woman in the story might not be the most generous person was, after all, raised in the *Filocolo*. Chaucer's text perhaps briefly directs our attention to the imposition of masculine decisions on her when in V, 1509–13 he isolates tellingly the facts of Arveragus's command and his principle of 'trouthe': as she leaves one man and bumps into the other, she tells him 'half as she were mad':

'Unto the gardyn, *as myn housbonde bad*,   *ordered*
My trouthe for to holde'.

(V, 1512–13; my italics)

No longer self-directed in any sense, she repeats like an automaton Arveragus's decisions, made for her, seeming not to recognise the man she is addressing as the potential rapist. Unlike Boccaccio, Chaucer depicts the lover as struck by her sorrow, as well as by the husband's nobility (V, 1515–20).

We have been prepared for Aurelius's lust to turn to ashes at this point by the mood-music of the set-piece that introduced this whole act of the drama: the description of winter in V, 1239–55 (perhaps in the decision to use changing landscapes, symbolically appropriate to the mood of the story, Chaucer was inspired by Boccaccio's much simpler motif of the summer–winter garden). The May garden of the beginning of Aurelius's love (V, 901–41) gives way to barrenness (V, 1250–1);

Phoebus descends from high to low, grows old (V, 1245–9). Winter is presented as a season of doubleness: the double-faced god Janus and a combination of dearth and merriment – fit prelude to an event which will bring hope and happiness to Aurelius and despair and abjection to Dorigen, who is, in the reality he cannot yet see, not his love but his victim.

The multiplicity of meanings with which Chaucer invests most turning-points in his plots is evident in the last dénouement, the Clerk's generous act. We have seen that it signifies, for him, a sort of moral entry into the knightly class. It also asserts the doctrine that true *gentillesse* is created not by birth but by virtuous action. It typifies, in a way the other men's *fre* actions do not, the Squire–Franklin Link's theme that money does not matter compared with high-minded principles. But there is an extra theme, which Chaucer inserts into the wording of the Clerk's declaration of the reasoning behind his decision, and it is to do with his professional skills and payment for them:

> For, sire, I wol nat taken a peny of thee
> For al my craft, ne noght for my travaille.
> Thou hast ypayed wel for my vitaille.
> It is ynogh . . .
>
> (V, 1616–19)

Even at this moment when Chaucer's plot unites all protagonists in acts of gloriously unworldly nobility of spirit, he introduces awareness of just what is the economic basis of this speaker's rank: the clerk earns his money from his 'craft' and 'travaille' (it is the professional class to which Chaucer himself belonged). The theme of the economic base, first raised in the Squire–Franklin Link, returns thus at the tale's end: part of a characteristically Chaucerian sober reminder of economic mechanisms in this otherwise fantastical milieu. Another instance is the insertion of practical detail about how Aurelius will pay his debt (V, 1570–84): he will ask for an arrangement to pay 'upon sueretee'. When considering the *General Prologue* portrait of the Knight, we saw how Chaucer's evocation of the chivalric myth there evades any reference to the power structures, the possessions and financial resources that made participation in such expensive military campaigns possible, but when we come to the Squire–Franklin Link and *Franklin's Tale* this issue of the relationship between wealth, rank and *gentil* qualities comes to the surface.

The unresolved issues and aporias in the text – Arveragus's departure, for the sake of honour, the unqualified beauty with which

Aurelius's disastrous love is described, Dorigen's unanswered questions to God, the absence of any suicide after her speech about suicide, the capacity of virtuous love to bring misery, the differing nature of honour and power between ranks and sexes, the phenomenon of fierce extra-marital passion among virtuous, well-meaning people, and of physical dangers in a benignly ordained Creation – all these help to create a text which challenges comfortable assumptions about the order of things.[4] The clerk's rejection of a fabulous fee challenges social order, showing there is nothing innate about *gentil* behaviour. The tale is an issue-raising fable, not just because it ends with an explicit question but as a result of the way it uses language and literary forms throughout. The opening passage, for example, the marital arrangement that is supposed to solve tensions between husband and wife, is introduced through a passage that is a *tour de force* of dialogic writing. Doubts about whether the formulas for strife-free marriage outlined in the opening lines can ever work, or can even be formulated in terms that make sense, in a hierarchical society, arise as the language begins to jangle, and chop and change, terms like *servant/lord*, *servant/love*, *lord/marriage*, *lordshipe/ servage*, *lady/love*, *lady/wyf*, in V, 791–8. Of the answers to conflict which Chaucer gives, the one which he makes sound most convincing is not this curious conceit of unequal equality but rather his usual solution to the strains and inexplicable dilemma of human life: that of *suffrance* and self-*governaunce*. The passage is a dazzling revelation of paradoxes within contemporary social and literary discourse of sexual love and marital power-relations. The overall effect is not self-cancelling, however, but an awareness of unresolved and irreducible incompatible value-systems co-existing.

The passage contains, notwithstanding, admirable principles and practical good counsel. There is no more useful advice about marriage than the lines about tolerance in V, 776–86. The theme of freedom, in the modern sense, is presented as a mutually shared aspect of human nature and love:

> Wommen, of kynde, desiren libertee,
> And nat to been constreyned as a thral;
> And so doon men . . .

> Whan maistrie comth, the God of Love anon
> Beteth his wynges, and farewel, he is gon!
> Love is a thyng as any spirit free.

(V, 768–70, 765–7)

'Free love', however, in the tale threatens disaster. The plot is one where each character finally binds him or herself to an obligation, and the resolution of the incompatibility and conflict of their desires and rights is through self-governance. This is *fredom* in the sense of 'generosity'.

The Tale as Breton *Lai*

Chaucer calls the *Franklin's Tale* a Breton *lai*. The most famous Breton *lais* are twelve Anglo-Norman short romances by Marie de France, *c*.1160. They were known, and some were translated, in fourteenth-century England. Chaucer may have been familiar with them and perhaps they provide a model of the type of narrative he had in mind when designating this tale a Breton *lai*. Love is their main subject. Most of Marie's *lais* centre on a passion which is mutual and irresistible. Occasionally she shows a passion begetting treachery and ruthlessness where the lovers are selfish and lack self-mastery. She also shows husbands who act with possessive, cruel domination. The kind of love she celebrates above all is a shared passion accompanied by sensitivity to others, generosity, sincerity and devotion. It is these personal qualities, rather than the presence or absence of marriage between the lovers, which act as the moral restraints in her vision of sexual relationships and define a love as virtuous. Her tales often involve magic, and magical motifs symbolise both love's power and some of the moral issues concerning passion which her *lais* explore: in one *lai* a magically propelled boat and a knot which only the beloved can untie symbolise the notion of a unique and fated union; in another, a man's transformation into a werewolf makes the reader question not just differences distinguishing men from animals but the almost more decisive differences that separate the *gentil* behaviour of humans who are sensitive and loyal to others from the voracious savagery of other humans who lack these qualities. The *Franklin's Tale*'s black rocks and their removal fit this model and are perhaps a symbol of this type.

It was perhaps because it centred on magic and the power of human generosity that Chaucer decided to recast the Boccaccio tale as a Breton *lai*. Marie's *lais* are central documents in the literary tradition which has been labelled by modern critics 'Courtly Love' – a concept as complex and fraught with problems of definition as 'feudalism' (see Burnley 1998: 148–75). Marie's *lais* and this tale present a passionate love as a supreme force in the lives of two people, a source of moral dilemmas but also, at its highest level, providing a moral strength which equals or transcends the influence of conventional sanctions such as marriage or chivalric honour. The *Franklin's Tale* finds perfect love within a marriage, but that is because it is a marriage centred on freely given and shared love.

Like the *Franklin's Tale*, Marie's *lais* portray extramarital love not as an inevitable sin or doomed folly, but as the birth of a second love, coming into existence in parallel to a marriage relationship, and as posing problems and challenges to human beings to act with faithful emotions, pure motives and charity. It is personal self-sacrifice which provides the dénouement and resolution of problems in *Eliduc*, where a wife gives up her husband when she perceives the strength of his love for a young girl, and *Le Freine* where a poor girl allows, with generosity, her lover to marry a high-born woman. In Marie's *Guigemar* a husband, like Arveragus, leaves his wife to win knightly renown abroad and as a result of this honourable action a love-triangle develops. Marie's *lais* created, then, a very distinctive genre: celebrating *gentillesse*, magic, love and delight, but also seeing human experience, emotional and moral experience, as inevitably incurring perils, difficulties and pain, some of which are caused by actions that in themselves are honourable, and which are irresolvable – except by magic or unselfishness. Chaucer develops the genre into new areas, however, by introducing philosophical and social topics which problematise questions of divine order, honour and sexual desire, and marital and social hierarchy, more urgently and directly than anything in Marie's *lais* and their successors.

Why did Chaucer allot this tale to the Franklin? His interest in *gentillesse* and money are perhaps presented as typifying a mixture of social standing and social insecurity in the contemporary position of a franklin of his type, taking up local government and acting as part of the regional squirearchy – which would make a tale about encounters on class-boundaries appropriate for him. His hospitality in the *General Prologue*, in its own way, prefigures the tale's theme of generosity, and its archaic word *vavasour* links him – like the Squire's talk of Gawain and Lancelot as bygone heroes of an 'olde curteisye' (V, 95, 287) – to old romance, the literary location of 'Thise olde gentil Britouns' (V, 709). Perhaps Chaucer was intrigued by the fact that literary forms, like humans and human social rank, can have lineage but need constantly to be made anew.

13
The *Physician's Tale*

The *Physician's Tale* is another story of a virtuous woman who undergoes unmerited suffering. Virginia's father kills her rather than let her fall into the hands of a lecherous judge. Like the *Clerk's* and *Man of Law's Tale*, this is a kind of secular saint's or martyr's story and it culminates in the vindication of virtue and the defeat of evil. It is also a tale that exemplifies the late medieval (and Chaucer's own) taste for pathos. Virginia's horror, tears and swoons at the proposal for her death are shown (VI, 231–45), but she recovers herself and goes forward unflinchingly to death, endorsing the values of virginity and obedience to her father and to God's will, at the cost of her own young life.

There seems no obvious link between the tale and the narrator's profession, though Chaucer adds medical jargon to the Host's coarse joking after the tale. The Host transfers the language of illness and medicine to his own game of story-telling: the tragic *Physician's Tale* has almost given him a heart attack, and he will need the remedy either of good beer or of a cheerful tale.

Honour and Dishonour

The story is from Book VI of Livy's *History of Rome* (*c*.AD 17), which also includes the story of Lucretia, retold by Chaucer in the *Legend of Good Women*. Both depict wronged women dying to protect their chastity, and powerful men abusing their power for corrupt ends. Chaucer may have known Livy's account, but probably took the story from the *Romance of the Rose*, 5589–658, where Reason tells it to illustrate the need for justice in an imperfect world and the importance of kings and judges administering justice rightly.

The *Canterbury Tales* shows incompatibly varied approaches to the imposition of unwanted sex on women. The *Wife of Bath's Tale* presents rape as an un*gentil* act of oppression by a powerful male; in the *Man of*

Law's Tale Custance is married off and sex is presented as a necessary trial she has to accept obediently. The *Physician's Tale* illustrates the traditional assumption (challenged in the *Franklin's Tale*) that for a woman her honour resides totally in her sexual purity and her sexual reputation. A woman's lost honour brings dishonour also on her family. The idea that death is the only honourable course for a woman facing this type of dishonour is voiced in the *Franklin's Tale* in Dorigen's grandiloquent speech listing women who have died rather than incur sexual assault, but the tale overturns this assumption: Dorigen's husband deems female sexual honour less important than other kinds of honour, common to men and women. Here Virginia's father in beheading her is preserving not only her but himself from shame. In ancient and medieval society, legal, ethical and social attitudes towards rape saw it, to a considerable extent, as a theft, depriving a woman – and her menfolk – of a possession in which honour, status and financial prospects resided. A virgin deflowered lost her worth in the marriage market – the student who leaps on Malyne in the *Reeve's Tale* has ruined the plans of her socially ambitious parents for an advantageous marriage for her. Rape of a virgin was a more serious crime than rape of a married woman. Modern western views of rape centre, however, on respect for the individual's feelings and the belief that sensitivity and mutuality are the guiding moral principles in sexual encounters. The tale which comes closest to modern moral assumptions is in fact the *Merchant's Tale*, with Chaucer's vivid evocation of January's sexual exploitation of May; it diverts the reader's moral judgements away from her subsequent adultery, though May's sexual subjection to January is presented there within the parameters of comedy not tragedy.

Cultural change is gradual and cumulative: old and new attitudes overlap in the practices, literature and subjective responses of any era. None the less, the *Physician's Tale*'s attitude to what is morally at issue in the story clashes with the dominant assumptions of modern western readers about female sexuality, paternal power, and the plight of a child ensnared into sex-slavery. Furthermore, the tale itself operates morally and emotionally, as Cooper's illuminating account (1996: 250–6) shows, in two somewhat different cultural worlds: one inherited from Roman society and the other more distinctively Christian. Though set in pagan Rome, it is also filled with Christian references and it combines in its approach to virginity a Roman concept of public family honour (a concept with currency still in medieval Europe), where it is appropriately the father's decision that honour requires a beheading, with the more personal, interior, value placed on purity and affection in

Christian literature. Cooper (pp. 250–2) links this addition of Christian cultural assumptions with Chaucer's decision to move the scene of Virginia's beheading from the public court to the private family home. When the two cultural worlds come together in this scene (VI, 207–55), style and content become discordant: Virginius summons his daughter 'With fadres pitee stikynge thurgh his herte' to tell her he must kill her (VI, 211); the murder is an act of love and not hate, he declares (VI, 225).[1] Chaucer saturates this scene between father and daughter before the beheading with emotive language, especially repeated *deere*, making it both the tale's central moment of intimacy and affection and the moment of murder. As in the *Clerk's Tale*, he seems to seek a deliberate conflict of values to construct a narrative enigma.

The *Romance of the Rose* version concentrates on the men: the wicked judge, his henchman and his plot, and the honourable knight Virginius. Chaucer gives somewhat more attention to Virginia, bringing out not only the pathos of her death but, in a long encomium (VI, 30–71, 105–16), her maturity, wisdom and virtue. She is not, like the 'litel clergeoun' of the *Prioress's Tale*, merely a pathetic young victim, nor is a fatal attractiveness presented as her only attribute; this is one of Chaucer's portraits of women with a range of qualities – gifts of beauty, self-control, discretion, intellect, eloquence and sincerity, seriousness, hard work, sobriety, and modesty. She may not have power but she has strengths. Chaucer's long opening section (VI, 1–118) not only depicts Virginia as an impressive fourteen-year-old but also increases our sense of her as a precious treasure for her guardians; first among these is her father, whose only child she is, but the most prominent is Nature who made her a creature of 'greet excellence', to the glory of God, her ally in the work. The story begins with Virginia accompanying her mother to worship at the temple. The long passage of advice to governesses and parents to protect daughters from moral laxity links to this theme of protection. Virginia's may be a story of a young life thrown away but Chaucer injects a sense of parental care and nurture paradoxically from the beginning.

Chaucer's interest in tales of virtuous women, and particularly of virtuous women with the capacity to suffer nobly, perhaps sprang from his work on the *Legend of Good Women*, an unfinished collection of stories showing that women can be faithful in love and be prepared to die for their fidelity. He was probably still engaged with the *Legend* while producing the *Tales*. One of his sources, for parts of the *Wife of Bath's Tale* as well as the *Physician's Tale*, was Jean Le Fèvre's *Livre de*

Leësce, a defence of women against antifeminist slander (Phillips 1995), which contrasts historical records of their virtue with misogynist fables and myths about their wickedness. Virginia is among Le Fèvre's historical examples, which probably explains Chaucer's description of his tale as 'historial thyng notable' (VI, 155–7). Dorigen's list of chaste women who killed themselves, and the *Wife of Bath's Prologue*, are other texts exemplifying Chaucer's interest in how literary tradition and written record present women's experience, to vilify or praise. On the surface this tale takes a simpler, less nuanced line than either of those tales, approving of the death of a sexually compromised woman, but – as so often – it is Chaucer's verbal handling, its discordancies of emotion and values, that raise doubts and complexities, challenging the monologic vision, offering the potential for questioning the ancient cultural sanctions that support it.

14

The *Pardoner's Tale*

The *Pardoner's Tale* belongs to the genre of sermon *exemplum*. *Exempla* (in English *ensamples*, VI, 435) were stories to illustrate a lesson. The *Pardoner's Prologue and Tale* teaches at least three lessons and they are all, in different ways, about death. First, sins will be punished, here or in eternity (see VI, 879–940). Secondly, avarice – which brings about death in the story – is the root of evils (*Radix malorum est cupiditas*, 1 Timothy 6:10: the Pardoner's constant sermon theme), leading to damnation, and avarice also brings a kind of spiritual death (see VI, 423–34). Thirdly, death is always close at hand and humans should be prepared for death and God's Judgement by confessing their sins and performing some form of compensatory penance (see VI, 680–4). The Pardoner declares that avarice makes him himself ineffective at reforming people or living a moral life (VI, 400–6), and the *General Prologue* association of him with homosexuality or effeminacy may also be a metaphorical prefiguring of spiritual barrenness. The tale's image of drunkenness as an entombment of *wit*, intelligence (VI, 558–9), is another instance of the recurrent and multi-faceted theme of death in the tale.

The *Pardoner's Prologue* is long enough to constitute an element in the *Canterbury Tales* in its own right, like the *Wife of Bath's Prologue*, but it contains no narrative and is more directly related to its tale. His address to the pilgrims, before and after the tale, makes a frame for the tale itself. Its preliminary section, the *Prologue*, concerns his sales of false relics; the second part (VI, 895–968) moves on to the sale of pardons as well – allegedly with the power to absolve the soul from its sins and ensure salvation after death (VI, 906–18). These two framing sections show him in action trying to make money: avarice using religion deceptively, and perverting in particular the doctrine of forgiveness of sins that gives people their chance of eternal life. In one sense, then, the tale is a sales trick: its themes of death, sin and punishment are used by him to incite listeners to give money for relics or pardons. A critical issue this raises is whether an author's purpose controls the meaning or the moral worth of a text; can a 'ful vicious man' tell a 'moral tale' (VI, 459–60)? Is a text – rather like a relic – dependent on its origins for what it can do in the world?

The Physician–Pardoner Link introduced this issue of the relation of the author's intention to the meaning of his text, though in the indirect fashion typical of the Links: the Host, having offered his own idiosyncratic interpretations of the previous tale (as an attack on false lawyers or a warning of the perils to women of being too beautiful), proposes the Pardoner's tale should be 'myrthe or japes'. *Jape* at this period meant primarily a 'trick', as well as a 'joke'. The upper-class pilgrims, however, demand 'som moral thyng'. The ensuing tale seems to have the potential to be both a deception, a *jape* to earn money, and an efficacious moral text with the power to teach and reform its listeners. Chaucer puts into the Pardoner's mouth the statement that a *gylty* speaker can nevertheless persuade people to turn from wickedness to penitence (VI, 429–31). Since repentance was the prerequisite for receiving God's mercy and therefore the chance of eternal life, this is not just a literary issue: the immoral Pardoner's moral tale also supports the Church's teaching that fallible people, its ministers, can pass on the gift of salvation to people.

The *Pardoner's Prologue* resembles the Wife of Bath's in taking the form of a rogue's 'confession' of the tricks of the trade, manipulating other people for personal gain (the Wife's trade is marriage). Self-revelatory speeches of this type, voiced by personifications of sins, are found in Langland's presentation of the Seven Deadly Sins in *Piers Plowman*, Passus V, and in the Vice characters in medieval morality drama. Thus, though a modern reader might initially assume the *Prologue* could be read as fictional autobiography, painting an individual character, it has affinities, like the Wife's *Prologue*, to a common medieval type of writing where an *exposé* of a vice is put into first-person confessional format. There is a parallel in the speeches of Faux Semblant, a personification of 'False Seeming', in the *Romance of the Rose* (see lines 11053–238). Like the the alchemist-Canon, the *Summoner's Tale* friar, or the *Reeve's Tale* miller, the Pardoner is a cheat; the text, like the *Canon's Yeoman's Tale*, contains – almost like a documentary – revelation of the fraudster's tricks. He is also, travelling the length of England from Berwick to Ware, one of the mobile money-makers Chaucer seems particularly to abhor: free of scruples, hard to control, and a threat to settled society (see p. 112). His most serious sin, however, is to play fast and loose with Christians' deepest priority, their chance of going to heaven. As the *Prologue* goes on, the revelations get grimmer in tone: the Pardoner describes his words as stinging a victim, and spitting venom out to intimidate anyone who criticises pardoners (VI, 412–22); there are recurrent declarations that his aim is 'to wynne', 'to profit', rather than turn people from 'synne' (neatly rhymed together in VI, 403–4); and he uses the evocative metaphor of souls 'going blackberrying' for all he cares. Since the devil traditionally owns blackberries after November this conjures up a picture of his victims being allowed to wander off like unprotected children, lured by distracting temptations (sweet fruit that can hurt the picker), away from safety to damnation.

The demonstration of typical preaching, up to line 422, is a three-cornered piece of dramatisation, with the Pardoner re-creating for one audience, the pilgrims, what he says to another audience, his congregations. Taking the pilgrim-audience into his confidence is itself a seductive alliance between trickster and listeners with potential dangers – which appear at the tale's close when he moves into the relic-selling spiel again, but this time with his pilgrim-audience as the victims. This sudden twist and the Host's alarmed, defensive reaction to it, raises for us, his third audience, the issue once more of the effect of an author's words on their recipients. He moves from using speech to amuse them to using it to get what he wants out of them – he moves from *myrthe* to *jape*.

The beginning of the *Prologue* (VI, 319–422) displays his speaking style and body-language, his addition of Latin words to 'saffron with my predicacioun' (saffron, a very expensive spice, was a fashionable ingredient in many dishes). The revelations arouse a mixture of disgust and pleasure in the reader. His text invites us and the pilgrim-audience to surmise for ourselves the gullibility of that other audience: they are obviously peasants obsessed with fears of animal diseases and poor crop-yields; the text lets us guess it would be unfaithful wives who would buy charms to put in husbands' pottage (again, a peasant staple food) to prevent jealousy, and that those who give money may do so because they are caught by his warning that those who have serious sins unconfessed will find it hard to come forward and pay. As we make these deductions the dramatic irony is enjoyable, and it induces a morally seductive sense of social and intellectual superiority over the audience depicted – who are clearly, we feel, *lewed* ('uneducated'), lower class, and sin-concealing dupes. There is also an element of roguish triumph in the *japes* and *gaudes*, and anarchic comedy in the absurd claims. The text thus constructs us within a complicity with the Pardoner, rather than with his audiences, which is morally disconcerting. The speech in the *Prologue* includes techniques with powerful realist effect, especially colloquialisms (*jape*, *gaude*, *bekke*), idioms typical of spoken discourse: 'And, sires, also . . .', 'Nay, nay!', 'But herkneth, lordynges', etc.), and a plentiful sprinkling of *I*, *I wol*, *my* and *myself*. Yet these realist devices and the first-person mode are obviously at times being used for statements that could never be, in novelistic manner, a believable speech of autobiographical confidences from a fully conceived character, but are really external observations, visual and moral, about the methods of typical pardoners, which have been put here into first-person form:

Thanne peyne I me to strecche forth the nekke,	*take pains*
And est and west upon the peple I bekke,	*nod*
As dooth a dowve sittynge on a berne.	
	VI, 395–7

I wol noon of the apostles countrefete.	
	(VI, 447)

I wol have moneie, wolle, chese, and whete,	
Al were it yeven of the povereste page,	*even if*
Or of the povereste wydwe in a village,	
Al sholde hir children sterve for famyne.	
	(VI, 448–51)

Faux Semblant voiced similar statements: 'However much I pretend to be poor, I have no regard for poor men' (line 11200), but he was much more a personification than Chaucer's Pardoner, and he also says things like 'At one moment I am a knight, at another a monk': which is clearly a definition of falseness rather than a description of a typically false person.

The *Pardoner's Prologue* presents a satirical picture of typical pardoners' tricks, dressed up as the revelations of a particular Pardoner, but the presentation has such realistic speech and recognisable psychological patterns that it seems on the verge of offering a coherent character. And many critics from Kittredge on (1915: 180) have interpreted the various elements in the *Pardoner's Tale* and the *Prologue* as an external expression of a complex individual consciousness, though arriving often at very different assessments of that character. Pearsall (1985: 91–100) surveys several such 'psychological' readings. He argues that, on the one hand, they have often been naive and neglected aspects of the text that do not fit a 'character' reading, yet, on the other hand, the alternative critical approach, which regards the Pardoner simply like the personifi-cation of an abstract vice, fails to acknowledge Chaucer's skill in creat-ing the illusion of psychological links between different parts of the performance, and the sheer strength of its effect on readers. Pearsall suggests the absence of any indication of motivation, background life, or capacity for change in the presentation creates the impression of a man who is empty, merely a performer. And this relates emblematically to the lesson the text teaches, which is that avarice and deceit atrophy the moral and living self (pp. 100–1). This argument hangs on to the 'psychological' approach while interpreting one of its drawbacks – absence of indications of inner life – as emblematic of the lesson that avarice kills the soul.

Concentrating too much on the relationship between the Pardoner's characterisation and his tale, or on the Pardoner as another of Chaucer's clerical fraudsters, can have the danger of obscuring the fact that thematically this text also has links with the *Parson's Tale* in its concern with sin, penitence and the journey to the eternal life, and also with the *Second Nun's* and *Man of Law's Tale*, in its sense of a total divide between materialism and the needs of the immortal soul.

The *Tale*

In the tale greed for money is linked to death, as in the *Prologue*, and death takes many forms. Money leads to the revellers' deaths literally and on a moral level: making them dead to spiritual awareness or concern for their fellow humans. Their stupidity about the 'theef men clepeth Deeth' (VI, 675), shows an absence of full human understand-ing, caused by worldliness. The *Tale*'s sermon-like first part (VI, 483–657) condemns gluttony and oaths in terms that associate them with death: gluttony brought damnation into the world (VI, 498–511); obsession with eating is a spiritual death, drunkenness a tomb of the mind (VI, 517–48, 551–72); drinking causes deaths (VI, 579–82). 'Great oaths' refer to Christ's death and also bring damnation, *cursednesse*; and often lead to violence and homicide (VI, 629–58).[1] They all also involve trivialisation of serious matters. These are three sins associated with *riot*, undisciplined, indulgent behaviour: a particu-lar temptation of 'yonge folk' (VI, 464). Preachers linked gluttony, gambling and swearing, particularly with taverns.

The tale of three rioters' search for death, the mysterious guide, and the deaths of the three would-be murderers, come from a folktale widely dispersed in Asian, African and European versions. In other versions the Old Man is a benevolent guide; he may be Jesus or a sage. Chaucer chose to make him a mysterious old man who, despite great age, cannot die and is forced by some strange coercion to walk the earth for ever. The description of the Old Man suggests several different identities: is he the Wandering Jew, a personification of Old Age, the Devil, God's Will, or Death, or Sin? One source is a Latin elegy, which also influenced some Middle English verses, in which an old man begs the earth to receive him because being old is so miserable.[2] But Chaucer's presentation of his old man's speech and actions has too many metaphors and connotations for one literal old man. He is represented as benign but rejected by the young men; he points them to *money* as death, to gold as the danger: the really destructive force. He seems, if only the worldly would pay attention, therefore, to represent the revelation that worldliness is spiritual death and that amendment of life is required to win salvation (VI, 765–7). This makes him like the medieval concepts of mutability and mortality, an encounter with which was believed to teach humans to see the spiritual perils of worldly pleasures and take pains to amend their lives and confess their sins.

The Old Man could clearly personify death itself, since death certainly never dies and, in this medieval tradition, the thought of death can teach wisdom. That the Old Man points the way to Death, a different Death under a tree, might seem to dislodge that hypothesis. Yet we already have in the poem more than one concept of death: physical death and the death of the soul and morals engendered by excessive love of the things of this world. The old man might therefore represent the first and show the second to be true. For the critic, however, the most important significance of this figure is that Chaucer's presentation makes a simple, certain interpretation difficult; each reader has to ponder the elements and try to read them, and here lies some of the moral–didactic value of this text. Chaucer's ambiguous presentation may also reflect the fact that worldliness involves, itself, many of the concepts suggested above: transience, aging and mortality, sin and the Devil, and death in various forms. Symbolically Chaucer links the money they find to sin rather than death: it is found down a 'croked way' and by a tree, reminiscent of the Fall of Adam. But, as this tale reminds us constantly, sin is death – to the soul. The man's wrapped form, though it may suggest a shroud, also veils him in mystery: garb leaves us with unanswered questions. Chaucer's use of questions (VI, 717–19) also puts the reader in questioning mode.

The other larger-than-life figure, one described but never seen on the stage of the action, is Death personified as a thief. This is, in contrast, a figure with a clearly established image and significance in medieval art and literature. The visual representation of death and of human beings unexpectedly encountering death was extremely common in late medieval Europe. The doctrine behind these representations was that the shock-tactics of being reminded that death lies ahead for everyone, with God's Judgement to follow, encouraged Christians to take measures to try to put themselves into a state where they might receive grace, forgiveness of sins and eternal life in heaven. Some examples may help to illustrate the kinds of association Chaucer's Death might have had for his contemporary audience. Sometimes Death, depicted usually as a skeleton, is shown summoning people from their occupations and places of work, the rich and idle from their pleasures, the lady from her mirror. In the fifteenth-century play *Everyman*, Death summons Everyman, who is startled to discover nothing he owns can go with him to help him except Good Deeds. Another popular motif in both art and literature is that of the Three Living and the Three Dead: three rich young kings out enjoying themselves hunting encounter three dead kings, their own dead fathers, who warn them of the need to change their lives. Some late medieval tombs depict the deceased as a corpse; an alarming reminder of what we all come to serves to teach the onlooker the lessons of penitence and distrust of this world. The image of Fortune and her wheel taught the same message. Chaucer introduces a reference to her just after the revellers see the gold which is Death, but they fail to draw the right conclusions from their perception (VI, 779), that it is Fortune (that is, the mutability of this world) which has given it to them.

The *Tale* does offer its readers a mystery, something whose identity is hidden. But the central mystery of the story is not who we think the Old Man is; it is the truth which is veiled from the revellers, the truth about the dangers of avarice and worldliness, to which they are blind. We never misunderstand the nature of the thief as they do and the absurdity of their setting out to kill Death underlines our own sensation of seeing things accurately. Through dramatic irony we also foresee that the selfish plots of the three are going to end in mutual destruction. The perceptions the *Tale*'s literary devices thus put into the readers' possession, but not into the characters', give readers the sense of discovering and making their own the moral lessons the text teaches: awareness of the inevitability of death and the futility of greed. Equally, however, these same elements in the presentation of *Prologue* and *Tale* can provide us with a discovery about gender identity: the text has the potential to speak of the medieval situation of a homosexual within the Church. As McAlpine's perceptive analysis argues, the pervasive mystery of parts of the text, its recurrent motif of failure to recognise actualities (the identity of the 'privee theef' or the secret, unconfessable, sins of the church-members in VI, 377–84, the picture of its speaker's alienation from the Church and from the sacrament of confession he purveys) can be read as Chaucer's study of homosexuality in the form of 'a deliberate intention to explore the inner reality of an outcast especially despised by his society and especially misunderstood by his Church'. We have, then, another concealment implicitly in the tale: the Pardoner's explicit besetting sin of avarice screens or parallels his sexuality; both make him a pardoner who cannot, himself, confess (McAlpine 1997). Harry Bailey's attack on the Pardoner's tricks and his relics, with its use of the insult of sodomy, is on the literal level a typically personal reaction to the immediate suggestion that he himself might have special need for the sin-absolving power of relics, but indirectly it may suggest a sexual reading of the text's central conundrums of the confessor who cannot confess, and the obvious truths that – to some characters – are not obvious. At the same time, the Host's reduction of the false relics to worthless excrement and genital impotence: turds, old breeches, and castration, symbolically identifies a truth behind superstition: that they amount to materialism, and that – like the Christian view of money in the tale – is dead matter.

The tale ends with another alienation: the Pardoner will not speak, the Host is too angry to communicate socially any more with him. After so disturbing a performance, with the potential to disrupt our confidence in ourselves as shrewd listeners, as well as dealing in the deepest human fears – death, guilt, sex, deceit – the Knight's insistence on simply imposing social harmony, refusing to countenance any conflict, dramatises one more concealment: the denial of social tension inherent in social authority.

15

The *Shipman's Tale*

Several of the tales link love and money, but here the whole plot is built on a direct equation between sex and cash. A wife offers sex in return for money to pay off her dressmaker's bill, a monk gets sex by promising a hundred francs, and there is a parallel between the resolution of the main plot and the outcome of the financial subplot: the monk makes pure profit on his deal with the wife (a night of free sex), just as the husband makes pure profit through his credit and exchange dealings. The equation is summed up in the wife's final pun: her *taille*, 'tail', private parts, is a *taille*, 'tally', account book. In the last episode she uses marital sex to get her financial debt with her husband cancelled. It is a cynical but also lighthearted study of worldliness: none of the characters is innocent and none of them has the capacity to be hurt.

It fits its teller generally because of its commercial theme but also because a Shipman transports commodities for profit from one place to another. In this story a commodity, sex, is moved round from one person and one negotiation to another, and exchanged for money at each point. Each of the characters feels superior in particular bargaining-skills to others: the businessman smugly pompous about his professional skills ('us chapmen') as he talks to the supposedly financially inexperienced wife and monk, the monk with his smooth manners plays off husband and wife against each other to his own profit, and the wife, confident that the power feminine sexuality exerts over men will enable her to triumph over both of them – as it does in the end. Critics have speculated whether Chaucer originally intended this fabliau about a faithless wife for a female narrator, perhaps the Wife of Bath. Lines 12–19, which are spoken from the point of view of a married woman, might seem to indicate that. Alternatively this could be a form of medieval Free Indirect Style, where the narrative is endowed with the viewpoint of a character, here that of the bourgeois wife – a device more convincing in oral performance than it looks to a modern reader assimilating the text only from the page. And, as suggested above, there is

157

more appropriateness between the Shipman's profession and the tale's plot than might initially appear if we view the relationship only from the criterion of naturalistic characterisation.

We start with a cynically observed bourgeois world (VII, 3–19), where corporate entertaining and investment dressing are the norm and, despite their pleasures, bring their headaches – 'all that party-giving, *salutaciouns and contenaunces*: sometimes it yields nothing solid, for all the effort that goes into it; and dresses: we wives need them, but the husband has to pay – or some other man – *and that is perilous*!', is a summary of VII, 5–18. The shift into Free Indirect Discourse here makes us suddenly privy to the thoughts, and the economic base, behind the 'compaignable' executive lifestyle we have just been introduced to. The stylistic shift almost prepares us for the *sub rosa* goings-on of the plot, as much as the content of these musings by the merchant's wife prefigure the veiled preoccupation with money and gain which will motivate all that the characters do in this narrative. Behind this wife's dilemma over the hundred francs she owes for clothes, as with the Wife of Bath's 'curtain lectures', lies a society where husbands have control over marital money. The theme of wives manipulating their husbands specifically for expensive clothes was also a standard anti-feminist topic (see examples from St Jerome and the *Romance of the Rose* in Blamires 1992: 70–1, 162–3).

Delicately Chaucer also introduces into this first paragraph a hint of a profounder theme, the transience of all earthly things: the 'salutaciouns and contenaunces' all pass – 'as dooth a shadwe upon the wal' (VII, 8–9). Moralists commonly compared the pleasures of this world to a fair, here today and gone tomorrow: Chaucer does it at the end of *Troilus and Criseyde*.[1] But the momentary hint of sombreness passes: this is not a tale like the *Merchant's Tale* where materialism is seriously and consistently set in contrast with religious ideas about eternity, mutability, sin and salvation.

The Plot: Credit and Exchange

The tale uses a popular, much-used old plot (Benson and Andersson 1971: 282–311). The basic plot-pattern is labelled by folklorists 'The Exchange of Winnings'. There is a succinct Latin version:

> A cleric once seduced a knight's wife for the payment of a cloak, and secretly he took away a pepper-mill from the house. The next day he

returned, bringing back the mill, in the presence of her husband. He said 'Give back the cloak to me: I have brought back the mill.' 'Give it back to him,' said her husband. 'I will give it back,' said the woman, 'but he won't be grinding in our mill any more.'

Boccaccio's *Decameron* 8.1 has a version which can be summarised thus:

> Gulfardo, a German mercenary soldier, finds it easy to get credit from merchants in Milan because he is regarded as financially reliable. He writes secretly to a merchant's wife, Madame Ambruogia, with whom he is infatuated, imploring her favours. She offers sex in return for total secrecy and two hundred florins. He is so disgusted by her mercenary attitude that he devises a strategem: he borrows the sum from her husband and returns it to her publicly, with the words that it is a debt he owes her husband. She grants him her favours but he then announces to her husband that he did not need the loan after all and asks for the money he put into her hands to be returned. She has to give the money up, and return it to her husband.

The basic plot all three stories have in common is about a chain of exchanges, and the trick hinges on the fact that one of the objects is an invisible object that has to be kept secret from the husband: the sexual favour which is exchanged for a loan or pledge. The wife is defeated by her own strategem when the lover reveals to the husband that he has given her something. In Chaucer's version, however, the ever-resourceful unfaithful wife contrives to regain the upper hand – as Proserpine predicted, correctly, May would do in the *Merchant's Tale*.

Chaucer introduces the subplot of the business-dealings in Bruges and Paris and reformulates the financial element in the old plot in thoroughly modern terms of contemporary credit transfers and exchange dealings. Chaucer's writing shows full awareness of the commercial and banking operations of his time (he was the son of a merchant, a civil servant working with major commercial operations: the wool trade and royal building commissions).

The terminology of modern commerce and commercial legalities is everywhere in Chaucer's writing. This is the jargon of *chapmanhede*, *chaffare* and *rekenynges* – words like *reconyssaunces*, *chevyssaunces*, *creauncyng fee simple*, *achaat*, *purchasynge*, *Lumbardes*, *seuritee*, *dette*, *wynne*, *taille*, *scrit and bond*. The language of business supplies him with images for many other things: for sex – *dette*, *tally*, *score* – and for religion:

reysen a rente, *duetee* and *purchasyng* used for salvation and damnation in the *Friar's Tale*. The idea of profit-making inspires Chaucer to creative wordplay: alchemy is *multiplying* in the *Canon's Yeoman's Tale* (see p. 209), the *General Prologue* Miller has a golden thumb and the Physician's favourite prescriptions involve gold. Chaucer comes across as a man who is aware of the price of everything as well as the value of everything. Typically he points out that the wayward student Nicholas in the *Miller's Tale* is not just wasting time on a hobby that should be spent on his BA work: he is also wasting money, the funds and income his *frendes*, 'sponsors' and family have provided (I, 3219–20).

The *Shipman's Tale* contains ironic parallels between profiteering and the more natural human experience of love. Money here is fertile – the merchant husband describes credit for merchants as a plough (VII, 288); the plough is often also a sexual metaphor in medieval literature (it is not by chance that the hot iron in the *Miller's Tale* was the pointed blade of a plough). Like the *General Prologue* Merchant, he has to keep his credit situation secret (VII, 230–8) – just as the illicit love deal is the secret commodity being credited and exchanged in the main plot (secrecy is a recurrent theme in the text). The monk borrows the hundred francs to 'buy cattle' in a secret deal (VII, 269–80): it is really to finance his enjoyment of the wife's body. And it is when the tension of his business deal is over that the husband's sexual energies return (VII, 369–82). The wife's final speech uses the concept of debt, as the Wife of Bath does, both for money from the husband and for the sexual relations that, according to the medieval theory of marriage, spouses owe to each other within the contract of marriage (VII, 413).

The Language of Bargaining

The tale has two fabliau stereotypes: the faithless wife and lecherous cleric (another of Chaucer's over-mobile, over-commercial, rogues, a monk riding about, outside his cloister, overseeing the farms that belong to the monastery). Chaucer's method of dramatising the wife and monk's treachery and hypocrisy, however, is far from stereotypical: as so often he employs his skill in presenting speech and response in dialogue to create a *tour de force* of verisimilitude, full of twists and turns which are morally and psychologically expressive. Each character enters into negotiation with the other cynically clear-eyed about what they want to get out of it. The garden scene (VII, 89–211) shows only a thin veil of respectability spread over the striking of their bargain. The Monk crosses the boundary early on into forbidden sexual territory, in an exploratory way (VII, 103–9), and then retreats into a laugh and blushing; but the wife has understood 'his owene thought' perfectly well and is ready with the assurance that she is open to offers: her marriage is sexually so unfulfilled, she declares, she has considered suicide or leaving the country. The monk's next move is to ask her if she feels she might benefit from a little counselling from him: this piece of clerical hypocrisy is also a coded message that they are talking in confidence to each other (VII, 125–41). They then proceed briskly, though still in code, to the problem of her husband: is he not, after all, the monk's oldest friend, his 'cosyn', and the wife's spouse? The monk rapidly denies all 'cousinship' – it is her he always wanted to get to know: that is why he cultivated her husband's friendship – and she readily denounces her husband. They have both now cut themselves loose from all the moral ties that might have restrained them. This brings the wife to the issue of money, the bargain is struck, and then the monk can move in on the first instalment of what he has bought. Chaucer employs a telling rhyme:

'. . . I wol brynge yow an hundred frankes.'
And with that word he caughte hire by the flankes.

(VII, 200–1)

Soon she, now playing the part of the fluffy-headed little wife who does not understand business, is chiding her husband for staying away so long worrying over their business affairs. The tale is a drama of three totally selfish individuals; and the words *we, us,* and *oure* abound in it, ironically since they are not interested in plural concerns.

Cosyn, which can mean 'cheat financially', is a key word in the tale: natural and virtuous social relationships are replaced by mercenary strategies. There is much else in the characters' words which has a thematic and satiric rather than naturalistic function: the wife's allusion to Ganelon, the traitor of the *Chanson de Roland,* at VII, 194, marks her own surrounding speech as marital treachery. Her exclamation 'Peter' as she knocks at the door of the counting-house is probably a reminder to the reader of St Peter guarding the entrance to heaven: this 'countour' is a materialist's version of heaven. The merchant, with the reversal of spiritual values that characterises the irredeemably worldly man, calls turning aside from successful money-making playing at a 'pilgrymage' (VII, 234), wasting time: this world is so 'queynte', complicated, and subject to Fortune, that he has to concentrate on the really important things: canny, secretive business enterprises (VII, 230–4). This passage not only shows his blindness towards spiritual priorities but may mimic an excuse contemporary merchants made that the uncertainty of business life justified large profit margins.[2] The characters often use cautious and ambiguous speech: when the husband wants to get his loan back from John (VII, 335–48), the text (using Free Indirect Style) tells us that what he said was that of course he had not come to ask for money, and then shows him getting round indirectly to the issue only at the end of the social visit, ostensibly confiding friend-to-friend his joys, hopes and fears (VII, 345–8). He juggles sexual and financial modes in another way when he delays mentioning the contentious matter of the hundred francs with his wife until after he has enjoyed her welcome-home embraces (VII, 300–99).

This management of words fits with the two plots in which one currency is exchanged for another: sex for cash and francs for 'sheeldes'. The financial subplot is a symbolic parallel to the main plot. Its financial mechanics are not in essence as complicated as they appear: the merchant goes to Bruges and buys a commodity on credit, calculated in *écus* or 'shields', a coin of exchange. Then having collected what money he has at home in St Denis and borrowed up to the hilt in Paris to pay back the credit bond, he can go to the French Lombards, a bank, and pay what he owes. By repaying in francs he makes a thousand francs profit because of exchange rate differences. The Lombards, an international organisation, would transfer his credit bond from Bruges to Paris, making it possible to buy on credit in one currency and pay back in another. The money keeps moving around from one city to another, but invisibly, in the form of credit not coins – just as the hidden item of sex moves round in the other plot.

The tale is full of sharply observed social, and socio-economic, details as well as large-scale satire on the topsy-turvy values of a materialist worldview: the two men who have come far – in worldly terms – from their village upbringing together (VII, 20–42); the merchant, who is popular because he is a generous host with an attractive wife (money and sex again), the monk, because he is 'fair', 'manly', tips the servants well, and brings a handsome present for his hosts (VII, 43–52; sex and money again). And finally there is the wife's protestation, with the unanswerable logic of the inveterate clothes-buyer, that she has spent the money prudently:

> . . . by my trouthe, I have on myn array,
> And nat on wast, bistowed every deel . . .'

(VII, 418–19)

'I haven't wasted it', she insists: 'I've spent it all on clothes!'

16

The *Prioress's Tale*

The *Prioress's Tale* is a 'miracle of the Virgin': a story in which Mary miraculously helps someone who has shown devotion to her. Miracles were a popular medieval genre: 'read, copied, and listened to by all levels of society, ecclesiastical and lay; ... recited in church and monastery in celebration of [Mary's] feasts; translated into dramatic form they entertained and instructed crowds of spectators' (Meale 1993: 115–16).[1] They are tales of wonder and magic. The religious values they express are generally limited and naive, and though the dénouement of their plots shows the pattern of virtue rewarded, normal morality is often disregarded: the virtue they reward is faith, devotion to Mary, regardless of whether her devotees are thieves, outlaws or religious men and women who have broken their vows. The people Mary helps in this tale are innocent, a child and his mother.

Antisemitism is not uncommon in Marian miracles: the level of religious experience to which they appeal is typically a low one, marked by superstition and bigotry, and they are frequently sensational narratives; if Jews appear it is usually as bogeymen, perpetrating cruel and blasphemous crimes (see Chaucer, *Variorum*, Boyd 1987: 3–22, on sources and background). The subgroup of antisemitic Marian miracles also reflects the adoption of Mary as the special patroness of the Church's increasingly intense war against heretics and non-believers from the eleventh and twelfth century on (massacres of Jews followed the announcement of the First Crusade in 1096; in England the antisemitic child-murder story first appears around 1144).[2] The doctrines with which Mary, as the mother of the God's son, is associated – the incarnation of the Messiah and the revelation of God as a Trinity of Father, Son and Holy Spirit – are doctrines particularly at odds with Judaism and Islam. On a less abstract level, the cult of Mary is also one of the distinctive, exclusive markers of medieval Christianity, and many miracles, including the *Prioress's Tale*, demonstrate the almost mechanical efficacy of specific rituals – here it is a hymn which the singer does not even understand. These, unlike deeper and more widely shared religious principles, such as love of God and love of one's neighbour, operate as cultic signifiers which mark off the cult and the adherent: they turn Mary in the miracles into the special champion of those who pay her special honour.

Critical examination of the *Prioress's Tale* produces questions rather than unequivocal answers. Critics, reluctant to believe Chaucer could have perpetrated a tale of this type (and its presentation of the Jews is more savage than in many analogues), have often interpreted it as a parody: either of antisemitism (Schoeck [1956], repr. 1960: 246), or of the naiveties and grotesqueries of the miracle genre, or as a parody of the Prioress, a damning expression of her personality as a combination of sentimentality, cruelty and shallow religion (see the summary in Chaucer, *Variorum*, Boyd 1976: 31–50). Sadly, there is no strong critical evidence for it as a parody, certainly not a straightforward parody, though arguably there are tensions and psychological pathologies discernible in it which indicate awareness at some level that the cause of antisemitism lies in the gentile observer and not in Jewish culpability. Its tension between cruelty and pathos, centred on maternal feelings, and the disconcerting combination of body-images that runs through it – privies, entrails, mouths, sucking babies, 'ravishing' (see VII, 470), throats and tongues – together with the sense of adults reduced to inarticulate childishness (the Prioress's self-image as a baby and the Abbot's tearful collapse), are as powerful as they are resistant to a unified critical reading.

The main argument against the parody theory is the unlikeliness of Chaucer designing as a parody a work with so much fervent, biblical and liturgical imagery in praise of Christ and Mary. Some critics, notably David (1976: 205–14) and Cooper (1996: 163–4), however, see Chaucer presenting the tale as genuine religious piety yet allowing the naive limitations of both the genre and the Prioress to come through at the same time.

Miracles celebrate faith as an exclusive – and potentially excluding – magic; that is why they can be prone to antisemitism, and why Mary's dispensation of divine mercies in them is so partisan. They are sensational, not just in the supernatural nature of her assistance but in the often desperate human situations it solves: life-threatening illness, violence, debt, or heinous sins like theft, incest, child-murder, or a nun's pregnancy. They are extreme human disasters though their setting is often a familiar one of home, street or monastery. Her intervention suspends the course of normal consequences, whether of natural cause and effect or of legal punishment. Meale (1993: 116) shows there is some evidence, particularly from France, associating manuscripts containing miracles with an aristocratic or female readership, and this is not the only miracle which focuses on family relationships and on the emotional experience of mothers or wives. In one type of miracle Mary helps a mother escape punishment who has borne an illegitimate child and killed it: there is a version where the mother has committed incest with her own son and thrown the baby's body in a privy. Does Chaucer's tale introduce this motif, but transposed now as the action not of a guilty Christian mother but of guilty enemies – Jews? Guilt, horror, and their opposites, innocence and protection, are the poles on which the *Prioress's Tale* is constructed.

There are many versions of a miracle story in which the Virgin reveals the whereabouts of a Christian boy murdered by Jews who were enraged by his hymn in praise of the Virgin. These are part of wider network of antisemitic propaganda myths, the so-called 'blood libel', which depicted Jews murdering children, often involving ritual insult to Christian belief. What is disturbing to a modern reader is not just the appearance of this evil, cynical and dangerous mythology among Chaucer's works, but the intense emotionalism his literary handling brings to it: a combination of sentimentality in his presentation of the child and brutality in his depiction of Jews. The word *litel* recurs, as do a set of words that call forth a protective tenderness from the audience: *yong*, *sely*, *tendre*, *swetnesse*, *sweete*, *innocent*; and the death is surrounded with expressions of pathos from the narrator and observers: *pitous*, *wepynge*, *salte teeres*, *swownynge*, *cried*, *preyeth*, and so on. The emotional assault is not just sentimentality but is expressed through writing unsurpassed in the *Canterbury Tales* for its tight control and its skilled manipulation of a set of interwoven images and patterns. The prologue and tale are built on several image-clusters which belong to the realms of liturgy, theology and psychology. These include motherhood, language, inarticulacy, feeding and orality.

The tale is also structured on a completely programmatic designation of the Jews as alien beings: totally separate from and opposed to 'cristen folk'. We have already noticed how Chaucer's handling of the tale divides innocence and guilt utterly into two peoples: one 'folk' wholly pure and vulnerable and the other wholly wicked. The text's spatial imagery places the Jews in their own enclave, a dangerous street down which a lone Christian child walks and is trailed by a murderer, open at both ends and with a pit and latrine nearby – giving it the air of being both a frightening trap and an image of a human gullet. It has a 'privee place in an aleye, a pit bisyde'. Of course this picture of Jews and Christians inhabiting different spaces reflects the fact that in much of the East and continental Europe in Chaucer's time Jews were in literal ghettos. (England never had ghettos, though Chaucer rented from 1374 to 1386 a house over Aldgate in the City of London which abutted what had been a Jewish street before their expulsion in 1290.) But Chaucer treats the spatial pattern as psychological symbolism, and the physical separation of Jews and Christians parallels other ways in which Jews are depicted as not sharing in common humanity: they are presented as really the residence of Satan (VII, 558–64); their hearts are like wasps' nests (VII, 559); they do not act with recognisable human or moral motives, conspiring with maniac fury against childish innocence and Christian piety (VII, 565); from the outset they hate Christ's people (VII, 491); and repeatedly Chaucer calls them 'cursed', referring to a line in Matthew 27:26 which had been interpreted over centuries as justifying Christian oppression and exile of Jews (on the pretext that they had been cursed by God for Jesus's death). At the end the accused Jews are bound and destroyed, whereas in many such stories they are converted. Chaucer did not, I think, design the work as a parody, but it does demonstrate, despite its own implication in xenophobia, how the psychology of xenophobia works: fear and guilt are projected onto others, who are associated with bodily disgust and allotted attributes which appear to justify their punishment, and these repositories of phobia have to be destroyed.

A Freudian critical approach might see the stress on inarticulacy and on the maternal themes (motherhood, suckling and mother–child separation, the image of the narrator as a baby) as exemplifying Kristeva's theory that both phobia and the desire for literary closure reflect a symbolic loss of the Mother and involve distress and loss that cannot be fully defined or named, because recovering one's identity as a subject goes together with finding that language and the symbolic world go together (see Kristeva 1982: 32–5).[3] As David (1976: 208) says, 'The "cursed Jews" represent a psychological rather than a historical reality.'

The Jews are hanged and drawn by horses, a torture of legendary horror (not actual contemporary legal punishment) associated in literature specifically with treason. Perhaps Chaucer envisaged it as fitting their separation from the true faith – as quasi-treason. Anti-infidel feeling here and in the *Man of Law's Tale* perhaps links with the *General Prologue*'s idealisation of a crusading Knight. Chaucer's allusion to the St Hugh of Lincoln legend (VII, 684–90) is perhaps trying to harness historical force to his own tale, but – continuing the knightly line of thinking – may reflect princely religious attitudes. Chaucer's wife and members of the family of the Duke of Lancaster, in whose households she served, belonged to the Fraternity of Lincoln Cathedral, where St Hugh was venerated.

It has been argued that, Jews having been banished from England since 1293, Chaucer had never met real Jews and used them here without specific animosity, employing an antisemitic convention: 'unthinkingly . . . as a convenient monster when such a character was needed in a plot' (Bowden 1964: 50–1). But Chaucer had travelled to countries which still had Jewish populations and ghettos. It is true that Jews and Saracens did figure as inhuman villains in popular forms like ballads and folkplays, right up to the nineteenth century. The points Chaucer selects in presenting his Jews, however, as illustrated above, are not simply building up a vague image of villainy; they are as carefully targeted as Chaucer's selection of details usually are, to slant the image a particular way: these are topics with a long history of use as arguments to justify oppression and exclusion (see Frank 1982). It can be argued that Chaucer was only reflecting the bigotry of his age. Yet Rex (1995: 13–26) shows that contemporary enlightened opinion, clerical and lay, included quite a widespread perception of Jews as fellow-believers in God, with a strong moral code, whose conversion rather than death Christians should seek. Some contemporary preachers and writers, including Langland in *Piers Plowman* (e.g., B.IX.83–7, B.XV.383), presented Jewish faith and morality as something Christians would do well to imitate.

Chaucer might, then, have been one of the bigots rather than the enlightened. On the other hand, he also lived in an era of Wycliffite disapproval of superstition, including miracles. His own Pardoner is a satire on superstition and the corruptions it engenders. If this miracle tale is not parody, was there some reason why this superstitious genre was admitted into his *Tales*? Perhaps he welcomed the opportunity to pen a tale of *pathos*. It might express personal devotion to the Virgin, or reflect Lancastrian or royal religious tastes. Chaucer wrote three powerful prayers to Mary: the one in the *Prioress's Prologue*, the Prologue to the *Second Nun's Tale*, and his *ABC*, a lyric prayer. Do the *Prioress's Prologue* and *Tale*, both in praise of Mary, stand like an invocation to a Christian Muse ('Gydeth my song', VII, 487) or prayer to the Virgin-Mother for help, in front of his own two tales?

Chaucer's general anxiety about questions of credit and financial profit might underlie the inclusion of the explicit attack on Jews for usury (VII, 491–2). In the thirteenth century, only Jews were allowed to lend money on interest, and they were brought into England by kings to supply governments with money, through special taxes on them, as well as through lending, but by the fourteenth century gentile banking and credit systems had developed. The association of Jews with money-lending perhaps links with the financial themes of the preceding *Shipman's Tale*.

As David (1982) says, 'To dismiss the anti-semitism in the tale as "conventional" is to beg the real question why it should have become conventional, for Jews were not always so despised in the Middle Ages.' Fradenburg's important article (1989) shows that it is precisely because the changing cultural language of different medieval periods repre-sented authority and control through a variety of legitimating strate-gies, that the critic needs to use different critical languages from those which would have been approved by contemporary antisemites. To conduct cultural analysis, 'one cannot rely exclusively on how the later Christian Middle Ages would have understood the question . . . confus-ing the "Middle Ages" with the ways in which the Middle Ages (mis)represented itself' (pp. 197–8).

The Mother, the Child and Speech

The mother in the story has a parallel in the Virgin who, mother-like, imparts sustenance and love to her devotees, and protects both the 'cler-geoun' and the narrator, enabling each to bear witness by their 'song' to her power. It is through mouths, particularly passive or inarticulate mouths, that divine power is channelled into this world: the praise of wise men of 'dignitee' (VII, 457); the narrator's inadequate words (VII, 481–7); the uncomprehended song of the child; the bodily rever-ence of sucking babies (VII, 458, 514–15); the grain on the tongue; the wordless weeping of the abbot and monks (VII, 673–8); the effi-cacy of the boy, with throat cut, and later dead, to bear witness as a martyr and increase faith. It may be that Chaucer prefigures these oral and maternal motifs in the Prioress's tender feeding of soft white bread to her little dogs in the *General Prologue*.

The opening prayer, structured on the themes of speech and inad-equate speech, is an intricate interplay of references not only to words, knowledge and infancy, but also to key doctrines of faith, especially the Trinity and the Incarnation. It praises Jesus and Mary within meticulously defined terms of their relationships within these two doctrines: Mary's power to ask for mercy for humanity is secondary to her son's; she conceived by the Holy Spirit, and the Son is the Wisdom of the Father. Her conception was the revelation of the Trinity to humanity (the mystery plays sometimes take pains to represent Jews repudiating the doctrines of the Incarnation, of Jesus as the Godhead, of Mary as a virgin-mother, and of miracles, partly no doubt to strengthen Christian adherence to these most difficult matters of belief).[4]

Though the text is theologically adept, its central meaning lies in the little *clergeoun*'s virtually pre-verbal, bodily, grasp of the words he sings, which constitute an unsurpassable *laude*. Like Mary, ravishing down motherhood (VII, 469–73) from heaven, the narrator will become heavy with the 'weighte' of her/his 'song' of praise (VII, 482–7). The tale becomes a hymn of praise and centres on one: *Alma redemptoris mater*, which begins:

> Beloved mother of the redeemer, who remain ever the gate through whom we may pass to heaven, and the star of the sea, who is concerned to help her people when they fall to rise up. You who gave birth to your own holy parent, to the wonder of Nature, a virgin before and afterwards, taking up the 'Ave' from the mouth of Gabriel, have mercy on sinners.

The child becomes one of the virgin saints who, according to Revelation 14:1–4, sing the 'new song' in heaven, following Christ the Lamb (VII, 579–85), and is linked with St Nicholas, expressing devotion by his manner of suckling (VII 5,14–15). The image-cluster is based on words from Psalm 8, part of the liturgy for the Mass of the Holy Innocents (the boys slaughtered by Herod, Matthew 2:13–18), honoured by the Church as martyrs:

> Out of the mouths of infants, God, and of sucklings you have perfected praise because of your enemies, O Lord our Lord, how admirable is your name in the whole earth.[5]

This tale at several points shows the body as speech: the boy's voice sings, with great significance, though without intellectual understanding; his blood 'crieth'; sucking babes praise Mary; swoons and tears express recognition of Mary's power. Conversely the narrator's speech in the *Prologue* gives way to physical experiences: guidance, conception, going before, light, and infant-like passivity and reception. The *Shipman's Tale* also treats body as document: the wife tells her husband he has 'my joly body' as a pledge or contract (VII, 423); he can *score*, 'mark', 'write up', his debts on her body (VII, 416).

Earlier twentieth-century criticism focused on the tale as expression of the Prioress's personality as suggested by the *General Prologue* (see Collette 1990: 97–8). This evades the question of how far it expresses Chaucer's own attitudes. The question of relationships between the tale and its adjoining tales is at least as important: the contrast between its piety and the *Shipman's Tale*'s worldliness; the parallel themes of faith and infidelity, infidels and traitors, running through each; the patterns of exchanges and reward at the centre of each plot; their negative images of financial profit and interest. The *Prioress's Tale*, starting and ending in prayer, may cast a formal blessing over Chaucer's entry, in the form of Chaucer the Pilgrim, into the story-telling arena. Cooper suggests (1996: 168) that, in the sequence of fabliau, miracle and minstrel romance between the *Shipman's Tale* and *Thopas*, Chaucer marks the status of the miracle as popular fiction and demonstrates some of its limitations. Like *Melibee*, this tale depicts a supremely wise and nurturing female guide. If the *Prioress's Tale* also makes its own contribution to an exploration of the role of authorship discernible in the tales of group VII to X, it is (like most things in the tale) a disconcerting image of the devout Christian as one who cannot speak anything of value except through repeating words of praise, like a pre-verbal infant: the uttering of words by a human is best done either by singing a hymn, like the *clergeoun*, or repeating a naive tale of simple faith – like a miracle.

17

Sir Thopas and *Melibee*

The two tales Chaucer gives to the narrator who represents himself
offer something unexpected even within the great variety of the
Canterbury Tales: both texts move beyond the expected definition of
story. The first, *Sir Thopas*, is a parody of story-telling – at least for the
real-life reader it is clearly parody and, though within the pilgrims'
fictional world it is presented not as a parody but as a genuine attempt
in the story-telling competition, it is none the less rejected as unsuc-
cessful story-telling by the literary arbiter, the Host. The second tale,
Melibee, though provided with a slight narrative frame (the assault on
Melibee's household and judgement on the thieves), is essentially a
moral treatise and its predominant genre is dialogue, not narrative.
Thopas is offered as a tale to be taken less seriously than other tales;
Melibee is more serious than the norm. As with the final *Parson's Tale*,
these tales stand apart from the sequence of stories and genres and
implicitly provide commentary on the whole business of fiction. *Thopas*,
being parodic, is metafictional: it observes a genre and style rather than
entering within them. *Melibee*, like the *Parson's Tale*, is differentiated
from other tales by being in prose and being directed, despite its use of
allegory, towards the external world, the arena of real-life moral action
beyond fiction.

The *General Prologue* sets up competition as the overarching motive
for the *Tales* and they are full of contentiousness, masculine competitiveness, conflicts between ranks and the sexes, the tragedy of warfare,
and the fabliau comedy of one character outwitting another. Yet in his
own tales Chaucer removes his representative from that competitive
arena: with his first attempt he fails, and the other preaches a pacific
attitude to conflict and shows the domination of masculine by feminine
in a triumph not of competitiveness but of reason and nurturing solic-
itude. In theme as well as genre, these tales move outside both the
fictional game of the competitive series and the game of literary entertainment. The *Parson's Tale* will also disrupt both, but more aggressively

and purposefully. The *Monk's Tale* will also dramatise a breaking up of the series of stories when it, like *Thopas*, is disrupted by another arbiter, the Knight.

Thopas and *Melibee* initiate a final series of tales concerned with literature itself, and with signs and meaning. At first sight Chaucer in various ways deprives 'his' tales of significance or dignity. Both fail the requirement to tell an acceptable story and he prefaces them with assertions of their lack of originality, one the only story he knows, an old 'rym', the other based on a 'tretys lite'. He does not allot himself the significant position of first or last story-teller in the *Tales*: his tales come somewhere in the middle. In his initial offering, *Thopas*, he declines to offer a message or any special dignity of genre, subject or technical brilliance, and his *alter ego* is presented as incompetent at authorship and as over-ruled: devices which develop the pose of modesty and lack of leadership or assertiveness discerned in the narrative voice in the *General Prologue*.

There is something more complex here than mere characterisation of Chaucer the Pilgrim. Though these tales fictionally discredit him as an adequate teller of tales, paradoxically they can also be read as demonstrating and commenting on the role and duties of a writer. They exemplify two medieval concepts of the purpose of literature, summed up in the Host's dual criteria: 'solaas' and 'sentence' (I, 798), *Thopas* being literature as *solaas*, entertainment (a 'tale of myrthe', VII, 706); *Melibee* representing *sentence*, didactic literature ('a moral tale vertuous', VII, 940); and their two genres embody two well-established assumptions about the function of the writer: as minstrel and also as adviser to lords. *Thopas* invokes the traditional address of a minstrel to his audience – the author as oral performer: 'Listeth, lordes, in good entent' (VII, 712), and *Melibee*, as an educational dialogue, incorporates the voice of the teacher. For a court author there is appropriate deference in both genres: the minstrel style of *Thopas* sets up its narrator as entertainer of 'lordes' (VII, 712) and – since it is so absurd – as a jester. *Melibee*, confining him to the serviceable mode of prose, is a Mirror for Princes, one of the guides to good government and morality often written for and presented to royal patrons. The genre of advice to princes, as Fradenburg (1985) and Hasler (1990) have argued, could be a genre which was particularly close to the court poet's own self-image.[1]

The Host's words (VII, 695–706) mark Chaucer the Pilgrim off from the other pilgrims – the fictional characters created by the real Chaucer, the author. No profession was allotted to him in the *General Prologue*. Now Harry's question 'What man artow?' – never answered within the text – foregrounds for us the issue of the nature and position of a narrator in relation to the fiction the author creates. This one is visually separate from the characters: he does not mix with them or speak with them; his gaze is away from them. That corresponds to the fact that Chaucer does not completely fictionalise his narrator – as one character among other characters, in Victorian mode. Without profession like the others, since he represents their creator, he is mentally abstracted, apparently belonging to a different realm from theirs: almost as if he belongs to fairyland, 'elvyssh', as the Host remarks (VII, 703). This is a reversed image of the actual relationship of a writer to his literary creations: they are in fairyland and imaginative fantasy, while their inventor belongs to the world of real life. Seen here from the Host's point of view, Chaucer seems to be in fairyland, while his fictions are the more confident, slightly contemptuous inhabitants of a real world. They have their feet on the ground; this fellow hasn't.

This description of the narrator is not, however, just a narratological symbol. Presumably to the original audiences, perhaps listening to Chaucer reading this aloud, the plump man – the armful which Harry Bailey teasingly imagines a slim pretty woman embracing – who is so absent-minded, was recognisably like Chaucer himself. The question of where the author is, in relation to his or her text, must have been raised in a particularly literal way in an era when the author might read a first-person narrative text aloud. The Host's enquiry, 'What man artow?', and the many puzzling aspects of Chaucer's self-presentation here (described by someone else, separate from the other characters, as an inadequate story-teller, lacking any creative originality) raise the deepest questions about authorship: Where is the author *in* the text? Who is the author in the text? The issue is not just about autobiographical writing. Chaucer creates a recognisable and enjoyable gap between our picture of this dreamy fellow who cannot tell stories and our sense of the author writing the whole text: there is an element in this part of the *Tales* like the gymnast dressing up as a clown and pretending to be about to fall off the high wire in sensational dives and stumbles. The author's self-presentation is also a link with the tale: as an unimpressive man, 'elvyssh', always in a dream, he prefigures his absurd hero Thopas who sets off for fairyland after dreaming of love for the elf queen.

Sir Thopas

Sir Thopas parodies several types of English romance. Its metre resembles a tail-rhyme romance. These often had a twelve-line stanza, but the six-line stanza which is the staple of *Thopas* is also found, for example in *Bevis of Hampton*, an old romance whose opening Chaucer perhaps echoes in VII, 833–5: *Bevis* begins 'Lordinges, herkneth to me tale! Is merier than the nightingale.'[2] It uses tags or 'bobs' – those almost meaningless two-syllable formulas like *in towne*, *in londe* (VII, 793, 887). These occur in several kinds of English narrative, including tail-rhyme romances and poems in alliterative stanzas like *Sir Gawain and the Green Knight*.

The text, like the *Miller's Tale*, includes words which for sophisticated Londoners by Chaucer's time were probably reminiscent of popular lyric and romance: terms such as *lemman*, *rode*, *bright in bour*, *gent*, and *child* in the sense 'knight'. To use a word like *lemman* in high romantic style, as here, when it was acquiring for sophisticates *déclassé* and even immoral connotations, would be laughably old-fashioned or provincial. Thopas is also described in dainty terms more suitable for a woman than a hero: his lips are 'red as rose' and 'He hadde a semely nose'. Burrow (1984) observes that calling a hero 'Sir' Thopas, common in contemporary English romances, would have seemed unfashionable to a court audience used to modern French romances. Chaucer only uses it for this knight (see Cooper 1996: 306).

It is not uncommon for romance heroes to enter a magic world or have a fairy-mistress: *Sir Launfal*, a tail-rhyme romance based on a Breton *lai* by Marie de France, and *Thomas of Erceldoune* are two examples. Guy of Warwick fights two giants, one called Amoraunt, in the popular romance of that name dating from the thirteenth century. As in the *Nun's Priest's Tale*, Chaucer uses bathos, combining these exotic motifs with unheroic details. Thopas's face is compared to *payndemayn* (VII, 725), delicate white bread – the equivalent of 'baguette' or 'croissant' – and his prowess is in wrestling (VII, 740), a lower-class sport (the Miller is a champion wrestler, I, 548). Thopas also excels in archery, another unaristocratic skill. Like the phrase 'His myrie men' (VII, 839), this brings in echoes of a widely popular genre, the Robin Hood ballads.

Chaucer's attitude to English minstrel romances is deeply ambiguous. As the main native model of narrative, it is clear they influenced his own technique enormously in many areas, including specific details like his use of stock phrases and traditional rhyming words. Yet he was brought up at court and employed in royal households where French romances were the fashionable reading. He mocks vernacular styles in their two most distinctive manifestations: minstrel romances, especially tail-rhyme romances, in *Sir Thopas*, and alliterative verse, which the

Parson dismisses as a northern peculiarity with an uncouth sound 'rum, ram, ruf' (X, 42–44), though the Parson's contempt is based on other criteria than London fashion. *Thopas* is classed as an oral performance by a minstrel with the traditional minstrel-phrases that begin each section: 'Listeth, lordes, in good entent' (VII, 712), 'Yet listeth, lordes, to my tale' (VII, 833), and the bathetic 'Now holde youre mouth . . . And herkneth to my spelle' (VII, 891–3). Just as one aspect of the *Canterbury Tales* design is as an anthology of genres, so Chaucer scatters literary terminology through this text: *spelle, tale, geestours, romances, minstrales, fit,* and the names of the heroes of just the popular romances he is imitating, King Horn, Bevis, Percival, and so on.

Burrow (1984) and Patterson (1989) argue that, since Chaucer learnt much from English romance, he cannot be expressing contempt for it in *Thopas*, especially as he allots it to Chaucer the Pilgrim.[3] The situation is clearly complex. Parody, of course, does not imply total contempt. That Chaucer owed much to native romance is as inevitable as the fact that contemporary novelists learned their art largely through, and against, the traditional novel: English romance and ballad – English verse fiction – would not have been an idiosyncratic taste of Chaucer's but an inevitable language of narrative. What *Thopas* declares about Chaucer as artist characteristically combines ostensible self-deprecation, in the absurdity, and covertly ambitious self-presentation, with the respects in which *Thopas* is a symbol of narrative itself and the *Canterbury Tales* in particular. For *Thopas*, an oral tale filled with many ever-popular elements of fiction – fantasy, love-longing, monsters, heroic quest and courage, natural beauty, and even the myth of wilderness authenticity – metonymically stands for the telling of tales. This remains true although its stylistic realization is absurd. The dream of setting out to possess the elf queen is, after all, a manifestation of that pursuit of desire and construction of desire that characterises both romantic love and the reading of fiction.

The pleasure of *Sir Thopas* does not lie only in its parodic laughability or the topical critical comment this could be seen as making on traditional English minstrel performances. The writing has its own appeal: the emblematic scenery, lists of names and exotic words. The hero may be mock-heroically unheroic, but his particular unheroism lies not in crudity but prettiness, and that ensures a pervasive decorative charm in the narrative. The pink and beauty of the hero who is named after a jewel, and the wistful romance of his longing for an elf queen, also have their own attraction (the narrator who looks like a 'popet', a doll to hug and hold, prefigures this cuteness). As with a drag-queen act which is also genuinely glamorous, the entertainment partly resides in the literal visual delight of the illusion and the stylistic display involved in it – apart from the mocking fracture of that illusion by revelations that the protagonist fails to live up to the high style in which he has been located.

The *Miller's Tale* also contains an effeminate hero depicted in part through parodic use of a more elevated literary vocabulary than his actions. That is Absolon, also described as a *child*, as if a hero of old romance, and also described as *fetis*, with a rosy *rode*, and garment 'whit as . . . blosme on the ris', now as if a heroine of old romance. Male competition in the tales is not just in mayhem and *quiting*: it is also in the effortless dominance of men who embody stereotypical masculinities, like Nicholas and the Host, and the foredoomed failure of those who do not, like Absolon, Chaucer the Pilgrim, and Thopas. This is the fear – of appearing a 'daf, a cokenay' – which spurs John in the *Reeve's Tale* to masculine action (I, 1408–9). Chaucer draws a lot of comedy out of attributing to characters details inappropriate to their sex, touches of stylistic cross-dressing – the Wife's spurs, the Pardoner's hair, the thickset Trumpington Miller's daughter – but a sense of conventional gender boundaries as power-boundaries, in terms of the social relations of each sex as well as between men and women, is recurrent in the *Canterbury Tales*. Part of Thopas's charm and interest for the reader, as well as the reason why he can never go on to win the elf queen, is that in many respects he is the elf queen.

The *Tale of Melibee*

The *Tale of Melibee* is a fairly close translation of the *Livre de Melibée*, itself a version of Albertanus of Brescia's *Book of Consolation and Counsel*, written for his son. It is a dialogue, a common medieval genre. More specifically, like Boethius's *Consolation of Philosophy*, it belongs to a type of dialogue where an authority figure, often female, argues someone who faces adversity or a problem into a wiser understanding. For Boethius this is Lady Philosophy, whose teaching shows Boethius a more philosophical viewpoint than the anger and misery he initially feels about the harm he has suffered at Fortune's hands. Prudence, the authority figure here, advises her husband Melibee not to take vengeance on his enemies. She personifies the virtue of prudence, and 'Melibee' means 'honey-drinker': he personifies the process of imbibing wise guidance.

His daughter Sophie, meaning 'wisdom', has been assaulted by thieves. She symbolises his own wisdom, which is damaged: allegorically the attack on Sophie denotes that in succumbing to passion and planning vengeance people destroy their own wisdom; prudence encourages more thoughtful reactions. The true dramatic interest of the piece lies in the evolving argument and debate; the frame-story of Melibee's enemies attacking his family is really a just symbolic representation of the state of mind which, at the outset of the discussion, is damaged and needs to be put right.

Melibee and Prudence symbolise the widely held medieval theory of the moral function of literature: Prudence in this allegorical reading is a writer, a speaker promoting wisdom, while Melibee is the ideal audience. The tale is filled with what medieval writers call *sentence*, the statement of wise truths, in the form of numerous quotations from the Bible and proverb-like aphorisms from writers on moral topics. Having posed in *Thopas* as a failure as an entertainer, offering literary *solaas* and fiction, Chaucer in *Melibee* takes on the role of the writer as purveyor of moral teaching – truth wrapped up in fiction – a guide to virtuous action, though he does this in a typically indirect, unassertive way: here wisdom does not come from the writer's own voice, but from someone else, a woman, Lady Prudence. Personifications of abstract virtues (and vices) are often female in medieval literature, partly because abstract nouns, like *Prudentia* or *Philosophia* have feminine gender in Latin. This etymological tradition was probably strengthened by certain role models in medieval culture which – going against the other, misogynist image of women's vice and unreason – could associate female gender with virtue and benign guidance: the models of female saints, good queens, women as teachers of children, and above all the Virgin Mary. Though the interest of *Melibee* remains in its arguments rather than in action, personal drama or interaction, Chaucer introduces some of the gender issues found elsewhere in the *Tales*.

The first topic Prudence discusses is whether men should listen to advice from women. Cooper (1996: 320) observes that at times the stance and style of Prudence's speeches resemble the *Wife of Bath's Prologue*, even though the Wife is an aggressive, capricious debater and Prudence the epitome of self-control and reasonableness. Her arguments about women's capacity for wisdom (VII, 1055–70) provide a counter to the anti-feminist element in the *Wife of Bath's Prologue*. She moves on to discuss good and bad counsellors and the issue of vengeance. The ideas about female counsel, in particular counsel towards mercy and forbearance, reflect, Strohm (1992:

95–119) shows, common late-fourteenth-century ideals about the role of queens.

The debate perhaps attracted Chaucer because it addressed, in safely indirect, fictional fashion, some issues relevant to Richard II's style of government. Richard was prone to vengeance, punishing those who opposed him in the 1386 parliament and in the late 1390s took terrible delayed revenge on the Appellant Lords (see p. 11). Yet *Melibee* could also reflect Richard's views positively, for in foreign policy he saw himself as a peace-maker. There was a growing opinion in late fourteenth-century society that war was both unchristian and imprudent (Saul 1997: 205–34). So, though, like many of Chaucer's works, this is a translation and not wholly his own invention, the choice of subject might be linked to royal policy, whether as a warning against vengeance or in tune with Richard's preference for avoiding French or Scottish wars. The importance of lords distinguishing between good and false counsellors is a major theme of *Melibee*, a tale which is itself an instrument of counsel. It perhaps indicates sensitivity about the text's potential for topical interpretations that one of the few passages Chaucer's translation omits is a biblical reference to the miseries that follow in a land whose ruler is a child. Richard came to the throne as a boy: this omission may suggest that Chaucer wrote *Melibee* with a consciousness of its applicability in the contemporary context to a monarch who was unwarlike abroad but could be capricious and vindictive where his own domestic power and royal dignity were threatened or criticised.

Prudence's speeches show her correct on all issues, but deferential; she is primarily an authority figure and a personification of prudence, not a character, but Chaucer allows her just enough of the verbal style of a ideal medieval wife, respectful but helpful, to give the debate some interpersonal drama and link it to other husband–wife exchanges in the *Tales*. Melibee personifies the capacity to learn reason and morality: he dramatises a change from blind, unreasoning aggression to a more prudent and peacable attitude. This is why his wounded daughter Sophie, impaired 'wisdom' – is never heard of again after the opening paragraph: the debate restores his wisdom and so the wounded daughter disappears.

The debate is animated by the drama of change, of turning the expected on its head. The limited references back to the opening episode later in the text reflect that fact that the concepts have been revolutionised. Prudence redefines the meaning of 'vengeance', reformulating the ancient medical theory of curing things by contraries to mean that true vengeance is loving your enemies and seeking peace.

She, a woman and a respectful wife, becomes the 'head' of her husband, who comes round to being led and guided by her superior reason, a reversal of contemporary theories about the relative authority of husbands and wives, and of men's superior rationality. Melibee's name is reinterpreted: the image of a 'honey-imbiber' meant one who is oblivious to anything except worldly pleasures (VII, 1410–25), applicable to his initial state, but it is used also of someone receptive to wise teaching (VII, 1110). The moment he begins to take in Prudence's advice, the new meaning for 'honey' delights him: 'I se wel that the word of Salomon is sooth. He seith that "wordes that been spoken discreetly by ordinance been honeycombes for they yeven [give] swetnesse to the soule and hoolsomnesse to the body" ' (VII, 1110). Medical images recur (Albertanus' son was a doctor); Sophie's wounds represent the threat to wisdom from the senses; the counsellors include doctors, and they and Prudence offer different interpretations of the doctrine of curing by contraries; Melibee's search for a cure for his daughter's injuries through vengeance and domination (VII, 1010–15) gives way during the dialogue to a transformed worldview: Prudence redefines victory as harmony with one's enemies and as repaying evil with goodness (VII, 1265–1325). Boethius had used illness and blindness as symbols of mental dullness at the beginning of the *Consolation of Philosophy*; as in *Melibee* these allegories are forgotten as the debate develops. In both works it is the dialogue that constitutes the cure.

18

The *Monk's Tale*

Medieval Tragedy

The *Monk's Tale* is a mini-version of the *Canterbury Tales* itself, a collection of tales, and unfinished, but these tales, unlike the *Canterbury Tales*, are all on a single theme: the fall of great men. The Monk's stories are *exempla*: didactic stories illustrating a lesson – or rather two lessons – that prosperity in this world is transient and that we should put no trust in it. For medieval writers this was the definition of tragedy. In IV, 1991–7 the Monk names his work as a *tragedie*, presenting those who were in 'heigh degree' and fell into misery; it illustrates the inevitable power of Fortune in this world and teaches:

> Lat no man truste on blynd prosperitee
>
> (IV, 1997)

The blindness here is, of course, in the person who does not recognise the transience of *prosperitee*.

The medieval concept of tragedy belongs essentially to a religious worldview in which ultimately nothing is tragic in the classical or modern secular sense – irremediably harmful – since worldly misfortunes can have the beneficial result of turning human thoughts towards the other world of eternal and spiritual joy, and teach contempt for material things that do not last.[1] The Monk's tales may be implicitly religious in that sense, and in the cases of Belshazzar and Nebuchadnezzar they do present royal pride explicitly as an affront to the honour due to God, but generally the Monk's focus is on this world: most of his tales end with a warning about Fortune's power and the inevitable instability of *heigh degree* and *prosperitee* within society, but without reference to the next world or spiritual values.

Though scholars in the Middle Ages were aware that classical tragedy had been a theatrical genre, the normal medieval concept of tragedy is as narrative (see Minnis 1982: 26–9). Boethius's *Consolation of Philosophy* was the text that established for later writers the link between Fortune and the genre of tragedy; the *Consolation* 2.2, says that what tragedies are about is the action of Fortune in overturning happy kingdoms. One example of Fortune's power Boethius cites is that of King Croesus, who also appears in the *Monk's Tale*. The pattern of the Wheel of Fortune, the fall of a great man, shapes many medieval narratives about rulers, including several about King Arthur.[2] Boccaccio's *De casibus virorum illustrium* ('The Falls of Famous Men') is a collection of stories showing how Fortune overthrew great men. This was a general inspiration for the *Monk's Tale* and supplied some of the details, but Chaucer is eclectic in the sources for his tales and original in his treatment of them. For his Nero and Croesus he drew partly on a passage about Fortune (inspired by Boethius) in the *Romance of the Rose*; Ugolino is based on an account in Dante (*Inferno*, XXXIII); several of the great men are biblical, and Zenobia appeared in another story-collection by Boccaccio, *De claris mulieribus* ('Of famous women'). Four of Chaucer's examples were medieval (critics call them the Modern Instances): Bernabò Visconti, the tyrant ruler of Milan, murdered in 1385; King Pedro of Castile, murdered in 1369, whose throne John of Gaunt attempted to win, having married Pedro's heiress Constanza; Pierre de Lusignan, a military commander, murdered in 1369; and Ugolino of Pisa, who starved to death with his children in prison in 1289.

The stories are well told, enlivened with rhetorical variety, and have plenty of interest of their own: Zenobia, for instance, is that rare thing, a politically powerful woman, portrayed as a warrior-queen with intelligence and bravery, an exotic wildness in youth and ruthless control over her empire later. The rarity of power of this kind in a woman presents as dramatic a spectacle as her eventual fall. The *Monk's Tale*, like *Thopas*, offers us a rapid conspectus of several types of literary pleasure. If, however, we explore the language and Chaucer's selection of details in each tale, patterns and emphases emerge which suggest some specific meanings and ideas in this set of stories, apart from the general lesson about the mutability of the world.

The *Exempla*

The series begins at the start of Creation with the two originary Falls that brought sin and misery into the world: the Fall of the angel Lucifer who became Satan, and the Fall of Adam. Their stories appeared, with the Creation, in the opening scenes of medieval mystery cycles. Writers usually stress the themes of pride and rebellion in Lucifer's story, but Chaucer's version concentrates on his suprahuman status as an angel (a word appearing thrice in the eight lines). His separateness, as angel, from the human species is paralleled in Adam's uniqueness among humans through his direct creation by God and his unprecedented rank and power – ruling all paradise except one tree. This theme of *rule* is repeated when Adam's sin is called specifically 'misgovernaunce'.

The second pair are men whose glory resided in their physical strength and each was brought low by something physical: woman, regarded in medieval tradition as inherently more fleshly, sensual and earthbound than man. Another pair follow: Nebuchadnezzar and Belshazzar, father and son, both kings of Babylon, but singled out here above all for the blasphemy against God represented by their over-weening concept of the 'magestee' due to earthly kings. The first commits literal idolatry, the second blasphemy by using sacred vessels for his own banquets, but the deep affront to God, in both cases, lies in their pride and misconceptions about kingship. The language repeat-edly emphasises the theme of kingship and kingdoms. The Belshazzar episode speaks for both reigns and spells out the lesson of the true rela-tionship of human kings to God. Firstly, kingship is the gift of God to the king:

> . . . 'Kyng, God to thy fader lente
> Glorie and honour, regne, tresour, rente; *income*
>
> (VII, 2210–11)

Secondly, God's is the real rule, the 'domynacioun', over kingdoms: 'Over every regne and every creature' (VII, 2219–20). Thirdly, this tale ends by specifically warning that *lordshipe* provides no guarantee against Fortune's power to take away 'regne' as well as wealth and friends (VII, 2238–43). These two tales began with the portrait of Nebuchadnezzar enthroned; he is proud and 'elaat', raised up, in his own perception of kingship (VII, 2167), but he misapprehends the real power of 'God, that sit in magestee' (VII, 2168). His punishment is appropriately to be lowered not only from his 'dignytee' but below the level of the human species, like an animal (VII, 2170–82). Perhaps Queen Zenobia's ascent above the bounds normally set for women is a parallel example of hubristic boundary-infringement. Certainly Holofernes' sin is to mistake human power as divine: he declared the king was a god. His mental blindness is represented as a seductively hidden force which will bring him down: Fortune 'likerously' kisses him and leads him up and down, and another, human, woman finally finishes him off.

Another pair are Alexander and Julius Caesar, both winning wide territorial power: Alexander over 'This wyde world', Caesar over 'th'occident by land and see' – and Caesar is called an emperor. Both are praised for their softer, elegant qualities too: 'gentillesse', 'franchise', 'estaatly honestee': the motif of friends who turn into betrayers, including Fortune, unites them also. The loss of the loyalty of kin and friends recurs in many tales, including Belshazzar, Pedro of Castile, Bernabò, and Pierre de Lusignan.

By this point the *Monk's Tale* raises the question of how far these *exempla* of the traditional theme of Fortune could, or should, be read as having topical applications. There were in the late 1390s, for example, plans for Richard II to become Holy Roman Emperor (the title of emperor comes specifically under disapproval at VII, 2525). Like Alexander and Caesar (and three of the Modern Instances) he was overthrown, in the coup by his cousin Henry of Lancaster, by those close to him. Richard was accused specifically of tyranny from 1397 on, and Nero turns from a good ruler into a tyrant (VII, 2511, 2508, 2537), overthrown by his people. Bernabò Visconti was, of course, notorious as a tyrant. Richard was a gourmet, with extravagant tastes in fashion and especially jewels. Food and drink – but more specifically the sophisticated luxury of 'delicacye' – recur in the tales, especially with Nero who like Richard has clothes embroidered with rubies, sapphires and pearls (VII, 2468–70; see Saul 1997: 353–5). Belshazzar's banquets are literally blasphemous in their conflation of royal elegance and sacred honour, but can also be read as metaphors for the sin of extravagant feasting. To the disapproval of many, Richard began in the 1390s to cultivate, through a deliberate programme of court rituals, art, and styles of address and language, an elevated ('elaat') concept of quasi-divine royalty not previously promulgated by English kings. The word 'majesty', previously associated with God, began – in imitation of French and Vatican fashion – to be used of and to the English king (Saul 1995). It is repeated at VII, 2144, 2168, and 2576.

'Kyng of kynges' (VII, 2167), a title of God, indicates Nebuchadnezzar's false self-image as a god-king. Croesus' 'roial trone' did not save him (VII, 2760) and the Nebuchadnezzar passage opened with the image of the king on his throne: it is not unlike the portrait Richard had made in 1397, enthroned with sceptre and orb.[3] This portrait is taken by some historians as a declaration of precisely that new claim to 'majesty' Richard was promulgating in his last years. The front-facing portrait of Richard enthroned mirrors iconographic traditions for representing Christ enthroned, the so-called 'Christ in Majesty' depiction of Christ. The Monk's reference to St Edward may reflect Richard's personal enthusiasm for the cult of the king and saint, Edward the Confessor and his interest in promoting the cult of his murdered ancestor King Edward II (Gordon 1993: 54–5).

Chaucer omits crucial information in the Modern Instances: he claims he does not know why Barnabo was imprisoned and murdered (VII, 2206). There are signs of evasiveness: the indirect reference to Pedro's murderer's name (VII, 2389), and they draw attention to what they omit (the technique Chaucer used with May and Damien in the tree). The tale of Croesus, which goes back to Boethius's well-known definition of the Tragedy of Fortune, ends with the quotation from Boethius cited above (p. 181), which creates the impression with this last Croesus stanza that we are being moved back into the safely literary, archetypal, and hallowed truisms of the idea of Falls of Great Men. That could also be a device for deflecting attention away from any topical applicability the *Monk's Tale* might have had. Chaucer had – boldly for his place and time (the period of the *Canterbury Tales*, *c*.1385–1400) – used contemporary figures as *exempla* for the insecurity of rulers' hold on power. There were precedents in Dante's *Inferno* for combining recent politics with timeless truths. Yet it would not be surprising if Chaucer retreated into quoting axioms from a Late Latin philosopher (albeit one imprisoned and murdered by unjust rule), and then allowed the greatest man among the pilgrims, the Knight, to cut short his Monk's moment of glory. If, like *Melibee*, the tale has indirect potential as a Mirror for Princes, it also includes the cautionary tale of an author, royal teacher and adviser who was killed for his pains, Seneca, a moral philosopher who influenced Chaucer's outlook on life deeply (Burnley 1979: 17–20, 67–9, 174–9).

In some manuscripts the four 'Modern Instances' are the conclusion, in others they are in the middle; did Chaucer vacillate about giving them particular prominence, rising to a climax or seeming to point towards the present day? While all his modern examples are safely foreign, a contemporary reference would be easily inferrable. If moving them suggests that at some point the *Monk's Tale*'s applicability to kingship seemed too clear, the additional fact that some manuscripts (including the early and authoritative Hengwrt Manuscript) lack the Knight's protest after the tale (VII, 2771–90) might indicate also changing decisions about how direct to make the *Monk's Tale*'s challenge to secular power and privilege, since this is a protest from the local fictional representative of Great Men. Much depends on the dating of the text, or more pertinently its latest date. Chaucer perhaps worked on the material over a period (the manuscript shifts suggest a rethinking). It has often been seen as an early work. The topical hypothesis presented here assumes a date at least as late as the development of Richard's new concept of kingship and his so-called 'tyranny': at least post-1395. The inclusion of so many men who do not simply fall from prosperity and happiness, perish in battle or lose power, but specifically are rulers who are overturned (often by associates), imprisoned and suffer ignominious fates, could suggest a date after Richard's deposition, imprisonment and probable murder, perhaps from starvation. In its final form the *Monk's Tale* may have been a Lancastrian poem.

As so often, Chaucer's Links are teasingly oblique or opaque in their relevance to the ideas in the tales. The *Melibee–Monk* Link starts (VII, 1890–1923) with a typical pilgrim misreading: the Host takes *Melibee* as a lesson for wives. His speech also provides an example of Chaucer's technique of letting themes, tones and instincts which have been exiled from one tale sweep back into the *Tales'* larger totality immediately after it finishes (the *Clerk's Tale* is a good example). Here, after the depiction of an authoritative and admirable woman, the anti-feminist strain of caricature of women's *maistrie* reasserts itself. If *Melibee* was in some sense a Mirror for Princes, Harry's response deflects attention from this, applying it instead to his own very ungrand and un*ruly* homelife. It is also an instance of Chaucer's pleasure in crossing stereotypical gender images: Goodelief is martial, her husband reluctant to fight. The Host's next speech rather similarly clads the Monk in unmonkish identities: as a virile 'tredefowel', a sleek *bonviveur*, a ruler of men: a 'governour'. There is not much Poverty, Chastity or Obedience in his imagined picture of the Monk. At first sight the Monk's dignified declaration that he will tell tragedies turns its back on this irreverent characterisation of him. But Harry's words not only capture what many contemporaries felt about worldly clerics: they also depict the Monk as very like one of his own worldly rulers who stand 'in greet prosperitee'. The Endlink shows us the two men with power over the pilgrims coming in suddenly to end the Monk's moment of authority in the story-telling realm.

19

The *Nun's Priest's Tale*

The *Nun's Priest's Tale* is very clearly a tale with multiple meanings. It is a funny story about animals; it is also about human sin, temptation and Adam's Fall; like the *Monk's Tale*, it teaches the lesson of mutability and the dangers of earthly ambition, glory and pride; and like the stories in the Monk's Tale it is also a medieval *tragedie*, a fall from Fortune's wheel (though here Fortune lets the victim rise again: a twist that reverses it into a comedy).[1] The tale can also be read as a rhetorical *tour de force*, a mock-heroic parody. Whether, additionally, it had contemporary political applications is an issue to which we shall return.

Chaucer, as often, uses the periphery to the tale, its Links, opening passages and conclusions, to challenge the reader into interpretative alertness by setting up confusing and even contradictory signals for interpretation. Before the tale, Harry Bailey insists it is to be an amusement with no solemn message, but the Priest's conclusion counters that, asserting that all stories are told 'To oure doctrine' (VII, 3442), and introducing another concept: that readers can choose their own interpretation. This narrative, he says, can either be frivolous entertainment – a tale of a cock and a hen – or teach an ethical lesson (a *moralite*). 'Taketh the moralite, goode men,' he says, employing the words *fruyt* and *chaf*, terms traditionally used since St Augustine for allegorical interpretations that find more than one level of meaning: *fruyt* referring to a symbolic reading and to deeper truths, *chaf* to a literal reading and less valuable meanings. Within the tale the Cock and Fox add two readings of their own: that it is a lesson about the folly of talking too much, and the need to keep your eyes open. Like most interpretations offered within the text of the *Tales*, these are manifestly red herrings, simply not adequate to the elaborate narrative Chaucer creates here with its complex networks of religious, philosophical, social and literary themes. Like the short warning against carelessness, negligence and flattery which follows these over-trite moralisations (VII, 3436–7), they are the type of simple 'moral' given in Aesopian fables,

and these homely proverbial interpretations act as a tease and challenge
`· ~· to work out their own reading of a far from simple or homely
's concluding address shifts us, with its citation from St
l terms *fruyt* and *chaf*, and the final prayer for moral
more sophisticated and religious concepts of literary
ose. But it provocatively evades telling us what the
· extractable lesson – should be.

al outwards to its readership at its close (like the
and the Host's declaration that no text is anything
eaders (VII, 2799–802), the tale raises questions about
eption as well as interpretation. It also poses a central ques-
about the whole *Canterbury Tales*: is its purpose ultimately *sentence*,
morally valuable truth, or *solas*, simple entertainment? The Nun's Priest
employs a literary form, equally suitable, it seems, for both the plans
that jostle together in the *Tales*: a journey to a Cathedral and a journey
ending back at dinner in the Tabard inn. And there are other ways in
which the tale is almost a microcosm of the *Canterbury Tales*: it
contains, like the *Monk's Tale*, tales within a tale in Chantecleer's speech
on dreams, and includes many of the *Tales*' major themes: the relationship of men and women, the relationship of secular and sacred art, ideas
about mutability, tragedy, sin and salvation. The aspect of authorship
with which this particular tale is concerned is authorship in relation to
interpretation and reception, and the issue of how far the very existence
and meaning of an author's text lies in the hands of his readers – and
depends on his ability to attract them. It is an issue central to the use of
words by a preacher.

The *Tales* are an anthology of genres – a genre is itself a mode of
interpreting – and this tale belongs to several genres, including the
beast-fable, religious allegory, and mock-heroic spoof (among other
things it is a spoof tragedy of Fortune).

The Tale as Beast-Fable

Medieval beast-fable had two main forms. One consisted of short
animal stories teaching a moral, a tradition going back to Aesop's
fables.[2] Two such fables are sources for the *Nun's Priest's Tale*. In one
(teaching the dangers of vanity and flattery), a raven is flattered by a fox
into opening his mouth to sing, thus losing to the fox a piece of cheese
he had in his beak; in the other (teaching the dangers of talking too
much), a cock, having been flattered by a fox into shutting his eyes to

sing and thus being captured, turns the tables by persuading the fox to shout defiance at their pursuers – and let loose his prey.

The other type of beast-fable was the great French comic epic cycle of stories about Renard the fox. In one, Renard catches 'Chauntecler', a cock, who has a wife, Pinte, and is sent a warning dream. Chaucer's fox is 'Russell', the name in the French stories of Renard's son. In twelfth- and thirteenth-century classic Renard stories, the fox is the hero: a rogue, thief and master of disguise, but a lovable and resourceful trickster. Two later developments perhaps influenced Chaucer's approach: the fox becomes more of a representative of evil or the Devil, and more social and political satire enters the tales. Chaucer makes Chantecleer, for all his foolish arrogance, the character with whom we sympathise, and in the religious symbolism he represents ourselves and all human kind as an Adam-figure, the archetypal human who falls victim to the Devil's snares through his own folly, conceit and pursuit of worldly pleasures.

Rhetoric and the Mock-Heroic Style

The French 'Renard and Chauntecler' story begins with references to heroes of medieval romances: Paris and Helen, Tristan, and Yvain. Cooper (1996: 341) observes that, unlike simple Aesopian fables, the Renard stories, with their quite elaborate human-like characterisation and imitations of elegant genres like romance, tended towards the mock-heroic. Chaucer takes these tendencies further. Chantecleer's vainglory is matched by an overblown style: his capture is presented with rhetorical devices like the *apostrophe* (address: 'O Destynee . . .', 'O woful hennes . . . '), repetition ('Allas . . .', 'Allas . . .') and the rhetorical question ('Why woldestow suffre hym on thy day to dye?'). There are echoes of a famous rhetorical handbook, Geoffrey de Vinsauf's *Poetria Nova* (*c*.1200), which gives a lament on Richard I's death as an example of how to write a tragic lament. This included an apostrophe to Friday, the day Richard died, and references to Venus, to whom Friday was sacred. Many parallels from the world's great literature create further mock-heroic inflation: the fox is compared to Judas, Ganelon and Sinon (respectively, traitors from the Bible, the Old French epic *Chanson de Roland*, and the *Aeneid*), the hens' cackling being compared to lamentations at the destruction of Troy, Carthage and Rome. The cock is presented like an epic hero through allusions to the *Chanson de Roland* (VII, 3227), the Arthurian tradition (VII,

3211–13), and the *Aeneid* (VII, 3228–9, 3355–9). His head and feet are visualised in chivalric and heraldic terms (VII, 2859–67). An absurd dignity hangs round Chantecleer and Pertelote's command of medieval science and learning: medical jargon in VII, 2946–67, astronomy in VII, 2855–8, and VII, 3190–9, dream-theory in VII, 2970–83, and VII, 3123–3148. Cock and hen are also described in the literary register of elegant romance: 'Madame Pertelote' is an elegant 'damoysele', described in courtly French terms, 'curteys', 'discreet', 'debonaire', 'compaignable' (VII, 2870–2). The resemblance of Chantecleer's mishap to a medieval tragedy of Fortune, teaching the transience of worldly glory, is also mock-heroic: this tale could be read as a parody of the Monk's tragedies. We could also read the parallels with Adam and the introduction of contemporary philosophical topics such as predestination or conditional necessity and philosophers like Boethius and Bradwardine (d. 1349) as primarily mock-heroic in purpose.

The Priest's conclusion, however, allows that some readers may seek *doctrine*, some kind of teaching, in the tale, and they will discard its outer rhetoric to look for *fruyt*, allegorical meaning, and to that we now turn.

Christian Symbolism and Allegorical Interpretations

Chantecleer's situation resembles Adam's: medieval art represented Eden as an enclosed garden and Chantecleer lives in bliss with his wife in a fenced yard with his enemy lurking around trying to entrap him. Chantecleer, letting his infatuation with Pertelote cloud his brain, and disregarding his own deductions about his dream's serious message, resembles the medieval view of Adam as blinded by his own sensuality and the dangerous attractions of Woman into following Eve's advice rather than his own (superior, male) reason. The text, from the moment Chantecleer decides simply to enjoy himself to the point when the fox catches him, is full of allusions to the Fall of Man and the general mutability of earthly joy: 'evere the latter ende of joye is wo', 'Wommannes conseil broghte us first to wo' (VII, 3205, 3257), and so on.

Medieval biblical interpreters taught that Adam fell because of gluttony, lust and pride. Chantecleer is absorbed in all these worldly distractions, which blind him from being vigilant about danger. Lines VII, 3230–51 introduce philosophical questions linked to the Christian theology of sin: is damnation predestined or do humans have free will? The popular story of the fox and cock was already commonly used by sermon-writers and in church carvings to symbolise Christian ideas: the Devil ensnaring the Christian soul, or hypocrisy, especially of false churchmen. Exegetical critics (see pp. 15–16), including D. W. Robertson (1962: 213, 251–2), have applied such allegorical interpretations with typical rigidity. Exegetical criticism takes this tale's allusions to St Paul, and *fruyt* and *chaf*, as indication that Chaucer wished all his tales to be interpreted as allegories whose real, theological meaning must be sought by stripping off the surface meaning, the literal *chaf* (see Rigby 1996: 91–108).

One does not need to be a thoroughgoing Robertsonian, however, to accept that the tale demonstrates an important Christian truth, shown also in the *Merchant's Tale*, that a man's fall into sin is caused by mental blindness born of his own worldliness and sensuality as much as by the Devil – or by female attractions. The tale abounds in moral and philosophical messages: about Fortune, free will, worldliness, vigilance, pride, *mesure*, the influence of women, flattery, mutability, and so on. This does not necessarily mean we have to find one single *fruyt* interpretation or even assume that finding an interpretation is the response the tale demands from us. Cooper (1996: 352) wisely says of the tale's multiple themes:

> It is a tale, then, that encompasses practically everything . . . too much of its proclaimed morality is contingent on the animal nature of its characters to stand independently, or to stand at all. . . . However urgent the same issues may be in other tales, when projected onto the farmyard they lose any absoluteness they ever possessed.

Some critics, among them Muscatine (1957: 238–43), Donaldson (1958: 941–3) and David (1976: 223–30), see the tale's central philosophical revelation lying not in one 'correct' extractable interpretation, but within its texture in the play of rhetorical virtuosity, its shifts of perspective and its potentiality for multiple meanings. For them, throwing this *chaf* away to secure a unitary kernel of 'message' misses the tale's deepest truth: its presentation of apparently incompatible points of view in human life, its mockery at attempts to understand the world through learned theories, and its affectionate attitude towards earthly ambitions and intellectual pretensions even while recognising their ultimate mutability and inadequacy.

In a way, the style, with the enormous gap and misfit between form and content, parallels the reader's task of fitting interpretations to the text. Hussey (1981: 191–3) and Knight (1973: 232–3) have stressed the text's rhetoric, not as a means to some other end, but as a subject in its own right with its own significance: against interpretation, and against readers' and humans' tendencies to take themselves too seriously. Mann (1974–5: 277–8) shows that the reference to 'Daun Burnel the Asse' (VII, 3312) connects Chaucer's tale to a tradition of mock beast-fables which satirise intellectuals' pretensions. The mockery of large areas of medieval learning and culture encourages moral focus on the frugal and contented peasant widow and the Priest's simple prayer for virtue and our heavenly destiny:

> As seith my [L]ord, so make us alle goode men,
> And brynge us to his heighe blisse! Amen.
>
> (VII, 3445–6)[3]

In this world the answer is that people should find virtue and contentment in their lot, but the *Canterbury Tales*' ultimate answer is to transfer the whole issue to a spiritual level as the *Parson's Tale* approaches.

Style and Politics

Does the style, with its inflation and the gap between form and matter, relate to the themes of social order and peasant protest that are discernible in the tale? These political themes do not amount to a consistent political allegory – nor yet another allegorical reading for interpreters – but they reveal a pervasive post-1381 political anxiety running through the text. The cautionary tale of the cock who gets above himself, presenting this as folly, danger and unnatural behaviour for one of his species (rank), can be read as a fable against social mobility and aspirations.

Certainly Chaucer's telling of the tale keeps reminding us of social disparities: of where people and creatures come on the vertical scale of rank and how much relative power they have. This is clear from the start when the Knight and Host dominate the other two story-tellers and the Nun's Priest deferentially obeys after a passage of concentrated verbal bullying by the Host, and where the Knight expresses a preference for hearing about people on top of Fortune's wheel, not its reversals – about rising to power not falling down.[4] The perspectives of the *Nun's Priest's Tale* are, from the beginning, vertical ones.

The focus on the narrow sooty cottage of the poor, presented in insistent verbal contrast to the halls and bowers of upper-class luxury ('poynaunt sauce', 'deyntee morsel', 'apoplexie', 'wyn', 'whit and reed', etc.) stresses the gap between lord and peasant.[5] And the Nun's Priest matches the widow in falling below the lifestyle of the well-to-do: his horse is 'a jade . . . foul and lene'. She is a demesne servant, a 'deye' or dairy-assistant, contented with her lot; he readily obeys instructions from the Host. Both are located relatively low on scales of power, then praised for being compliant. A merry heart, patience, obedient acceptance and 'hertes suffisaunce' are their appropriate responses to lowly position.

The cock's mock-heroic treatment contrasts with these two humble humans and a confusion of dimensions and proportions begins to set in. In relation to more powerful humans, the priest and widow are socially low, but in contrast to her birds the peasant woman has towering superiority: of power, size and species. In relation to her social superiors her contented humility makes her admirable; in relation to his human owners Chantecleer's pretensions make him absurd.

The narrative is rife with disproportions. The little cock's Fall is framed by two Brobdignagian appearances by his human-sized owners, within whose power and fence of sticks his freedom is, in reality, totally contained and restrained. Inflated rhetoric makes him a grandiose hero of high epic, tragedy and romance, but the framing presence of the 'povre wydwe' and her 'narwe cotage', and the sudden inrush of this larger human world again later when the peasants pursue the fox, bring him suddenly down to size before our eyes, both by their higher status as large human beings and by their own low class. They are themselves only 'cherles' (VII, 3409).

The mock-heroic descriptions often stress a height, making the contrast with the birds' actual smallness specially disconcerting: Chantecleer is like an abbey clock, his comb like a castle wall (VII, 2854, 2860); he knows 'ascensiouns' of astronomical hours (VII, 2855–7), looks up to the ascending sun and Taurus (VII, 3190–203); struts up on his toes, not deigning to put his foot down on the ground (VII, 3180–1), and is caught by his readiness to stand on tiptoe and stretch himself up high with his eyes shut. His downfall is described in grand human political jargon as a 'heigh ymaginacioun', which means here 'high conspiracy' (VII, 3217), for he himself is a prince 'roial . . . in his halle' (VII, 3184, 3325–30). Leaving the safety of his 'narwe' perch to strut around in foolish negligence, sensuality and pride, is a flight downwards (VII, 3172, 3231). The device of bathos accompanies the mock-heroic: the text's sudden allusions, amid high-flown rhetoric, to cabbage-beds, perches, and hens bathing in sand, or Chantecleer clucking at finding a seed after his lordly translation of Latin (VII, 3175).[6] Is he, for Chaucer, as absurd as a peasant who gets above himself? This verbal verticality and bathos stylistically supports the religious theme of a Fall, but it also meshes in with some unexpected references that we find in this text to contemporary socio-political matters. That the mock-heroic/bathos seesaw of style and the dizzying effects of disproportion and shifts between high and low are not merely comic, allegorical or aesthetic, but have links with late fourteenth-century economic and political anxieties, is suggested by certain elements Chaucer introduces into his tale. Whereas the main Renard source makes Chauntecler's owner a rich farmer, Chaucer substitutes his elaborate study of the poor but contented feudal peasant widow: an ideological wish-fulfilment portrait equal to that of his *General Prologue* Knight. His brief portrait (VII, 2810–20) of the Nun's Priest is also of one deferentially eager to please those who order him about: that 'sweete' and 'goodly' man (reserving enough independence only to urge communal spiritual improvement at the end). Most striking are two distinctly political references. One is Chaucer's only direct reference to 1381 – the noise of Jack Straw, a rebel leader, and his bands as they attacked Flemish merchants during the invasion of London (VII, 3393–6). The reference is contemptuous about the rebels: they are conceived as an uproar of primitive noise and savagery (in actuality the 1381 rebels were generally well-disciplined). The other, as Justice (1994: 210–19) shows, is Chaucer's description of the peasants' chase, which echoes intertextually a satirical attack by John Gower on the 1381 rebels: Gower concentrates on rural names, wild noise and close association between peasants and their animals. Gower, in his *Vox Clamantis*, I, 783–98, much less ambiguous than Chaucer in his attitude to social conflict, compared the rebels to animals lacking human rationality (the chronicler Froissart reported that one of the 1381 protests was that hereditary serfdom treated peasants like animals, not like men equal to other men; see Patterson 1991: 262–4).

If Chaucer's animal fable about the absurdity and perils of lower beings getting above themselves has reference to the social conflicts that became visible in 1381, there was already a tradition available to him for drawing such a parallel. The phrase 'proude cherles' (VII, 3409) is perhaps therefore introduced to link this tale of an animal's dangerous pride to a conservative view of lower-class human protest and demands. The two descriptions of peasants at the beginning and end of the story would thus have different functions: the Gower-like hullabaloo of the peasants and animals at the end, accompanied by the description 'proude cherles', suggests Chantecleer's pride can be read as a negative image of obstreperous peasants, while the contented 'povre widwe' at the beginning is an image of how they should be. There is no consistently worked out political allegory in the tale but it can, all the same, be read as a fictional attempt to contain awareness of new social forces and tensions by translating them into ancient, universal patterns like Pride before a Fall, absurd animal antics, and the Christian concept of everyman's tendency to temptation and sin.

Gender issues link the tale to several others. The theme of marital power conflict, and its negative statements about 'Wommannes conseil' (VII, 3250–66), provide an anti-feminist counterbalance to *Melibee*: not a very powerful one, since Chantecleer is not a strong argument for male mental superiority, and one which will be eclipsed by the mental and moral superiority of the female hero of the *Second Nun's Tale* – if Chaucer intended that to follow. And as Dinshaw comments, Chantecleer's interpretation of *Mulier est hominis confusio* shows that here '"glossing" is a tool of masculine conquest' (1989: 15).

The tale is appropriate in its potential for a Christian message – and perhaps its misogyny – to a celibate priestly teller (though once the tale starts there is no sense that we are hearing a voice that is specifically the story-teller's). From a cynic's viewpoint its image of polygamous Chantecleer with his hen-harem could be seen as a caricature of the position of a priest serving a convent of nuns. Immediately after the Priest's prayerful conclusion comes, in nine related manuscripts, a bawdy joke at the Priest's expense from the Host, hinting at substantial sexual prowess. Whether this is scribal or a Link idea Chaucer wrote but decided to use for the Monk (VII, 1943–64) as the *Tales* evolved, the Host's disrespectful allegorical reading bears final witness to the multiplicity of readings the *Nun's Priest's Tale* can engender. Yet it also engenders much unintellectual laughter: the peasants' pursuit at the end is the classic chase scene that brings a rush of energy towards the end of so many stories and films, and the picture of Chantecleer gazing at a butterfly or harmonising 'My lief is faren in londe!' (VII, 2879) is genial, uncontentious comedy.

20

The *Second Nun's Tale*

Like the Nun's Priest, this Second Nun may be an afterthought as a story-teller. She scarcely features in the *General Prologue*: perhaps Chaucer felt the need as the later sections evolved for more religious narrators and also, after including only the medieval equivalent of the token woman among the *General Prologue* portraits – two token women, one secular/married and one religious/virgin – perhaps the need for more female narrative voices?

She is the Prioress's companion, called in I, 163–4 her *chapeleyne*, here meaning secretary and assistant, her second-in-command in running the nunnery. This is the most unified, the closest to being monologic, of all the tales: in the sense that, though containing oppositions (for instance between weakness and strength, female obedience and disobedience), these are wholly integrated into the all-ruling divine purpose. The Prologue's themes establish the tale firmly within the world of the convent: it centres, like the *Prioress's Prologue*, on a prayer to Mary, full of echoes of Marian liturgy and hymns. Its first topic, avoidance of idleness, also had conventual associations: nuns and monks were expected by the rules of the religious life to avoid idleness by regular work; the *General Prologue* Monk despised this regulation. Nuns might sew, teach, or in some houses scribe or decorate service books. Translations and hagiography were two genres in which women writers, including nuns, worked. The duty of virtuous occupation sometimes appears in prefaces to books by religious authors and is appropriate to a self-emptying cloistered writer: it justifies and sanctifies the otherwise potentially egotistical act of composition. This translation is offered as a labour of 'feithful bisynesse', dutiful and faith-inspired service (VIII, 24).

Its genre is that of *legende*, saint's life (VIII, 25); *lif* and *passioun* (VIII, 26) are also literary terms meaning 'saint's life' and 'martyr's life' – *passioun* meant 'suffering'. Chaucer's main source was a famous collection of saints' lives, Jacobus de Voragine's *Legenda Aurea*, 'Golden

Legend'. Its life of Cecilia includes allegorical interpretations of her name like VIII, 85–119. Chaucer also knew a French translation of Voragine which opens with a prologue about avoiding idleness.

The Female Saint: Cecilia as Hero

Hagiography (saints' lives) was a very popular medieval genre, especially interesting from the viewpoint of women's history and the history of women's interaction with books as virtually the only genre that regularly presents women as protagonists and as heroically brave figures, albeit in roles that retain their virtue, faith and obedience. Cecilia is the opposite of 'ydelnesse': her life is full of energy and vigour in the cause of God. Both the Prioress and Second Nun start with prayers which include requests for a divine power to fill them and for Mary to direct their writing. Cecilia herself is powerful not in herself but because she is filled with God's grace.

Cecilia was a probably apocryphal Christian virgin-martyr, killed, according to tradition, during the third-century persecution of Christians in Rome. The tale ends with a miracle, her preservation despite attempts to execute her by fire and beheading. The miracle has a three-fold function: to demonstrate the power of God and of steadfast Christian faith; to epitomise the martyrs' role as living witnesses who bring others to God (Cecilia continues to preach); and as an image of Cecilia's own separateness from this world. It is a sign acted out in her own body, that she has always been indifferent to the physical realm because her spirit is wholly given up to heavenly reality even while in this world. She is already a citizen of that 'bettre lif in oother place' (VIII, 323). The only judge she cares about is 'The rightful Juge' in heaven (VIII, 389), not the oppressive earthly judge she despises. Like Griselda and Custance she thus has strength amid earthly weakness and submits to suffering with calm obedience. Just as they remain undisturbed by adversity, she remains cool and untroubled in a bath of flames (this also functions as an image of her virginity). Unlike these two other heroines she is a bold speaker, both in teaching and inspiring others (e.g. VIII, 319–41) and in arguing against her opponents, constantly accusing her pagan judge of blind stupidity. Words like 'boldely', 'ful stedfaste' and 'wyse' are used of her speech; she speaks to her male companions of death as 'bataille' (VIII, 383–90), and laughs at her enemies (VIII, 461–5, 493–506). She voices explicitly a contempt for worldly forces which can hurt her that is expressed by Custance and Griselda only implicitly through meek endurance. Though this strength makes her a genuine female hero – she performs actions that are courageous and effective – it is also shown to be God's strength working through her (VIII, 275): the power of 'myghty God . . . in his hevenes hye' (VIII, 508). Chaucer's interest in strong women has been seen already in the *Tales*: female heroic endurance, exemplified in Griselda and Custance; female wisdom and guidance, exemplified in Prudence and the old woman in the *Wife of Bath's Tale*; and one might even add female temerity and scorn in argument, seen in the Wife of Bath and Pertelote: all these qualities are drawn together now in Cecilia and, in a fashion which becomes more common towards the end of the *Canterbury Tales*, they are subsumed within a religious perspective. This is a tale about female strength; it is, however, also a tale about choosing death and rejecting sexuality, fertility and life. Chaste marriage and brides who opposed sexual consummation are common motifs in medieval saints' lives; chaste marriage was adopted by some late medieval spouses, including the fifteenth-century English mystic Margery Kempe. Richard II himself may have admired the concept.[1]

The *Prologue's* prayer contains echoes of St Bernard's prayer to Mary, which is the climax of Dante's *Divine Comedy*. Dante's prayer opens 'Virgin Mother, daughter of your son, more humble and more high than any creature' (compare VIII, 36, 39). Chaucer's prayer to Mary as the Nun's merciful advocate and poetic Muse, though full of echoes of other authors' hymns to Mary, has its own unity through a chain of references to holy women: it links the tale's virgin heroine and its virgin nun-narrator with the supreme heavenly Virgin (VII, 29–35, 43–9) and introduces two other virtuous women, St Anne and the Canaanite woman from Matthew 15.22.

The Saint and Language: Cecilia as Image

The text moves from one traditional image of Mary to another, recalling familiar medieval prayers, concentrating on her female and merciful roles; as 'flour of virgines' she brought salvation (Christ) into the world; she pleads for sinners' forgiveness in heaven, and helps people on earth to keep themselves pure. The meditation on Cecilia's name is typical of medieval belief that names, like scriptures, could be interpreted to yield a range of allegorical religious meanings. These last stanzas of the

Prologue present the heroine already as a set of sacred symbols, and the name interpretations introduce key themes of the tale such as light, purity, heaven and selflessness.

The tale is one of powerful consistency, unlike the superficially similar *Prioress's Tale* where the tale itself, enclosed between two prayers in its Prologue and final stanza, is an explosive brew of moral and emotional contradictions and a site of disturbing psychological, even pathological tensions. Here the same confidently triumphant lyric unity of mood runs throughout the Prologue and tale. It is created primarily through the way the text is structured on images – of light, fire, crowns, roses and lilies, fragrance, heaven and angels – and full of repeated words and lexical sets: *bryghte, red, white, heaven, blisful/joye, clene/cleere, hevene, sweete, savour, deere*. Direct speech dominates the narrative but without colloquialisms. The style, while avoiding overt rhetorical show, abounds in rhapsodic, prayer-like exclamations and balanced verbal designs:

> 'O Lord, o feith, o God, withouten mo,   *summing up all*
> O Cristendom, and Fader of alle also,
> Aboven alle and over alle everywhere.'
>
> (VII, 207–9)

> 'With body clene and with unwemmed thoght   *unspotted*
> Kepeth ay wel thise corones,' quod he;   *for ever*
> 'Fro paradys to yow I have hem broght,
> Ne nevere mo ne shal they roten bee,
> Ne lese hir soote savour, trusteth me;
> Ne nevere wight shal seen hem with his ye.'   *man*
>
> (VIII, 225–30)

Devices here include chiasmus ('body clene' and 'unwemmed thoght' have the pattern *noun–adjective / adjective–noun*), alliteration, and lavish repetition, especially of doublets and triplets. The text is full of syntactic and lexical repetition, apostrophe and alliteration. Symmetrical designs, language more typical of lyric than narrative, continue even during ugly scenes:

> 'Of whennes comth thyn answeryng so rude?'   *blunt*
> 'Of whennes?' quod she, whan that she was freyned,   *asked*
> 'Of conscience and of good feith unfeyned.'
>
> (VIII, 432–5)

'Han noght oure myghty princes to me yiven,
Ye, bothe power and auctoritee
To maken folk to dyen or to lyven?
Why spekestow so proudly thanne to me?'

(VIII, 470–3)

Quasi-melodic verbal patterning, together with recurrent imagery of
beautiful things like light, flowers, cleanness and sweetness, and the
effect of closely rhyming stanzas, all convey an impression of human
events filled with an inner ecstasy, held in a heavenly harmony, despite
their literal violence and earthly deprivations. They create a sense of
stasis and stability within which the dynamic and dramatic events of
Cecilia's life are narrated and this combination corresponds to the
earthly and heavenly elements united within the saint.

The text is structured on spiritual counterparts to sensual and
worldly values. The spiritual 'bataille' with 'armure of brightnesse'
(VIII, 385–6) is willing submission to death by the faithful; the
'flambes rede' of the virgin's martyrdom (VIII, 515) are the cause of the
heavenly crowns of roses and lilies (VIII, 220–1); the love of an angel,
day and night (VIII, 152–4), replaces and transcends ordinary marital
love; chastity is paradoxically a 'seed' which has a 'fruyt': conversion
(VIII, 190–6). Roses and crowns were traditional Christian symbols of
the glory given to martyrs in heaven and Cecilia's ascetic choices in life
are contrasted with the *Romance of the Rose*, (*c*.1237), the greatest of all
medieval love-narratives, which centres on the sensual image of the
rose: the Second Nun's first three lines recall the scene in the *Romance*
where the gate to the Garden of Delight is opened by Idleness.
Paradoxes throughout the text's imagery express rejection of sensuality,
summed up in Cecilia's first appearance wearing both gold dress and
hair shirt, and singing a silent song (VIII, 132–3).

The Holy Woman and Society

The saint is presented as building on faith and building faith: her boldness comes 'Of conscience and of good feith unfeyned' (VIII, 434), and
draws others to steadfast belief. Her life is a social as well as a private
spiritual achievement. Towards the end the woman turns into the
church: she dies surrounded by the 'Cristen folk'; her last acts are to
preach the faith and donate her house to become a church building and
the poem ends appropriately with the Church of St Cecilia at Rome,

still a lasting memorial to the saint and a place where 'Men doon to Crist and to his seint servyse'. 'Servyse' is an appropriate last word: work, service to others, and the worship of the Church.

The tale speaks of harmony: in its evenly patterned style and its picture of lives lived in conformity with God's will – the Nun's as well as the saint's – but they are lives of energy, work, intelligent articulacy and service to a community. That is heralded in stanzas 1–4, the Nun's teaching on 'feithful bisynesse'. Harmony there may be, but not sleepy serenity or self-indulgence: work has both a spiritual value, keeping temptation at bay, and also a social value, creating 'good' and 'encrees', 'wealth and profit' (virtuous and material?), and ensuring the religious person does not simply consume what others produce by labour (VIII, 17–21). We could read this as a response to to those of Chaucer's contemporaries who criticised monks and nuns as idle parasites: it shows that those who turn aside from the mainstream assumptions of human society – virgins, the cloistered religious, martyrs willing to die – can none the less use life for service. The qualities the Nun celebrates are brisk ones though expressed with lyricism and imagery.

Martin (1990: 150–1) shows how Cecilia contradicts and transcends stereotypical social expectations of women. Whereas the *Prioress's Tale* is – at best – emotional piety, whose narrator presents herself as passive and childlike, the Second Nun stresses her subject's 'techynge','bisynesse', 'swift and bisy . . . werkynge' and 'charite' (VIII, 93, 98,116, 118), and her own desire to present usefully and clearly the straightforward 'sentence' of her material (VIII, 77–84). If this tale provides yet another aspect of authorship, it is that of writing as 'werk' (VIII, 24, 77, 84). Cecilia's sufferings, unlike those in the tale of the little 'clergeon', are not described with the language of pathos. No weeping, swooning or *pite* surrounds her deathbed; despite her torments the emphasis is on what she *does* while dying, not what she suffers. At the men's martyrdom, it is a man, Maximus, who reacts with 'pitous teres' (VIII, 371, 401); Cecilia's calm purposive cheerfulness stands out in contrast. Cecilia demonstrates both absolute conformity to authority – God's will – and disobedience to earthly authorities: defying patriarchal authority, frustrating her father's wishes, redefining her marriage, winning her husband over by argument, and confronting secular authority (see Johnson 1990). There was a tradition behind this vision of the holy virgin as bold rebel: against the background of medieval assumptions about the weakness of women, their legal subjection to their husbands and the inherent sinfulness of marriage, virginity put a woman in a position of relative strength. The women who made a positive decision to become nuns could in some ways go against the constraints of a society that tended to define secular women simply in terms of their biological role, as brides, wives and mothers, in relation to men. In *Melibee* too, Chaucer shows a woman reversing hierarchies through rational and moral argument.

Chaucer's women of authority operate, however, only within limits: Cecilia dies despite her moral victory, and in earthly society has moral respect but never the social authority of Urban, Maximus, Almachius or her father. Prudence uses all her skills, undoubted intellectual superiority and ethical maturity only as adviser to her husband, the man who has the civil authority. Chaucer's virtuous strong women are teachers (Cecilia, Prudence, the Old Woman in the *Wife of Bath's Tale*, re-educating her immature and worthless spouse) or mothers – the paradigm of female wise service to men: Custance, Mary in the Prioress's Tale, and the mother-wife in the *Wife of Bath's Tale*. Cecilia represents a religious resolution, an apotheosis, of the *Canterbury Tales*' long-running contention over 'Wommannes conseil'.[2] Her moral authority, her spiritual *maistrie*, is not contested by her virtuous male associates: there is companionable, brotherly and sisterly harmony between the members, male and female, of the Christian group; Valerian exerts no *maistrie* over his wife. As Knapp (1990: 112–13) points out, her story depicts almost a Golden Age myth of female defiance of oppression, female effectiveness and intellectual authority, and harmony between the sexes, but whereas it is easy to locate this in a pre-Christian era where civil authority is pagan, the tale does not explain how women can imitate the saint or resist oppresion in an era when authority is that of a Christian state.

21

The *Canon's Yeoman's Tale*

This tale is told by the *yeoman*, 'servant', of a canon who is an alchemist and confidence-trickster: his master's trick is to persuade people that if they give him money he can turn base metals into large quantities of silver. His clothes show he is an Augustinian canon. They lived usually in towns and under less fixed rules than other ecclesiastics. Though there were some large, well-run Augustinian houses in the late fourteenth century, others were poorly endowed and some were associated with financial and other scandals.[1] This canon, as was not uncommon, seems to be living independently in a parish. It was an order with a slightly dubious reputation, an association Chaucer exploits but then ostentatiously apologises about: his own rogue is merely an archetypal Bad Apple (VIII, 992–1011; compare 'infecte', 973). He does not figure among the *General Prologue* portraits: we have no prior account of his character; instead Chaucer's Link employs more realistic devices, positioning the reader as an onlooker picking out details as the new arrivals approach and listening to replies to the Host's questioning.

As with the *Prioress's Tale*, no discussion or comment follows the *Second Nun's Tale*. A mark of respect for the religious tale, as self-evident truth calling for no discussion? Or prudence in a time of religious controversy, to avoid admitting even in fiction the possibility of conflicting attitudes or lay discussion of religion (opponents of Wycliffism deprecated uneducated laypeople's growing taste for theological debate)? Or is this departure from Chaucer's established formula for the Links about narrative as much as religion? Though the Link turns immediately to the newcomers, connections back to the preceding tale will be made, as we shall see, but through thematic contrasts and parallels between the two tales rather than through conversation between pilgrim characters. The *Second Nun's Tale* created a harmonious, unified effect, one impervious, compared with other *Canterbury Tales*, to alternative worldviews. What follows is not other perspectives voiced from within the story-telling group, but an interruption of that fictional circle. The sudden statement (VIII, 554–61) that the group is being overtaken by the galloping canon, is a narratorial strategy directing readers' attention to new elements in the sequence of narratives and dramatising a development increasingly important in the later tales: a turning away from, and breaking out of, the enclosed world of the pilgrims' game of tales. In different ways all the last tales challenge readers to recall the existence of worlds outside fiction. Chaucer's story-telling company has set up expectations of closure, two of them in fact: cathedral or Tabard inn, but the actual end of the *Tales* as we have it will refuse to provide either of those closures, or any closure within the norms of fiction, for the *Parson's Tale* will reject *fables* entirely. If the little world of the pilgrims' story-telling game symbolises fiction, the Canon comes from somewhere else: a somewhere that is itself fictional but symbolises recognition of extrafictional consciousness, of a context outside the closed world of the pilgrim company.

The Canon's hurry and enthusiasm, and the curiosity stirred by the Link's gradual identification process and the Host's insistent questions, stimulate (and simulate) the reader's own eagerness to read on. These are outsiders to the original *General Prologue* group, lack prior identification and ride up from we know not where – though we later learn their home is in the *suburbes*, not salubrious 'suburbs' but the unregulated backstreet warrens of a medieval town: almost shanty towns. These newcomers have a maverick and free-wheeling air. In being mobile, urban, and an unconfined member of a religious order (one which was itself relatively unregulated), the canon has already characteristics Chaucer usually regards with suspicion. He is eager to join and flatter the pilgrims; is he hoping, like the Pardoner earlier, to prey on them? His Yeoman starts on the sales pitch that they will get *prow*, 'profit,' if they listen to what he has to say (VIII, 606–612). The initial mystery over their identity arouses readers' critical and judgemental faculties. And nothing turns out to be what it first seems: the Canon's Yeoman claims he can make fabulous amounts of silver, so why does he look so poverty-stricken? The Yeoman first praises him, then denounces him; the Canon is initially affable, then scampers off angrily.

Despite the abrupt transition between them, the *Second Nun's* and *Canon's Yeoman's* tales are linked thematically and through contrasts. Both are about transmutation: one about chemical transmutation and creating money out of nothing, the other the transmutation of the earthly into the spiritual, the flames and blood of martyrdom turned into eternal crowns of roses; human dross refined through the faith and the fire of martyrdom; victimisation turned into heavenly triumph.

Fire is central to both: Cecilia, marytred by literal fire, also burns 'evere in charite ful brighte' (VIII, 118); the Canon's fire of greed and avarice destroys others' wealth and his servant's natural complexion. One has real miracles, the other a fruitless quest, offensive to God, for a miraculous substance. One is about aggressive egotism, the other about selfless spirituality. One is about faithfulness and service, the diligent building of something eternally real; the other about cheating and exploitation, attempting to earn money without work.

Alchemy is an exotic topic but the tale may also represent more common anxieties about contemporary socio-economic developments. The horror the tale expresses about alchemy may symbolise Chaucer's unease about modern economic developments: early capitalism and the movement away from the communal and hierarchically controlled production of the feudal estate towards a world of individualistic money-making and the creation of profit from commercial dealing itself – not just financial scams but the type of respectable dealing on credit featured in the Merchant's portrait and the *Shipman's Tale*. The Canon's mirky backstreet milieu (*pryvee* and *fereful*), a thieves' district (VIII, 657–62), locates him in the same imagined region of sordid urban disorder and rapacity as the *Cook's Tale*. As an unprincipled, exploitative and materialistic cleric, dealing in false or forbidden beliefs, he is also an extreme symbolic epitome of the perils of worldliness, cynicism and superstition many saw threatening so wealthy an organisation as the medieval Church. Alchemy is vilified as a 'cursed craft' against Christ's wishes, destructive, and causing economic 'scarsetee' (VIII, 1388–1480): terms which could also be used to condemn both financial deception and profit-making. The evils of alchemy and profit are linked throughout the tale: *multiplye* means both performing alchemical fusions of different substances and making a profit. Silver was in short supply in the contemporary economy, which perhaps explains why silver is named as the alchemist's goal.

The *Yeoman's Prologue and Tale*

The canon is another of Chaucer's false clerics, abusing knowledge as well as holy office. The tale is of fabliau type, about one rogue outwitting another, like the *Friar's* and *Summoner's Tale*, with avarice the motivation for everything. The plot contains no sex but avarice is presented like an immoderately insane lust. It concerns an alchemist-canon who tricks a soft-living cleric, a London chantry-priest residing in luxury provided by a doting widow (a hint of scandal there). The priest is lured by his own 'coveitise' as much his naivety (VIII, 1076–7). The tale is framed by the Yeoman's damning revelations about how alchemists work, exposing the whole business as inimical to God as well as an opportunity for fraud and exploitation of the gullible. He ends with a solemn warning about delving into secrets God wants to keep hidden: a reappearance of the theme of 'Goddes pryvetee' raised humorously in the *Miller's Tale* (*pryvetee*, *pryvee* and *secree* recur in this text). The sections before the actual tale, VIII, 599–971 (called *Prologue* and *Prima pars* in the Ellesmere manuscript and modern editions), resemble the Pardoner's and Wife of Bath's Prologues in revealing the tricks of someone adept at conning money out of others. The Canon's anger at his servant's betrayal reintroduces the familiar motif of male conflict. As with the *Reeve's* and *Summoner's Tales* malice and revenge provide fictional motives for a tale.

Alchemy

Alchemy is a loan word from Arabic, from the same Greek root as 'chemistry'. Medieval and Renaissance alchemy was a mixture of genuine chemical discovery, occult mumbo-jumbo and money-making chicanery. Alchemists, sincere or fraudulent, taught that alchemical processes could discover the 'Philosopher's Stone', 'the secree of the secretes', an imaginary mineral that could create gold or silver from lesser metals (VIII, 862–971, 1428–71). An alchemist, Nicholas Flamel, claimed in 1382 to have made silver and gold from mercury. Chaucer himself had serious scientific interests: he wrote two works about astronomy and this tale shows knowledge of alchemical treatises. It mentions the treatise by Arnald of Villanova ('New Town'), *The Rosary of the Philosophers* (VIII, 1429–40), and a treatise by Senior Zadith sometimes attributed to Plato (VIII, 1450–71). Alchemy flourished in the fourteenth-century West. It included occult and pseudo-mystical rituals and beliefs and was condemned by the Pope as sorcery (it is 'elvysshe nyce loore', VIII, 842: foolish magic doctrine) – perhaps there is a contrast with the Christian faith which is the subject of the *Second Nun's Tale*. Those dabbling in alchemy are called men without divine grace, mentally blinded (VIII, 1076–80); the canon 'lurks' in 'blynde' streets that go nowhere (VIII, 658). In contrast Cecilia's name symbolised triumph over mental blindness (VIII, 92–3, 99–119).

Language and Deception

Like the *Pardoner's Tale*, the tale shows love of money brings loss and destruction, and like the *Pardoner's Prologue* it shows the power of words to deceive: the alchemists 'speken so mystily' men cannot follow them (VIII, 1394). This trickster is another juggler with words, be-dazzling and ensnaring his listeners: the Yeoman's story begins with his verbal power to beguile (VIII, 980–9).

The *exposé* of alchemists' frauds abounds in vivid detail. The effect resembles investigative journalism; line 897 declares '*Lo*, thus this folk bitrayen innocence!' and the tricks are shown in detail: the preliminary psychological softening-up as the con-man wins the victim's trust (VIII, 980–1051), then the technical mechanics of the hoaxes – silver, hidden beforehand in hollow coals, or in a hollow poker or up a sleeve, appears to be created by the experiment – and finally how the victim is persuaded to part with forty pounds, a vast sum, to buy the worthless recipe, whereat the fraudster rapidly absconds.

The Canon and Yeoman's arrival from outside the company of story-tellers fits with the tale's focus on factual details allegedly from real life (the more profoundly 'non-fictional' *Parson's Tale* is also set apart from the normal sequence of pilgrim-tales by certain devices: a shift into prose and a refusal by the character to provide a story). The *Pardoner's Prologue* intro-duced the spectre that skill with words could be falsehood, a theme contin-ued here, and tales after the *Pardoner's Tale* pose questions about the mysterious nature of literature with its illusion of reality, and the gaps between verbal signs and meaning, and about the status of all textuality in relation to external non-textual experience, including spirituality.[2]

There is no consistent characterisation of Canon or Yeoman, but Chaucer's writing here is a *tour de force* of realist technique. We have already noticed how Chaucer positions the reader as a surprised observer watching the Canon approach and gleaning scraps of infor-mation gradually from the Yeoman's replies to the Host: techniques of verisimilitude, creating an impression of figures operating in three-dimensional space and the illusion that a real-life hinterland exists beyond the text. The repetition of *I*, *me* and *we*, particularly in the first part of the tale, increases the sensation of listening to a witness and participant of what is described. Even when the Yeoman moves into the story itself its characters are introduced with phrasing and tenses (present, frequentative present, and perfect) that suggest they too have a non-fictional existence, at this very moment, in the solid real-life exis-tence of the speaker, out there back in London (my italics):

Ther *is* a chanoun of religioun
Amonges us . . .

(VIII, 972–3)

In al this world of falshede *nis* his peer   *isn't*
For in his termes he *wol* hym so *wynde*,
And *speke* his wordes in so sly a kynde,
Whanne he *commune shal* with any wight . . .

(VIII, 979–82)

Ful many a man *hath he bigiled er this*,

(VIII, 985)

And yet men *ride and goon* ful many a mile   *ride and walk*
Hym for to seke . . .

(VIII, 987–8)

It is filled with colloquialisms and spoken discourse features: 'Fy! Spek
nat therof . . .', 'ye woot wel how . . .', 'But taketh heede, now sires, for
Goddes love! . . .', 'A! No! Lat be . . .', etc., creating a strong sense of
the presence of a speaker ('I seye . . .','I yow praye . . .') inter-relating
with his listeners ('Sire hoost . . . Ye woot wel . . . I warne yow
wel . . .'). This is another three-dimensional effect: that of a speaker
talking to an audience physically present round him (see p. 95

for the same techniques in the *Wife of Bath's Prologue*).

In a text crammed with concrete detail and technical jargon the reader feels mentally baffled and bamboozled by the display of mysterious scientific terminology, much as the alchemists' victims do. Many words are rare and impenetrable: loan words into English from the languages most associated with science in the classical and medieval periods, Latin, Arabic and Greek): *orpyment, citrinacioun, sal armonyak, sublymatories* [Latin]; *alkaly, elixir, alambikes* [Arabic]; *porfurie, egremoyne* [Greek].[3] Others are mundane English words, though denoting chemical ingredients and equipment: 'brent bones', 'an erthen pot', 'mannes heer', 'salt', 'papeer'. Rare and everyday words cascade together:

> . . . watres albificacioun;
> Unslekked lym, chalk, and gleyre of an ey,
> Poudres diverse, asshes, donge, pisse, and cley,
> Cered pokkets, sal peter, vitriole,
> And diverse fires maad of wode and cole;
> Sal tartre, alkaly, and sal preparat . . .
>
> (VIII, 805–10)

('The whitening of waters, unslaked lime, chalk, and white of an egg, various powders, ashes, dung, urine, and clay, waxed bags, potassium nitrate, sulphate of iron, and various fires of wood and coal, potassium carbonate, alkaline, prepared salt')

In this passage (as with the Pardoner's disturbing description of human digestion as a kind of tomb, VI, 521–8) the ordinary familiar world and its vocabulary seem to supply merely the unsavoury relics of earthly life – ordure, urine, clay and bones – rather than evoking lively natural experience. There is a reminder here, amid the scientific substances, of mortality: of 'ashes to ashes', with a symbolic implication of the deathliness of materialism as a way of life. The pursuit of money engenders processes that produce only destruction, loss and misery, and words referring to those three toll through the text: *grame, destruccioun, faille, beggers, lese, smert, peyne, disese, grief*, etc. This 'cursed craft' (VIII, 830) is a pursuit of profit in which people lose everything, and its science is fruitless.

The terminology represents accurately chemicals used in alchemy and materials from which chemicals were isolated, as well as its paraphernalia and processes: the heating, boiling and distilling by which substances were extracted or one substance was transformed into another. The tale shows how alchemy (like gambling), by holding out the promise of a free supply of money, could breed a madness, a furious obsession: 'in oure madnesse everemoore we rave', says the Yeoman (VIII, 959). It is desire gone wild after a delusory goal: 'But al thyng which that shineth as the gold / Nis nat gold' (VIII, 962). The greedy folly of their dupes gives the fraudsters their opportunity to make gold – from their clients, not from alchemy. The alchemist-canon and his craft are called 'feendely', 'false' and 'cursed'.

The Yeoman's self-revelations are offered more as moral warnings than are the Pardoner's and Wife of Bath's:

'Lat every man be war by me for evere!'

(VIII, 737)

and the tale's language and imagery evoke central patterns of ideas about good and evil, natural and unnatural behaviour, found elsewhere in the *Canterbury Tales*. The pursuit of alchemy is described in terms of desire: *desir, luste/liste* and *multiplie*. Just as a commercial attitude to sex in the *Shipman's* and *Merchant's* tales appears a perversion of natural sexual love, so the language of the *Canon's Yeoman's Tale* makes the 'multiplying' of metals and money seem unnatural, a displacement of sexuality and 'breeding' onto dead money. The priest, eager to make silver, is described in an outburst of lover-like language in VIII, 1341–9 as like a bird singing at dawn, a nightingale in May, a lady lustily dancing and talking of love, a knight eager to please his lady.

The tale, as Cooper shows (1996: 378–9), is full of words for material objects, cluttered with *things*. Yet it also is full of restless instability and movement. Like the quicksilver, nothing stays still: the Canon rides up, the Canon rides away; the scenes described are full of heated and uncontrollable activity and the story is told with the accompaniment of much physical gesture, bustle, and rushing hither and thither. Like the transient world of Fortune all here is restless flux. The terms in which alchemy is presented include many associated elsewhere by Chaucer with condemnation of excessive cupidity for worldly gain: blindness, folly, madness, lust, beguilement; it is 'a bitter sweete' (VIII, 878); makes the eye 'blered' (VIII, 730): reveals 'al thyng which that shineth as the gold / Nis nat gold' (VIII, 962–3). The business of chemical transformation takes on through the words and metaphors used of it the image of this world with its mutability and delusive joys: it is a 'slidynge science' that leaves its seekers stripped 'bare' (VIII, 732–6):

> . . . it slit awey so faste.   *slides*
> It wole us maken beggers atte laste.
>
> (VIII, 682–3)

In a scene surely symbolic, the alchemists' boiling pot explodes leaving them nothing but 'mullok', rubbish, to sweep up (VIII, 932–59). Rubbish here, as in Dickens's *Our Mutual Friend*, equates with money-grubbing and its worthlessness.

The tale has no direct reference to the contemporary political context but its warning about alchemy can be read as fables about the development of both capitalist economics and Wycliffite reformist controversy in Chaucer's society. We may prefer to see in it no more than the timeless teaching that love of money is the root of evil, but through its imagery runs perhaps also the shadow of fear about new kinds of economic relations: capitalist economics are built on the creation of surplus profit and the creation of money (as in alchemy) from little or nothing, through credit and speculation. In contrast, feudal economics present a picture of an apparently more balanced relationship between the products of the land and the prices paid for them, of wealth created from nature, where labour is duty-bound and payment often in kind rather than cash. Economics and alchemy come clearly together in the word-play of lines 1402–25, which warns about an *increase* which will not yield *profit* for its practitioners:

> So faren al ye that multiplie, I seye . . .
> Ye shul nothyng wynne on that chaffare,   *profit, commerce*
> But wasten al that ye may rape and renne.   *grab*
>
> (VIII, 1417, 1421–2)

The tale's warning that those who delve into such secrets are God's *adversarie* (VIII, 1476) could similarly be read as an analogy to contemporary attempts to combat Wycliffism by discouraging laypeople from probing the scriptures for themselves or discussing theology: a contemporary preacher warned the laity: 'it is inowghth [enough] to the [thee] to beleven as Holy Church techeth the and lat [leave] the clerkes [clerics] alone with the argumentes'.[4]

Many details are clearly chosen for their contribution to symbolic structures, rather than to create characterisation in a realist mode. The Canon's sweating prefigures the heat of alchemical distillations; the Yeoman's discoloured face suggests the destructiveness of the practice (the image of a burnt man who cannot keep away from the fire returns as a metaphor for money-making at VIII, 1407–8). Despite the impression of a speaking voice, and the claim that it springs from the Yeoman's vengeful mood, the tale lacks a wholly consistent personal viewpoint or moral stance. The address to respectable canons (VIII, 992–1009) cannot be read as the Yeoman speaking naturalistically to the group of pilgrims; it is an address coming out of the text itself to a hypothetical audience for the *Canterbury Tales*. The Yeoman switches in his tale from boastfulness about alchemy to condemnation. A collaborator in the tricks constitutes a plausible narrator for an *exposé*, yet no naturalistic guilt for his own involvement appears. It concludes on a fervent religious note: the Yeoman's revelations have shown his own complicity but the speaker voices no naturalistic contrition. The 'confessional' style, though managed here and in the *Pardoner's* and *Wife's Prologues* with great panache and frequent psychological subtlety, is more a framing device for the presentation of certain types of material than the outpourings of a fully conceived personality in a crisis of self-examination.

The tale ends with a series of morals. First, VIII, 1402–25, the message that this business will bring loss not profit; next, VIII, 1426–66, that the great philosophers themselves opposed revelation of alchemical secrets. Here we get a taste of the side of alchemy involving pagan gods and planetary powers: a return to mystifying jargon but with a new, alarming addition of the quasi-occult and pagan, appropriately preparing readers for the final message which is that such investigations are against the will of a loving God. The final line is not just a conventional blessing to end a tale: it is a succinct declaration of the Christian alternative to seeking alchemical wealth: 'trewe' men can find in God happiness to relieve all earthly troubles:

God sende every trewe man boote of his bale!   *relief, misery*

22

The *Manciple's Tale*

After the *Canon's Yeoman's Tale*, as after the Second Nun's, and the *Manciple's Tale* itself, Chaucer dispenses with comment on the tale just ended. Did he get bored in these last tales with Links that centre on the responses of the characters, and focus more in the thematic juxtapositions between tales? Another feature of these last Links is reference to the passage of time and space: markers of how far we have gone on our journey to Canterbury. Now we are at Hambledown, only two miles from Canterbury (IX, 2–3), and it is morning (IX, 16). Real-life place and time impinge on the narrative more in these Links, but as we move into the final *Parsons' Tale* these will become pointers towards a spiritual awareness that time is running out, life does not last, and humans must think about their heavenly destiny.

For now, however, we are at the *Manciple's Prologue* and what emerges – another regular feature of the late tales – is a sense of breakdown in the story-telling, the fragility of the whole game. In the *Parson's Tale* all earthly fiction gives way before the imperative of preaching spiritual priorities, but here storytelling breaks down because the Cook – the next narrator – is drunk. 'Dun is in the myre', announces the Host (IX, 5): forward progress has halted and the Cook's powers of speech stop too (VIII, 48).

The animosity of Cook and Manciple evokes the contemporary social and economic London background: a manciple as catering manager would employ cooks, and the Host advises the Manciple to restrain his scornful words because the Cook might tell tales about his accounting (and we know from the *General Prologue* that he deceives his employers). The tale's theme of bridling incautious speech is thus prefigured here in miniature: the Manciple pretends his words were only spoken in jest and in his turn prevents the Cook speaking out against him (or even remembering the quarrel?), by filling him up with more alcohol. The topic of *rakel ire*, 'rash anger', will return in the tale (IX, 278–91).

The tale often turns away from the action to point a lesson or discuss an issue: women and freedom, euphemisms, tyranny, rash anger, and so on. It is the ideas not the tale's dramatic potential that have priority (this emphasis on rhetorical asides rather than human drama or vivid settings made the tale unimpressive to modern critics until the end of the twentieth century).

The tale of how the crow got its black feathers, from Ovid's *Metamorphoses* (AD 2–8), was well known; several medieval writers including Gower wrote versions of it. Several critics have seen Chaucer's tale as a fable about the dilemmas of the court poet (see Scattergood 1974), a fable of Chaucer's own position as real-life administrator and 'prince-pleaser' (Fradenburg, 1985), and exposer of social tensions in the earlier *Canterbury Tales* (Knight 1986: 152–3). On such a reading, the Manciple, as the upwardly mobile secular administrator, cleverer than the men who employ him, is a self-deprecating representation of Chaucer's own position as civil servant and official, while the caged crow represents his position as a court poet, dependent on patrons and obliged to take pains to please them and avoid offending them. 'Like the crow, the court poet is obligated to mirror his object, i.e. the subject-sovereign,' says Fradenburg (1985: 87). It is a picture of the medieval writer, far from glorying in any Romantic illusions about the freedom and sublime selfhood of the poet, as a pet bird, a parrot unable to speak independently. The prince may be in one sense the subject-matter of poetry but he is also its ruler, dictating directly or indirectly its nature, what it is prudent to include and omit.

The ruler, Phoebus, has two captive pets: his singing bird and his wife. They are presented as parallels. The wife, like a bird, cat or she-wolf, naturally desires liberty – a theme familiar from the *Franklin's Tale*: 'Wommen of kynde, desiren libertee' (V, 768), and from the *Miller's Tale* (I ,3223–33). The tale's attitude to relations between the sexes is ambivalent: partly anti-feminist, as the she-wolf simile suggests (IX, 183), but also demonstrating men's emotional instability: stealing other men's wives, sentimentalising the women who betray them, and hating to hear the truth. Phoebus dominates the bird more successfully than the woman. He speaks after the wife's death to warn against hasty judgements and unjustified suspicion, but then punishes the bird unjustly for a 'false tale' which was nothing but the truth and spoken with the ruler's interests in mind. That was the only time the captive bird spoke truly its own words, and it destroyed him: it cost him his role as singer, his comfortable home, and his voice.

The theme of treachery is a minor strand in the tale, with political as well as sexual implications. The medieval king was likely to label those who displeased him traitors; Richard II certainly did so. In a feudal culture, built on networks of lordship and loyalty, political opposition is itself treachery. This tale shows a master who thinks he sees betrayal and punishes it – in the bird, who is in fact his loyal servant – but fails to see the real treachery of another: his wife. The *Nun's Priest's Tale* (VII, 3225–80) had advised lords to be discerning about who in their courts offers truthful service and who cloaks treachery under a deceptive front.

The theme of poetry is introduced at the beginning with the description of the god. Phoebus is also presented there as a chivalric warrior: words associated with aristocracy and the chivalric myth are crammed into lines 123–7: *gentillesse, honour, parfit worthynesse, flour of bachilrie, fredom, chivalrie, victorie*. He has autonomy as well as poetic gifts. His crow has poetic gifts but only within limits: he is a copyist. He can utter only what his master teaches him to say and his skill is to 'countrefete the speche of every man / He koude, whan he sholde telle a tale' (IX, 134–5). Did Chaucer see himself in the *Canterbury Tales* doing just that? The artist is seen here as doubly dependent on others: he obeys his patron and is invisible behind his creations, the voices of his characters. Phoebus is like the aristocratic patron: the patron calls the tunes, the poet sings to order and is his master's voice.

Originally this is a narrative like a folktale or Kipling's *Just So Stories*: to explain how things came to be as they are. It tells us how the crow became black and got its harsh voice. But Chaucer makes it an exploration of speech, dependency and power: themes central to a poet's situation in a society before printing, where he depends on patronage. At the moment when the crow sees evil in the god's household but does not speak, the narrative is interrupted (IX, 205–36), and the intervening passage elaborates on two topics that shift away from classical gods and talking animals into contemporary society and point to hypocrisy, evasion and silence about scandals in high places. Those two topics are sexual scandals and tyranny. In medieval political thought, tyranny was associated not only with cruelty and oppression but also specifically with the extortion of money from subjects and excessive or unauthorised taxation. This passage points out that upper-class lechery and tyranny escape criticism because everyone is too frightened to call a spade a spade. A rich woman who is 'of hir body dishonest' will be described euphemistically as her lover's 'lady', whereas a poor woman would be labelled his 'wenche' or 'lemman' (wenche with the primary sense 'servant woman', also had negative sexual connotations; 'lemman' meant 'darling' and was lower-class register, and developing slight connotations of sexual impropriety in the late fourteenth century, see pp. 57, 60). Similarly the chivalric-sounding 'capitayn' veils the depredations of a high-born tyrant, though there is no real difference between a tyrant and 'an outlawe or theef erraunt' – a highwayman. Indeed the tyrant can do more harm, having more power and a bigger band of henchmen scouring the country to harm the population. Did Chaucer have in mind the Poll Tax tax-collectors whose aggressive visitations provoked the 1381 Rising, or the resentment in the late 1390s during Richard II's so-called Tyranny, when he imposed new forms of taxation and other revenue-raising impositions? Probably nothing so dangerously explicit – this is a tale about cautious speech – but giving moral advice to rulers was an honourable course for writers: *Melibee* belongs to that tradition. The theme of tyranny hovers also in the *Clerk's Tale* and even more the *Monk's Tale*. Robin Hood and his outlaw band – and there were plenty of real-life outlaws and highwaymen – forcing travellers to give up their purses, would be less harmful to the people than the soldiers and officers who terrorise the population to raise money for a ruler who acts like a 'titlelees tiraunt': a tyrant acting outside the law and claiming money to which he has no entitlement.

Whether Chaucer's purpose in this digression on tyranny was to warn or to criticise, and whether he was thinking of tyrants at home or foreign tyrants like the Visconti in Lombardy, at this point the text of the *Manciple's Tale* itself makes a striking retreat from bold honesty in speech: the speaker of this increasingly pointed and political protest jumps back from the political theme of oppression to the literary one of interpretation and denies any responsibility for the interpretation of what he has said:

> But for I am a man noght textueel,
> I wol noght telle of textes never a deel;   *nothing at all*
> I wol go to my tale, as I began.
>
> (IX, 235–7)

The text covers its traces here, and with an ingenuous paradox: 'textual' was a topical hate-word for preachers who wove elaborate interpretations from the text of scriptures, in contrast to presenting the plain words of the gospel. So this ostentatious retreat from speaking plainly about tyrants is saying 'I am a plain speaker: I don't intend to mention texts; let's get back to the story I had begun.'

This particular text, in fact, provides us with a variety of interpretations in its final section (IX, 309–58), and they are all less challenging than the disturbing topics that opened up in the centre of the tale about the role of the servant-poet and the upper-class immorality, robbery and oppression that go unreproved because sycophancy refuses to put into words the truth which all can see.

The first of these conclusions offers the original Ovidian message: this story tells us how the crow became black and got its croak. The second picks up the strand of man-to-man cynicism about marital relations in the text: it is a mistake to tell a husband his wife is having an affair: 'He wol yow haten mortally, certeyn' (IX, 313). The tale ends with a shower of old saws about the advisability of holding your tongue: rash speech can break friendship, no-one was ever harmed by saying little, restrain your speech unless it is to talk of God; if someone says something controversial or dangerous don't join in – just nod; you can never unsay your words; if you tell a man something he's got you in his power, and so on. These are small-minded, proverb-type dictums, and Chaucer marks them as the sort of instruction given to medieval children: books with titles like 'How the Goodwife taught her Daughter', 'How the Father taught his Son' were filled with homely precepts and Chaucer's insertion of 'thus taught me my dame [mother]' and 'My sone' in IX, 317–259 marks them as that kind of nursery instruction (it does not make the Manciple a richly conceived naturalistic character who loves his mother!).[1] The literary register of these concluding interpretations itself represents a further cautious retreat away from any suspicion that the tale could have contemporary relevance.

The *General Prologue* Manciple's portrait and his tale both focus on servant / employer relationships: the canny administrator who can run rings round those who employ him and the captive bird which cannot sing freely are two different images of the dishonesty of the prudent, worldly-wise servant. They provide an interesting comment on Chaucer's choice, for his own two tales, of a minstrel lay of embarrassing corniness or a Mirror for Princes which advocates moderation. The Portrait of the Artist that emerges is one with few pretensions. The anti-feminist element in the *Manciple's Tale*, with pessimistic images of wives as wild animals who, however pampered will run after their low pleasures, and the unfaithful wife whose husband refuses to believe her treachery, perhaps suggests another analogy for the poet: something between a discontented wife, who would prefer freedom to his gilded cage, and a whore? Whether we see the *Manciple's Tale* as a personal fable about being a court poet or a political fable about the inadvisability of speaking up about betrayals or oppression, or just a folktale with a set of homely morals about talking too much, it is undoubtedly, of all the tales the one most concerned with the medium of all stories: words. It ends with a warning to its narrator not to be 'an auctour', not to tell 'tidynges' whether truth or fiction to anyone, whether upper or lower class, and in all situations to hold his tongue (IX, 359–61). *Tidynges* in Chaucer's *House of Fame* stood for all sorts of literary activity.[2] If this is a self-reflexive composition it is of the most wittily negative kind: one that proposes putting an end to stories and speech.

Appropriately, in the next Link we learn this is the last tale before the final one – and it is the *Parson's Tale* which turns its back on the whole business of fictions. Already at the conclusion of the torrent of simple advice that ends the *Manciple's Tale* we have a precept that looks forward to the *Parson's Tale*'s substitution of serious Christian teaching for storytelling, when the advice is given that the only subject on which it is good to speak is 'To speke of God, in honoure and preyere'. At the end of the *Manciple's Tale* the parameters of Art are already closing down; this, the last proper tale, ends as a traditional series of proverb-like statements and a denial that any utterance is valuable except praise and prayer to God, which looks forward to Chaucer's Retraction.

The stance this narrative ostensibly takes is a cynical and despairing one: the truthful crow tries to help his master but the plot does not vindicate him. The Manciple does not articulate one truth that we all see: that the real fault lay with the master, Phoebus, for not distinguishing between his true and false subordinates, but it is not rulers who get a warning at the end. The final warnings vary between genuinely moral reasons for holding one's tongue and cynically expedient ones. The message seems to be that society is so ordered that underlings waste their time if they try to speak truth or give advice. And the text itself draws back from giving advice to rulers about showing judgement in who they trust: as the Manciple says, he is not 'textual' – he is keeping his mouth shut about extracting a full interpretation from his story. The tale's subject, of speaking and not speaking, has a social, political dimension, but it also contributes to the exploration of authorship implicit in the *Tales*; Chaucer, evasive as ever, does not endorse the Manciple's moral cynicism, but Scattergood (1974: 145) observes: 'Chaucer seems interested in the Manciple because the Manciple's handling of language bears some relationship to the poet's strategies.'

The notorious misogynist Mathéolus had cited the crow fable to complain that women did not change their vices so easily. Chaucer knew Le Fèvre's French translation of Mathéolus (extract in Blamires 1992: 184); this use of the fable may have inspired his passage about the stylistic registers which can disguise or expose sexual misdemeanors (IX, 204–22), as well as the misogynist *Romance of the Rose* material (IX, 163–95). But Chaucer's treatment extends and elaborates the fable's potential far beyond Mathéolus's narrow and bitter exploitation of it: words and their meanings, power and its abuses and self-deceptions, honesty and its dangers are some of his topics here, and it is notable they do not fall into any discrete moral category. The tale is both moral and cynical in stance, but as cynical in its observation of men's sexual proclivities as of women's. And the butt of the narrative's mockery is not those who deceive themselves about what they see, nor those who deceive or betray others, nor rulers who lack restraint – though the tale certainly includes these important *Canterbury Tales* themes. It is, ruefully, the author himself, and all those who try to tell people things they don't already know. 'Be noon auctour newe / Of tidynges', warns the Manciple, 'Kepe wel thy tonge and thenk upon the crowe.'[3] And with his words comes an end of the story-telling. What will follow next is not novel, but truths everyone always knew, but now made new – rather startlingly – in the context of the *Canterbury Tales*, and it is the message that life is short and that morality is humanity's most important concern.

23
The *Parson's Tale*

The *Parson's Tale* explodes like a hidden bomb, blowing apart the very fabric of fiction. For the Parson and his tale reject *fables*, fiction. The *Parson's Tale* is not a story but a treatise; it is not about either *sentence* or *solaas* but the most important choices human beings have to make: between good or evil, and its subject is humanity's ultimate destination, the Next World. Though it goes against the design announced in I, 798–801, that the *Tales* would end back at the Tabard inn, once we read the *Parson's Tale*, it is hard to think that Chaucer could have done anything different – like giving the Parson a conventional tale, even a religious one. It is an ending that refuses to offer literary closure and sends us back into the real world outside fiction, and to the supreme reality of spiritual priorities.

In many manuscripts it also takes us textually on to the author's Retraction, where Chaucer himself divides his works of a lifetime into those which are worldly or tend towards sin and those which are saints' lives or contain 'moralitee and devocioun'.[1] This is another kind of rejection of fiction, in the sense that the criteria used to divide the texts are ruthlessly non-aesthetic: no-one could call *The Book of the Duchess* or *Troilus* lacking in moral seriousness, unless we have come completely beyond art into a world of absolute division between what belongs to the Next World, and everything else.

Though it comes as a very effective shock, this dénouement of the *Tales* has, we see retrospectively, been foreshadowed potentially in the *Second Nun's Prologue*, with its lesson about not wasting time, and the *Manciple's Tale*, whose conclusion is antipathetic to story-telling: 'Kepe wel thy tonge' (IX, 362), and which teaches restraint of speech except when speaking of God (IX, 329–31).[2] The Manciple warned about the worldly inadvisability of speaking; the Parson gives a spiritual warning against speaking or caring about anything except our spiritual destiny. The *Parson's Prologue* begins with the sun sinking, and there are verbal suggestions of approaching mortality: the end of the day, the speaker's 'shadwe' (X, 7), entry into the 'ende' of a village (X, 11), and the end of the Canterbury journey and its story-telling. The passage moves to the issue of the *Canterbury Tales*' plan: Harry Bailey, the creator, guide and ruler of the long enterprise, announces that all is complete except the last act, one final tale:

> Fulfilled is my sentence and my decree . . .
> Almoost fulfild is al myn ordinaunce.
>
> (X, 17–19)

The Parson is to 'knytte up wel a greet mateere' (X, 28). There is something God-like in the Host's words, and they include his (typically flippant) blessing (X, 20). Mystery play cycles also ended as the sun sank, with a final drama, the *Last Judgement*, that looked ahead beyond death and the created world in time, to humanity's destiny in the next world, and divided humans into good and evil, according to their behaviour in this world, recalling to them the importance for salvation of the virtues, the Seven Works of Mercy.[3] The *Parson's Tale* ends by preparing its audience to meet Judgement, for that is the purpose of penitence:

> Men sholden eek remembren hem of the shame that is to come at the day of doom to hem that been nat penitent and shryven in this present lyf. / For alle the creatures in hevene, in erthe, and in helle shullen seen apertly al that they hyden in this world.   (X, 1063–4)

The *Parson's Tale* is not specifically about the Last Judgement nor are the *Canterbury Tales* structured like a mystery cycle – it is a human comedy which remains within time – yet Chaucer seems to recall that pattern in the decision about his last tale which 'knits up' his own 'greet mateere'.

The Parson's rejection of 'fables' (X, 31–8), and refusal to use literary forms such as alliterative verse or rhyme, and the determination to speak only 'in prose', may reflect Wyclif's condemnation not only of preachers who introduce fictions and pagan literature ('fables') into their preaching, but also of the use of rhyme for religious writings:

> Do we believe that they who beg immediately after the sermon preach the word of God from a sincere heart, or that they speak, as a rule, from God who lay stress upon apocryphal poems, fables and lies, such as will please their hearers?[4]

Some by rhyming, and others by preaching poems and fables, adulterate in many ways the word of God.[5]

This is an attack on preachers who do something other than teach Bible-based Christianity – ask for donations or include non-biblical material; Wyclif is not discussing the nature and moral potentialities of literature as such. If the Parson's attitude to storytelling sounded discernibly coloured by Wycliffite views to Chaucer's original audience it would seem more the expression of a fictional viewpoint, the Parson's, within the text and less an absolute one from outside the text. Yet Chaucer's subsequent rejection of many of his own Canterbury tales in the *Retraction* does seem to come from an absolute position.

Some critics have argued that this tale's subjects, sins and virtues, and the metaphorical journey to heaven, are the underlying design of all the *Tales* (see pp. 15–16). Some early critics saw sin and virtue as the basis of the *Tales'* design. Robertson (1962) saw them as an allegorical journey to the New Jerusalem, through choices between cupidity and charity. If, however, the *Tales* were already so attuned to the Parson's message, there would be no point, moral or artistic, in the dramatic rejection of what has gone before as *fables*, no sense of moving into a quite different realm of discourse and reality, in both the final tale and the *Retraction*. The Parson does 'knytte up al this feeste and make an ende', but does so by pointing the pilgrims out to another enterprise that lies ahead:

> To shewe yow the wey, in this viage,
> Of thilke parfit glorious pilgrymage
> That highte Jerusalem celestial.
>
> (X, 49–51)

This proposal, radically disconcerting to the critic trying to assess how the tale relates to the totality of Chaucer's *Tales*, is welcomed by the fictional pilgrims, and the Host gives a blessing which could itself symbolically refer to preparation for the Last Judgement:

> '. . . hasteth yow; the sonne wole adoun;
> Beth fructuous, and that in litel space,
> And to do wel God sende yow his grace!'
>
> (X, 70–2)

The idea of hurrying to become ripe fruit before Judgement occurs also in *Gawain and the Green Knight* in a penitential context.

Knot was a rhetorical term for the conclusion to which a text is point-ing (see pp. 133–4). The *Parson's Tale* on one level fails to do what the Host asks: it does not smoothly *knytte up* the pattern of the preceding tales, and it does 'breke . . . oure pley' (X, 23). Yet we can see the tale developing themes introduced earlier in the *Tales*. The Parson's pilgrim-age metaphor picks up an image from the *Knight's Tale*:

> This world nys but a thurghfare ful of wo,
> And we been pilgrymes, passynge to and fro.
> Deeth is the ende of every worldly soore.
>
> (I, 2847–9)

That was a Stoic view from a world without Christian revelation; now there is hope and a destination for the pilgrims: 'Jerusalem celestial' (the notion of heaven as a heavenly Jerusalem derives from the Book of Revelation). The rejection of 'fables' alludes to 1 Timothy, an epistle with affinities to the otherworldly values embodied in Griselda (see p. 116). It is accompanied by contempt for what was perhaps the most ornate contemporary poetic style, alliterative verse (X, 42–4), and a switch to prose (on Chaucer's prose, see Elliott 1974: 132–80). In a sense we could see this uncompromising reduction of the function of speech to that which serves divine purposes as the *Tales'* final commen-tary on aspects of authorship, texts and literary meaning to which all the tales contribute different perspectives. We cannot know whether ending the *Canterbury Tales* at Canterbury with the *Parson's Tale* would have been Chaucer's final decision, had he lived and had he finished the work (not necessarily concomitants: Chaucer had left many works incomplete). A religious ending is, on the literal level, as the pilgrims agree, appropriate: 'To enden in som vertuous sentence' [teaching] (X, 63); for an author who found it difficult to resolve the complexities and incompatibilities of human experience into simple monologic art or neat closures, the *Parson's Tale* solution, to move the discourse into another realm entirely, where the dichotomies are clear (good/evil, heaven/hell), was perhaps also the only artistic solution honest and profound enough to bring such a text to an end. The juxtaposition of incompatible or unresolved worldviews is a feature of some of the greatest medieval literature. There is a long medieval literary tradition of ending works with a *volte-face*: Andreas Capellanus' *De arte honesti amandi*, a frivolous twelfth-century guidebook to the art of love, ends with a rejection of love. The *Romance of the Rose* and Chrétien's *Lancelot* can be read as celebrations of illicit worldly passion or as condemnation of it. Several of Chaucer's contemporaries, including Le Fèvre and Machaut, wrote palinodes: texts countering views expressed in a previous work; indeed, his *Legend of Good Women* purports to reverse the view of women presented in *Troilus*. Boccaccio moved to writing only religious, Latin works in old age.

The *Tales* present inconsistent views on many things: women, warfare, poverty, and sexual purity, to name but a few. It would be reductive to search this non-tale for an answer on how to read previous tales or their stance on these topics (Cooper 1996: 404–7 discusses some parallels and the critical problems of relating the moral lessons of the tale to the moralities in the *Tales*). The fact that it is itself a fiction, though announcing the death of fiction, is a final irony, Chaucer's awareness of which is suggested by the absence of any pilgrim reaction after it; it behaves as if it has stepped outside the context of pilgrim-tellers and pilgrim-listeners by the time it has delivered its message.

The tale has sources – William Peraldus's *Summa vitiarum* (1236) and some related material for its central section on vices and virtues, Raymund of Pennaforte's *Summa de poenitentia* (*c*.1225) for the account of penitence which frames it (Bryan and Dempster 1941: 723–60). It perhaps translates a lost work based on both these, but appears to be an original construction (see Patterson 1978: 331–80, on its sources, structure and place in the *Tales*). The 1215 Lateran Council required Christians to confess at least once a year. The Church laid great stress on educating priests and laity about confession and examination of conscience. There are many penitential handbooks for priests; Brewer (1984: 241) observes that it was still rare for a layman like Chaucer to write a religious treatise. The teaching is orthodox and sometimes towards the strict end of the spectrum of opinion for its period. On the legitimate purposes of sex in marriage, for example, it names only procreation, paying the 'debt' and avoiding lechery; liberal clerical opinion had given marital affection more status than this account does. There is emphasis, however, on the effect sins have on other people, not just their spiritual harm to the sinner, as with the pride that leads to fashionable clothes whose trains trail expensive cloth through the mud: 'al thilke trailyng is verraily as in effect wasted, consumed, thredbare, and roten with donge, rather than it is yeven to the povre, to greet damage of the forseyde povre folk, (X, 419).

The tale's conclusion promises us a place where there is resolution of earthly contradictions and imperfections:

ther joye hath no contrarioustee of wo ne grevaunce; ther alle
harmes been passed of this present lyf; ther as is the sikernesse fro
the peyne of helle.   (X, 1076)

This is the opposite of much that characterises the *Canterbury Tales* as
a literary structure and picture of human experience: instead of sociable
pilgrim company, full of contest and conflict, there will be 'the blisful
compaignye that rejoysen hem everemo, everich of otheres joye';
instead of varied tales of the mutable world there will be 'no contrarioustee'; there will be no ambiguity, for 'but every soule replenyssed
with the sighte of the parfit knowynge of God'. The journey will be
over: 'ther alle harmes been passed of this present lyf'. The last sentence
explains that the destination will be attained by 'poverte espiritueel',
'lowenesse', 'hunger and thurst', 'travaille', and by death itself, but even
more by the death of sin, 'mortificacion of synne' (X, 1080).[6] There is,
in these last lines of the *Canterbury Tales*, a passing-over, as at the end
of the *Pilgrim's Progress*: verbally at least, though not in narrative, the
text looks beyond death to a place which is also beyond sin. It is not
surprising that, beyond this point, what follows is Chaucer's own rejection of those of the *Canterbury Tales* that 'sownen [tend] into synne'.

Though not in sermon-form, it does teach, and Chaucer himself, the
author not the pilgrim, becomes its responsive congregation in the
Retraction. The division of material into numbered lists is typical of
medieval preaching and pastoral teaching, as are the biblical citations,
little allegories and vignettes of human failings. The writing is sharpest
whenever Chaucer, characteristically, focuses on speech: he pinpoints
the euphemisms by which evil cloaks itself (fining serfs 'amercimentz',
'whiche myghten moore resonably ben cleped extorcions than amercimentz', X, 752), and notes the backbiter's unexpected *knotte* of criticism, the late 'but', that unexpected *volte-face*, by which a speech of
praise becomes blame (X, 490–7); he mingles everyday colloquialisms
with French/Latin words ('sompnolence, that is sloggy slombrynge', X,
706). The style relies for its effectiveness primarily not on showy vocabulary or description but on lively syntax: on varying different sentence
types, pithy one-liners and syntactic patterning. There are some vivid
passages reminiscent of scenes earlier in the *Tales*, for example, the
robust images of the condemnation of lecherous old husbands (X,
855–8) recall January's lust in the *Merchant's Tale*, and the attack on
unchaste clerics with a taste for other men's dinners and other men's
wives (X, 900–1) matches the picture of a flirtatious Friar bespeaking a
delicious dinner with the wife in the *Summoner's Tale* (III, 1836–5).

There are, however, moral perceptions that only literary narrative (fiction), and not penitential treatise, can express: the insensitivity of January to his wife and the oiliness of the Friar's contempt for the peasant, for example. And there are moral questions (or are they equivocations?) that comedy raises which solemnity cannot answer. The Parson describes how a man consenting to temptation 'feeleth . . . a flambe of delit', and if not self-controlled will seek if he may have 'tyme and place' to consummate it (X, 352–3); the *Miller's Tale*, from I, 3275 on, describes a particularly ingenious process of just such a contriving of a 'tyme and place' with a hilarity which seems to deprive it of anything but delight and exhilaration. How from the vantage point of the *Parson's Tale* do we judge the literary achievement of the *Miller's Tale*? The Parson's rejection of fiction leaves unaddressed the complex expression of ethical issues by fiction. Chaucer lived in an era when there was no concept of secular literature as a separate form of moral or philosophical discourse from the type of teaching the *Parson's Tale* represents, except as *fable*, which has the inferior senses of that which is untrue, frivolous and baseless. The decisive cutting free from fiction by the *Parson's Tale* can be seen as having the advantage of leaving that separate realm, of all the tales that went before, separate. That would not have been the case either if it had been itself merely a religious fiction (a tale of St Thomas, perhaps), or if the present material had been voiced by Chaucer the Pilgrim. We end with a final tale which destroys fiction, but in its own non-fictional terms, and in relation to the sin/virtue terms of the *Retraction* rather than to the equivocal terms in which even the most monological of Chaucer's tales, like the *Second Nun's Tale*, has presented human experience. Even the *Retraction*, after all, unless Chaucer died immediately after writing it (as Gardner imagined in his fictional biography), existed in time not eternity.[7] There remains, as at the end of Chaucer's *Troilus*, a question unanswered, and it is not so much whether earthly concerns are inferior to spiritual ones – since Chaucer clearly leaves it beyond question that are – but whether literature forms its own distinct realm of human activity, with its own dignity, which raises moral and philosophical issues as challengingly as the religious treatise can do. The *Parson's Tale*, whatever Chaucer originally planned, is where we arrive at the end of the *Canterbury Tales*, and it points us off somewhere else, in another direction, away from fiction and even away from the morality and spirituality that can be voiced through fiction. But meaning in art lies characteristically more in how we have travelled than where we arrive.

John Lydgate, in his *Siege of Thebes* (1412–21), continued where

Chaucer apparently left off, and described in his Prologue both the arrival of the pilgrims in Canterbury and his own journey back with them to London. The fact that Chaucer leaves unclear whether his destination is sacred Canterbury or secular Southwark in some ways matches the ambiguous mingling of sacred and secular impulses in the opening lines of his *General Prologue*. Both could have been occasions for moral conclusions, of course. Southwark, however, would mark more clearly the end of the closed world of the pilgrims' journey together. If Chaucer had ended the *Tales* back at the Tabard with the communal dinner, would that also in some way have figured the return of the pilgrims and ourselves to some larger social reality, some reality outside fiction – perhaps to the social, political England, at 'every shires ende', the contexts from which these varied pilgrims have come, of which directly we receive only provocative hints in the course of the surprisingly closed world of the story-telling journey? That it seems unlikely is less because Chaucer is (as some critics have believed) unconcerned with the political and economic imperatives of the world around him than because he had discovered ways of making them present, in fable form, in indirect and often verbal forms, and in the human conflict and conversation, throughout his *Canterbury Tales*.

Chaucer's text is engaged with contemporary social context and conflict on many levels: through its own diversity of social relations, philosophies, styles and values; through the tensions exposed when this most socially and economically sensitive of medieval observers presents a conservative, aristocratic, worldview; and through the creative discordances of much of his fiction. Though the importance of moral discernment is clear throughout the text, no unified message emerges from the fiction (though one does from the *Retraction*). Chaucer's perceptions of his own society do not find the unequivocal certainties and conclusions he reaches, in the *Retraction*, about his own soul. To the last, he explores his own role as writer, reversing and revoking his former enterprises (but never, it seems destroying them). Similarly, for his readers, interpretation remains a process, and a pleasure, without end.

Notes

Chapter 1   Chaucer and the *Canterbury Tales*

1   Executive Director, Jonathan Myerson; Executive Producer, Christopher Grace; an S4C, HBO and BBC Wales co-production, 1998. The chickens are, of course, Chantecleer and his wives in the *Nun's Priest's Tale*.

2   'Different people said different things but for the most part they laughed and enjoyed themselves', *Canterbury Tales*, I, 3857–8. Chaucer quotations are from The *Riverside Chaucer.*

3   Focalization is the stance or point of view from which a text seems to be written, whether this is explicit (a named narrator with a specific personality and life-experience, for example) or implicit (a set of attitudes, perceptions and assumptions which underlie the ways in which the narrative presents material to the reader. An example of very strong single focalization is John Buchan's *The Thirty-Nine Steps*, which is focalized, explicitly and implicitly, through the perceptions and attitudes of Richard Hannay, its first-person narrator.

4   Modern historians treat with suspicion the traditional concept of a feudal society, i.e. a society where lords hold land in return for military services to their overlord, where peasants living on an estate are obliged to give the lord periods of their own labour to work the land, and where both the wage economy and market economy are weak. It is hard to find such a neat structure anywhere in medieval Europe, especially after *c.*1200. Yet 'feudal' is still a convenient if loose term, and Chaucer's England was in many ways this type of agrarian peasant society, while at the same time commerce and production for the market were increasing, peasants and lords were moving towards economic relationships based on wages, rents and labour-mobility, and in both towns and countryside an economy of buying and selling, profit and credit, was developing. We can also see a feudal cultural ideology at work – in literature especially – which envisages loyalty and mutual benefit as binding the different classes together, deplores alike rebellion by the lower classes and exploitation by the rich, and is distrustful of commerce and profit-making. On the question of whether 'feudal' or 'capitalism' can be usefully applied to late medieval England, see Dyer 1994: 305–27.

5   On socio-economic background, see Dyer 1989.

6   Caxton: 'we ought to gyve a synguler laude [praise] vnto that noble & grete philosopher Gefferey chaucer, the whiche for his ornate wrytyng in our tongue may wel haue the name of a laureate poete. For tofore that [before] he by hys labour enbelysshyd, ornated and made faire our Englisshe, in thys royame was had [there was] rude speche & incongrue [rough and unpolished language]', Proem to *Canterbury Tales* (1484); Dryden: 'he is the Father of English Poetry. . . . Chaucer follow'd Nature everywhere, but was never so bold as to go beyond her . . . he has taken into the compass of his *Canterbury Tales* the various manners and humours [i.e. characters] (as we

227

now call them) of the whole English nation, in his age . . . 'Tis sufficient to say according to the proverb, that here is God's Plenty . . . for Mankind is ever the same', Preface to his translation of Chaucer, *Fables* (1700); in Brewer 1987, vol. I, pp. 76,164, 167.

7 See, for instance, 'Preface to the Lyrical Ballads (1800)', in Wordsworth and Coleridge, *Lyrical Ballads: Wordsworth and Coleridge*, ed. R. L. Brett and A. R. Jones (London: Methuen, 1963), p. 246.

Chapter 2 The *General Prologue*

1 In an agricultural economy sexual imagery carries wide associations, evoking the continuity and yearly renewal of economic life for the nation; it is not just an imagery of human private experience as it is in modern urban culture.

2 There is an initial reference to Deptford, 'the Wateryng of Seint Thomas', at the end of the *Prologue*, I, 826; then we have Sittingbourne, III, 847 (which geographically comes after Rochester and suggests that at some point Chaucer intended this part of the text to come later, after what is now VII); Rochester, VII, 1926; Boughton, VIII, 557; Harbledown, IX, 2. The Canon and Yeoman break into the pilgrim group from the outside world. The Canon returns to it. References to time and to the day is ending, at the beginning of the last tale, remind us that the magic enclosed world of the journey narrative cannot remain unbroken for ever.

3 On the difficult questions of the dating of the commercialisation of English society and the applicability of 'capitalism' to late medieval society, see Dyer 1994 and Britnell 1996.

4 Knight (1986: 93) argues there is a gradual move into a 'clericisation' of the text's vision as it moves towards its end, a form of evasion of the awareness of late fourteenth-century social conflict which underlies the whole *Tales*.

5 See Variorum *General Prologue*, A 3, 211–16 (includes texts), B 3–27, and Riverside notes.

6 See Gower, *Mirour*, pp. 278–83, on monks.

7 See Gower, *Mirour*, pp. 330-4, on merchants.

8 Dyer (1994: 15) says of the Three Estates model and its apparent revival amid the challenges to traditional authority and economic structures in the fourteenth century, 'The notion had, of course, been a myth from its inception, because the burdens and benefits were so unequal. The workers in particular were parties to a very one-sided social contract. The repetition of the idea . . . its revival in the fourteenth century, points to the disquiet felt by some clerical and aristocratic writers.' He believes Chaucer implicitly criticises the theory's remoteness from 'complex and sinful' social reality.

9 On medieval homophobia see Keiser (1997). See also Dinshaw (1989).

10 Several names are associated with the military careers of the future Henry IV and Pierre de Lusignan; in particular, Henry IV campaigned in the Baltic in the early 1390s, and Pierre's 1365 siege of Alexandria was celebrated in Machaut's *Siege of Alexandria*. On crusading, see Keen (1983).

11 See Pratt (1987); Keen (1983). Even so, the cost of providing such service was felt to be such an imposition that many born to knightly status tried to evade becoming knights, and governments found a fruitful source of revenue in fines for this evasion.

12 Thrupp (1989), p. 39, shows that throughout the fourteenth and fifteenth centuries virtually none of the men chosen as aldermen or sheriffs in London came from the ranks of tradesmen like Chaucer's group.

13 Middle English sentences could be more fluid than modern sentences, and the restrictions imposed by the modern system of syntactic punctuation were absent, so that Chaucer's series of reasons given for these men's social elevation, between lines 366 and 378, is a more telling mismatch of cause and effect than modern editions like the Riverside fully reveal: their silver knives, girdles and pouches, their `wisdom', their wealth, and their wives' pretentious visions are all offered as reasons.

14 See Platt (1996).

15 Register is a set of vocabulary associated with a particular socio-linguistic context – e.g. archaic, slang, scientific or religious registers: Chaucer uses medical register for the Physician, and a disconcerting register of masculine sexual vigour runs through the Monk's portrait.

16 Wycliffites often referred scathingly to friars as 'beggars'; as with *prelaat*, Wycliffite jargon for disliked ecclesiastical authority, Chaucer seems to be using the register of contemporary reformist polemic occasionally.

Chapter 3   The *Knight's Tale*

1 Boccaccio starts with the Athens–Amazons war; see Bryan and Dempster (1941: 93–4); translated text in Havely (1980).

2 Patterson shows how Chaucer associates Thebes with irrationality and conflict and Athens with wisdom and the harmonisation of conflict (1991: 47–83, 198–30).

3 A gloss (interpretative note) that Boccaccio provided to his Teseida identified Mars and Venus with two ruling appetites: for war, the irascible appetite, and for love, the concupiscent, Havely (1980: 131).

Chapter 4   The *Miller's Tale*

1 Song of Songs 4:9–14; 5:1.

2 'The angel, surreptitiously entering into the private chamber of the Virgin, soothing her fear, said "Ave. . . . Thou who art made the gate of heaven . . .". "How shall I conceive, who have not known a man? How shall I break what I have vowed so firmly?" "The Holy Spirit's grace will perform all these things. Fear thee not, but be rejoice and feel secure".' Music and Latin text (with a translation) in Dobson and Harrison (1979: 176–83, 261–8, 327).

Chapter 5   The *Reeve's Tale*

1   Knapp (1990: 32) views the Miller's unruly protest as reflecting an inter-
      pretation of *The Knight's Tale* that sees it as 'dominant ideology encoded in
      dominant discourse. . . . And . . . objects to it violently'.
2   There is another very similar fabliau, Jean Bodel's *Gombert et les deux clers*:
      see Benson and Andersson, 1971: 70–83.
3   David (1976: 116–17) points out that the reader is implicated in the atti-
      tudes of *The Reeve's Tale*.

Chapter 7   The *Man of Law's Tale*

1   It seems likely Gower's version preceded Chaucer's but it may be the other
      way round.
2   Obvious examples are the grail romances, especially the *Queste del saint
      graal*, where the values of Arthurian secular adventures are turned on their
      head and replaced with a Cistercian-inspired concept of chaste and spiri-
      tual knighthod. Among other Arthurian romances, *The Awntyrs off Arthure*
      introduces teachings about mutability, into a romance of magic and
      chivalry, and *Sir Gawain* has a hero who experiences temptation, sin and
      penitence.
3   The *Legend* heroines have much in common with those in Ovid's *Heroides*,
      a major source, but they are also presented as both noble lovers and 'saints'
      and 'martyrs' of love; like the *Man of Law's Tale*, this shows Chaucer's
      interest in combining the figures of the romance heroine with the female
      saint, uniting the two figures through the theme of faithful but suffering
      women.
4   Chaucer presents Jews and Moslems as enemies determined to destroy
      Christianity, and as aspects of the Devil. The Sultaness is identified with
      the Serpent of Eden (e.g. II, 404–6). On the psychological and political
      structures of medieval European anti-Jewish and anti-Islam attitudes, see
      Swanson (1995: 260–93).

Chapter 8   The *Wife of Bath's Prologue and Tale*

1   Aquinas's *Summa Theologiae* provides the classic illustration, designed to
      present the thesis, the antithesis (each supported by citations from the
      Bible) and the resolution.
2   These last lines are omitted in several important manuscripts, including the
      Hengwrt Manuscript (1400). The inconsistencies in the Wife's sexual
      mores may reflect either changes in Chaucer's plan for the text or scribal
      interference.
3   The critical collections edited by Wasserman (1986), Dor (1992), Evans
      and Johnson (1994), and Beidler (1996) include a range of approaches to
      the text; see also Rigby (1996: 116–66).

4 Dinshaw (1989: 112–31) analyses the implied criticism of scholastic exegesis of texts as a parallel to criticism of masculine violence against women's bodies: a link between 'patriarchal hermeneutics' and the rape in the *Tale*.
5 *On the Properties of Things* 7.13, quoted in Miller (1977: 387).
6 For a psychoanalytic critical approach to the 'imprisonment of criticism' in the *Prologue*, see Strauss, in Allen and Axiotis (1997: 126–44).
7 The works that seem the closest forerunners of autobiography, like Abelard's *History of his Calamities* or Guibert de Nogent's *De vita sua*, are framed as accounts of spiritual growth, on the model of Augustine's *Confessions*.
8 It rather oddly resembles the pattern in Dorothy L. Sayers' *Gaudy Night*, where the independent Harriet Vane, having finally decided to marry Lord Peter Wimsey, insists on retaining the bride's promise to obey in her marriage vows, just at the time the Church of England had made this optional. She is another independent woman with problem-solving abilities, and an unexpected attraction towards *gentil* husbands.

Chapter 10 The *Clerk's Tale*

1 See the satire in the *Summoner's Tale*, III, 1284–94, against a cynical friar using 'glosynge' rather than the literal word of the Bible, in order to justify donations to his order.
2 Boccaccio's marquis refers to the chains of marriage; Petrarch's subjects, to the 'lawful yoke': Chaucer unites in the wordplay, as in his tale, power with submission, and obedience with happiness.
3 See Phillips (1995). The reference to Petrarch's death perhaps prefigures the theme of mutability too.
4 Wallace (1997: 261–2), observing that Griselda absorbs Walter's tyranny in her own body, to the benefit of the body politic, sees her oppression as a metaphor for political tyranny and the Petrarchan poetics that endorsed it, and he argues that Chaucer, by restoring the tale to the vernacular, by showing (he believes) more strongly a clash of interests between the common people and Walter, and by concluding with the sequence of contradictory interpretations, challenges Petrarch's hegemonic use of the story.
5 Pearsall (1985: 272–7) argues that the humanising touches increase the strain upon the narrative of the exemplary [i.e. allegorical] reading, citing several critics who believe the tale, or the Clerk, fails to hold the exemplary and 'dramatic' readings together. His alternative is to see Griselda's willing acceptance of suffering, as if by the Christian soul to its God, as a force that eventually reforms her oppressor's mode of exercising temporal power.

Chapter 11 The *Merchant's Tale*

1 An established image for Fortune, like that of the covered monster a few lines later; Chaucer used both in the *Book of the Duchess* (628, 635), but in this context *deceyvable* suggests the serpent of Eden too.

2   Augustine (1951–2), *The City of God*, XII–XIII.
3   See David (1976: 170–81) on the discrepant 'mixed style'.

Chapter 12   The *Squire's* and the *Franklin's Tales*

1   Pearsall (1985: 44–38) steers interestingly among several theories: that the tale is finished as it is, that it ends absurdly, that the whole romance was perhaps meant to be ironically bad. He suggests the ending is deliberately absurd, and is the end – the Franklin interrupts – but that both the pathos of the falcon episode and the marvels of Part One are seriously meant, and this romance stands appropriately between the teller's father's tale and that of the Franklin, who would like to be his father.
2   On courtly language, literature and 'Courtly Love', see Burnley (1998), especially 1–22, 99–175.
3   Knight (1986: 117) sees the *Franklin's Tale* as developing more fully than the Squire can 'a fuller ideological answer to the types of disorder, familial and social' that have been raised in fragments III to V.
4   'Aporia' is a term made popular by Deconstructive criticism for aspects or elements of a text which defy satisfactory analysis, inconsistencies and absences which cannot be solved by the reader because they bring together irreconcilable meanings.

Chapter 13   The *Physician's Tale*

1   This echoes line 560 in the *Romance of the Rose* version, which is in the context of a wider discussion about love and whether love alone can rule human society without justice.

Chapter 14   The *Pardoner's Tale*

1   On oaths, see Elliott (1974: 56–70).
2   See Riverside note to lines 727-36.

Chapter 15   The *Shipman's Tale*

1   Book V: 1840–1, see Riverside note for related images.
2   See Riverside note.

Chapter 16   The *Prioress's Tale*

1   See Boyd (1964), Nolan (1990), Collette (1990).
2   The story of St William of Norwich, a murder usually dated to 1144, is

recorded in the *Peterborough Chronicle* under the date 1137. The entry was probably written in 1154. The motives were financial: William's canonisation benefited the Cathedral and religious community.

3　I am indebted to Sarah Kay for information on these and enlightenment on the relevance of Kristeva.

4　See especially *N-Town* (1991), where the Council of Jews and arguments of Annas and Caiphas and others before Pilate are used for lengthy didactic debate on doctrines.

5　Translation from Boyd (1964), notes 1643–9, pp. 118–19.

Chapter 17　*Sir Thopas* and *Melibee*

1　See Green (1980: 143).

2　A typical twelve-line tail-rhyme stanza appears in *Sir Launfal*: aabccbddbeeb. The shorter, three stress, lines (*b* in these schemes) are the tail lines.

3　Patterson (1989) summarises the critical arguments and presents an analysis of *Thopas* as a comment on and parallel to Chaucer's whole oeuvre.

Chapter 18　The *Monk's Tale*

1　See Kelly (1997).

2　See, for example, the *Alliterative Morte Arthure* (*c*.1400), where, just as he reaches the peak of his power, about to march on Rome, he has to return back to face a usurped kingdom, civil war and a final battle in which he and his great knights perish.

3　Richard II had a special interest in angels (Gordon 1993: 57–8).

Chapter 19　The *Nun's Priest's Tale*

1　Aristotle's *Poetics*, 1449, defined tragedy as the fall of a great man, comedy as a rise from low position to high, views which filtered indirectly into medieval ideas of tragedy. The Knight's taste for tales about elevations not falls seema naive but prefigures the Christian pattern the tale shows of a rise again after a fall, and the element of free will against destiny.

2　Aesop (*c*.500 BC) is regarded as the founding father of a long tradition of European fable-writing.

3　I take *Lord* to refer to God, and capitalise: the Priest ends with a prayer which is also a typically modest blessing, in which he includes himself with his audience/congregation, asking for the Christian basics: goodness and salvation. This implicitly contrasts lords in a socio-political context with the Lord, and earthly story-telling with a priest's true use of language.

4　Does this prefigure Chantecleer's final trick; an implicit statement of Christian and Boethian hope, against the philosophical pessimism of the

Monk; an expression of easy upper-class confidence; a signal that the coming tale is a comic counterpart to the Monk's tragedies, or a formal marker of the vertical motifs of the next tale in the sequence?

5   Knight (1973: 212–13) shows *catel*, *rente* and *sklendre* were upper-class register: the estate-owners' world, not that of the estate servants like the widow. *Repleccioun* and *apoplexie* are learned, grand words for aspects of over-eating.

6   Like a learned interpretor finding a *fruyt* of allegorical meaning in a text?

Chapter 20   The *Second Nun's Tale*

1   He had a special devotion to Edward the Confessor, who supposedly had a chaste marriage; Richard's own first marriage may or may not have been chaste: he and Queen Anne had no children.

2   Knapp (1990: 112) point out that her story is almost 'a straightened out, Christianised version' of May's in *The Merchant's Tale*.

Chapter 21   The *Man of Law's Tale*

1   For example, St Frideswide's in Oxford. I am grateful to Alison McHardy for advice about canons.

2   Fragment VIII appears in many manuscripts before Fragment VII, but in the most authoritative manuscripts, including Ellesmere, after it, perhaps representing Chaucer's later decision.

3   Muslim science and scholarship preserved and developed ancient Greek science and philosophy, which then re-entered western Europe from the twelfth century, often from Muslim and Jewish texts, commentaries and intermediaries.

4   The sermon can be found in *Middle English Sermons*, ed. W. O. Ross, EETS, os, 209 (London, 1940), p. 128.

Chapter 22   The *Manciple's Tale*

1   Chaucer may have got the idea from a single use of 'My sone' in Gower's *Confessio Amantis* version, though there the phrase reflects that fact that the speaker is a priest in the confessional. The effect here is quite different – but that is common with Chaucer's verbal echoes.

2   Lines 358–62 work as a cumulative set of short, distinct phrases (without originally, of course, modern punctuation restraints), and when read or heard sequentially it is legitimate to see them as a series of linked warnings: don't be an author, don't be the source of unexpected news – whether true or false, and don't utter it to anyone, whatever their class; guard your tongue in all situations.

3   The combination of the terms *auctour* and *tidynges* is eye-catching, and

probably deliberately so: *auctour*, probably here with the primary sense of 'originator', usually means in Middle English not just an 'author' but a revered, Latin one, and the concept of *tidynges*, suggesting merely talk of news, to the modern reader, was used in Chaucer's *House of Fame* in a very wide sense of all kinds of communication and written or oral record: together they suggest caution in the role of the poet as well as caution in bringing people bad news.

Chapter 23   The *Parson's Tale*

1   Twenty-eight manuscripts, plus Caxton's 1478 edition, have the *Retraction*.
2   David (1976: 131–4) relates it also to the *Man of Law's Prologue*.
3   See the York *Last Judgement* play.
4   *Polemical Works*, I, 41, cited in M. Deanesly, *The Lollard Bible and Other Medieval Biblical Versions* (Cambridge, 1920; repr. 1966), p. 244.
5   *Expositio super Matthaei XXIII*, quoted in Deanesly, ibid., p. 244.
6   I am indebted to Dee Dyas for pointing out to me that 'life pilrimage', moral reformation, had been preached by the Church from earliest times as the true meaning of pilgrimage; by making teaching on the Seven Deadly Sins and virtues the climax of a pilgrimage journey, Chaucer, like Langland in *Piers Plowman*, Passus V–VII, is entirely orthodox, replacing 'place pilgrimage' with 'life pilgrimage'; see Dyas (1998).
7   Gardner (1977: 202). Gardner's book is speculative, sometimes proved inaccurate by subsequent scholarship, but also thought-provoking.

Bibliography

Aers, David (1986), *Chaucer* (Brighton: Harvester).

Allen, Valerie, and Axiotis, Ares (eds) (1997) *Chaucer*, New Casebooks (Basingstoke: Macmillan).

Augustine (1957–72), *The City of God Against the Pagans*, ed. and trans.George McCracken *et al.* (London and Cambridge, Mass.: Loeb Heinemann).

Bal, Mieke (1985), *Narratology: Introduction to the Theory of Narrative,* trans. C. van Boheemen (Toronto: University of Toronto Press).

Baldwin, Ralph (1955), *The Unity of the 'Canterbury Tales'*, Anglistica 5 (Copenhagen: Roschilde and Bagger).

Beidler, Peter G. (ed.) (1996), *The Wife of Bath*, Case Studies in Contemporary Criticism (Boston and New York: Bedford Books of St Martin's Press).

Benson, David C. (1986), *Chaucer's Drama of Style: Poetic Variety and Contrast in the Canterbury Tales* (Chapel Hill and London: University of North Carolina Press).

—— and Robertson, Elizabeth (1990), *Chaucer's Religious Tales*, Chaucer Studies 15 (Cambridge: D. S. Brewer,).

Benson, Larry D., and Andersson, Theodore M. (eds) (1971), *The Literary Context of Chaucer's Fabliaux* (Indianapolis and New York: Bobbs Merrill).

Blamires, Alcuin (ed.) (1992), with Pratt, K., and Marx, C. W., *Woman Defamed and Woman Defended: An Anthology of Medieval Texts* (London: Oxford University Press).

Bolton, J. L. (1980), *The Medieval English Economy, 1100–1500* (London: Dent).

Bowden, M. A. (1964), *A Commentary on the General Prologue to 'The Canterbury Tales'* (New York: Macmillan).

Boyd, Beverly (1964), *The Middle English Miracles of the Virgin* (San Marino: University of California Press).

Brewer, Derek (ed.) (1974), *Geoffrey Chaucer: The Writer and his Background* (Cambridge: D. S. Brewer).

—— (1984), *An Introduction to Chaucer* (London: Longman).

—— (ed.) (1987), *Chaucer: The Critical Heritage*, 2 vols (London: Routledge and Kegan Paul).

Britnell, R. H. (1996), *The Commercialisation of English Society, 1000–1500*, 2nd edn (Cambridge: Cambridge University Press).

Bryan, W. F., and Dempster, Germaine (1941), *Sources and Analogues of Chaucer's Canterbury Tales* (Chicago: University of Chicago Press).

Burnley, J. D. (David) (1979), *Chaucer's Language and the Philosophers' Tradition*, Chaucer Studies, 2 (Cambridge: D. S. Brewer, Rowman and Littlefield).

—— (1983), *A Guide to Chaucer's Language* (London).

—— (1998), *Courtliness and Literature in Medieval England* (Harlow: Addison Wesley Longman).

Burrow, J. A. (1984), ' "Sir Thopas": An Agony in Three Fits', *Essays on Medieval Literature* (Oxford: Clarendon Press).

236

Capellanus, Andreas (1941), *De arte honesti amandi: The Art of Courtly Love*, trans. Parry, J. J. (New York: Columbia University Press).

Carruthers, Mary (1979), 'The Wife of Bath and the Painting of Lions', *PMLA*, 94, pp. 209–22; repr. in Evans and Johnson (1994), pp. 39–53.

The Chester Mystery Cycle (1974), ed. Lumiansky, R. M., and Mills, D., 2 vols, Early English Text Society (London and New York: Oxford University Press).

Chaucer, Geoffrey, *The Riverside Chaucer*, ed. Benson, Larry D. (London and New York: Oxford University Press, 1988).

—— *Variorum Edition of the Works of Geoffrey Chaucer*, gen. ed. Ruggiers, Paul, vol. 1 (Norman, Oklahoma: University of Oklahoma Press, 1982, continuing). *Nun's Priest's Tale*, ed. Pearsall, Derek (Variorum, 1984).

The Manciple's Tale, ed. Baker, Donald (Variorum, 1984).

The Physician's Tale, ed. Corsa, Helen (Variorum, 1987).

The Prioress's Tale, ed. Boyd, Beverly (Variorum, 1987).

Coleridge, Samuel Taylor and Wordsworth, William, *The Lyrical Ballads*, ed. Brett, R. L., and A. R., Jones, 2nd edn (London and New York: Routledge, 1980).

Collette, Carolyn (1990), 'Critical Approaches to the *Prioress's Tale* and the *Second Nun's Tale*, in Benson and Robertson (1990), pp. 95–107.

Cooper, Helen (1996), *The Canterbury Tales,* Oxford Guides to Chaucer, 2nd edn (Oxford: Oxford University Press).

Crane, Susan (1994), *Gender and Romance in Chaucer's 'Canterbury Tales'* (Princeton: Princeton University Press).

David, Alfred (1976), *The Strumpet Muse: Art and Morals in Chaucer's Poetry* (Bloomington: Indiana University Press).

—— (1982), 'An ABC to the Style of the Prioress', in Carruthers, Mary J., and Kirk, Elizabeth D. (eds), *Acts of Interpretation: The Text in its Context, 700–1600: Essays in Medieval and Renaissance Literature in Honor of E. Talbot Donaldson* (Norman, Okl.: Pilgrim Books, 1982), pp. 147–57.

Diamond, Arlyn (1977, 1988), 'Chaucer's Women and Women's Chaucer', in *The Authority of Experience: Essays in Feminist Criticism*, ed. Diamond, Arlyn, and Edwards, Lee R. (Amherst: Massachusetts University Press, 1977, 1988), pp. 60–83.

Dillon, Janette (1993), *Geoffrey Chaucer* (Basingstoke: Macmillan).

Dinshaw, Carolyn (1989), *Chaucer's Sexual Politics* (Madison: University of Wisconsin Press).

Dobson, E. J., and Harrison F. (1979), *Medieval English Songs* (London and Boston: Faber and Faber).

Donaldson, E. Talbot (ed.) (1958), *Chaucer's Poetry: An Anthology for the Modern Reader* (New York: The Ronald Press Company).

—— (1970) 'The Idiom of Popular Poetry', in *Speaking of Chaucer* (London: Athlone Press).

—— (1954) 'Chaucer the Pilgrim', *PMLA* 69, pp. 928–36, repr. in Schoeck and Taylor (1960), vol. 1 (19), pp. 1–13.

Dor, Juliette (1992), 'From Crusading Saint to the Polysemous Virgin: Chaucer's Constance', in Juliette Dor (ed.), *A Wyf Ther Was: Essays in Honour of Paule Mertens-Fonck* (Liège: University of Liège, 1992), pp. 129–40.

Dyas, Dee (1997), *Images of Faith in English Literature, 700–1550: An Introduction* (London: Longman).

—— (1998), 'The Image of Pilgrimage in Medieval English Literature', PhD thesis, University of Nottingham.

Dyer, Christopher (1989), *Standards of Living in the Later Middle Ages: Social Change in England, c.1200–1520* (Cambridge: Cambridge University Press).

—— (1994), *Everyday Life in Medieval England* (London and Rio Grande, Ohio: Hambledon Press).

Elliott, Ralph W. V. (1974), *Chaucer's English*, Language Library (London: André Deutsch).

Ellis, Roger (1986), *Patterns of Religious Narrative in the Canterbury Tales* (London and Sydney: Croom Helm).

Embree, Dan, and Urquhart, Elizabeth (eds) (1991), *The Simonie: A Parallel-Text Edition, ed. from MSS Advocates 19.2.1, Bodley 48, and Peterhouse College 104* (Heidelberg: Carl Winter, Universitätsverlag).

Evans, Ruth, and Johnson, Lesley (eds) (1994), *Feminist Readings in Middle English Literature: The Wife of Bath and All her Sect* (London and New York: Routledge).

Ferster, Judith (1985), *Chaucer on Interpretation* (Cambridge: Cambridge University Press).

Finke, Laurie (1996), ' "All is for to Selle": Breeding Capital in the *Wife of Bath's Prologue and Tale*, in Beidler (1996), pp. 171–88.

Fletcher, A. J. (1991), 'The Faith of a Simple Man: Carpenter John's Creed in the *Miller's Tale*', *Medium Aevum*, 61(1), pp. 96–105.

Fradenburg, Louise O. (1985), 'The Manciple's Servant Tongue: Politics and Poetry in the *Canterbury Tales*', *English Literary History*, 52, pp. 85–118.

—— (1989), 'Criticism, Anti-Semitism, and the *Prioress's Tale*', in Allen and Axiotis (1997), pp. 193–31.

—— (1996), ' "Fulfild of Fairye": The Social Meaning of Fantasy in the Wife of Bath's Prologue and Tale', in Beidler (1996), pp. 205–20.

Frank, Robert W. Jr (1982), 'Miracle of the Virgin, Medieval Anti-semitism and the "Prioress's Tale" ', in *The Wisdom of Poetry: Essays in Early English Literature in Honor of Morton W. Bloomfield*, ed. Benson, Larry D., and Wenzel, Siegfried (Kalamazoo: Medieval Institute Publications, 1982), pp. 177–88.

Gardner, John (1997), *The Life and Times of Geoffrey Chaucer* (New York: Knopf Random House).

Gastle, Brian W. (1998), 'Chaucer's "Shaply" Guildsmen and Mercantile Pretensions', *Neuphilologische Mitteilungen*, 99(2), pp. 211–16.

Gordon, Dillian (1993), *The Wilton Diptych: Making and Meaning* (London: National Gallery).

—— Monnas, Lisa and Elam, Caroline (1997), *The Regal Image of Richard II and the Wilton Diptych* (London: Harvey Miller).

Gower, John (1992), *Mirour de l'Omme*, trans. Wilson, W. B., rev. Van Baak, N. W. (East Lansing: Colleagues Press).

Gray, Douglas (1979), 'Chaucer and "Pity" ', in *J. R. R. Tolkien, Scholar and Storyteller: Essays in Memoriam*, ed. Salu, M., and Farrell, R. T. (Ithaca and London: Cornell University Press, 1979).

Green, Richard Firth (1980), *Poets and Princepleasers: Literature and the English Court in the Late Middle Ages* (Toronto: University of Toronto Press).

Hahn, Thomas, and Kaeuper, Richard W. (1983), 'Text and Context: Chaucer's *Friar's Tale*', *Studies in the Age of Chaucer*, vol. 5, pp. 67–101.

Hansen, Elaine Tuttle (1992), *Chaucer and the Fictions of Gender* (Berkeley: University of California Press).

Hasler, A. J. (1990), 'Hoccleve's Unregimented Body', *Paragraph*, 13, pp. 164–83.

Havely, Nicholas R. (1980), *Chaucer's Boccaccio*, Chaucer Studies, 5 (Cambridge: D. S. Brewer, Rowman and Littlefield).

Hieatt, C. B. and Butler, S. (1976), *Pleyn Delit: Medieval Cookery for Modern Books* (Toronto and Buffalo: University of Toronto Press).

Hines, John (1993), *The Fabliau in English* (Burnt Mill: Longman).

Hussey, S. S. (1981), *Chaucer: An Introduction*, 2nd edn (London: Methuen).

Johnson, Lesley (1994), 'Reincarnations of Griselda: Contexts for the *Clerk's Tale*', in Evans and Johnson (1994), pp. 195–221.

Johnson, Lynn Staley (1990), 'Chaucer's Tale of the Second Nun and the Strategies of Dissent', *Studies in Philology*, 89, pp. 314–333.

Jones, Terry (1985) *Chaucer's Knight* (London: Methuen).

Justice, Steven (1994), *Writing and Rebellion: England in 1381* (Berkeley: University of California Press).

Kaske, Carol V. (1975), 'Getting Round the *Parson's Tale*: An Alternative to Allegory and Irony', in *Chaucer at Albany*, ed. Robbins, R. H. (New York: Burt Franklin) pp. 147–77.

Kean, P. M. (1972), *Chaucer and the Making of Modern Poetry* (London: Routledge and Kegan Paul).

Keen, Maurice (1983), 'Chaucer's Knight, the English Aristocracy, and the Crusade', in *English Court Culture in the Later Middle Ages*, ed. Scattergood, V. J., Sherborne, J. W., and Burrow, J. A. (London: Duckworth, 1983), pp. 45–62.

—— (1990), *English Society in the Later Middle Ages, 1348–1599*, The Penguin Social History of Britain (London: Penguin Books).

Kelly, Henry Ansgar (1997), *Chaucerian Tragedy*, Chaucer Studies, 24 (Cambridge: D. S. Brewer).

Kittredge, George Lyman (1915), *Chaucer and His Poetry* (Cambridge, Mass.: Harvard University Press).

Knapp, Peggy A. (1990) *Chaucer: The Social Contest* (New York: Routledge).

Knight, Stephen (1973), *Rymying Craftily: Meaning in Chaucer's Poetry* (Sydney: Angus and Robertson).

—— (1986), *Geoffrey Chaucer* (Oxford: Basil Blackwell).

Kolve V. A. (1984), *Chaucer and the Imagery of Narrative: The First Five Canterbury Tales* (Stanford and London: Edward Arnold).

Kristeva, Julia (1982), *The Powers of Horror: An Essay on Abjection*, trans. Roudiez, Leon S. (New York: Columbia University Press).

Langland, William, *The Vision of Piers the Plowman: The B-Text*, ed. Schmidt, A. V. C. (London: Oxford University Press, 1978; rev. edn, 1987).

Lawton, David (1985), *Chaucer's Narrators*, Chaucer Studies, 13 (Cambridge: Brewer).

Mann, Jill (1973), *Chaucer and Medieval Estates Satire: The Literature of Social Classes and the General Prologue to the Canterbury Tales* (London: Cambridge University Press).

Mann, Jill (1974–5), 'The *Speculum Stultorum* and the *Nun's Priest's Tale*', *Chaucer Review*, 8, pp. 262–82.

—— (1991), *Geoffrey Chaucer* (New York: Harvester).

McAlpine, Monica E. (1980), 'The Pardoner's Homosexuality and How It Matters', *Proceedings of the Modern Language Association*, in Allen and Axiotis (1997), pp. 36–50.

Martin, Priscilla (1990), *Chaucer's Women* (Basingstoke: Macmillan).

Meale, Carole M. (1990), 'The Miracles of Our Lady: Context and Interpretations', in *Studies in the Vernon Manuscript*, ed. Pearsall, Derek (Cambridge: D. S. Brewer, 1990), pp. 115–36.

Miller, Robert P. (ed.) (1977), *Chaucer: Sources and Background* (New York: Oxford University Press).

Minnis, A. J. (1982), *Chaucer and Pagan Antiquity*, Chaucer Studies, 8 (Cambridge: D. S. Brewer).

—— (1984), *Medieval Theory of Authorship: Scholastic Literary Attitudes in the Later Middle Ages* (London: Scolar Press).

Muscatine, Charles (1957), *Chaucer and the French Tradition* (Berkeley and Los Angeles: University of California Press).

N-Town Play: Cotton Vespasian D.8 (1991), ed. Stephen Spector, Early English Text Society, Special Series, vols 11–12 (Oxford: Oxford University Press).

Nolan, Barbara (1990), 'Chaucer's Tales of Transcendence: Rhyme Royal and Christian Prayer', in Benson and Robertson (1990), pp. 21–38.

—— (1992), *Chaucer and the Tradition of the 'Roman Antique'* (Cambridge: Cambridge University Press).

O'Brien, Timothy D. (1997), 'Ars-Metrike: Science, Satire and Chaucer's Summoner', in Allen and Axiotis (1997), pp. 15–29.

Olson, Paul A. (1986), *The Canterbury Tales and the Good Society* (Princeton: Princeton University Press).

Patterson, Lee (1978), 'The "Parson's Tale" and the Quitting of the *Canterbury Tales*', *Traditio*, 34, pp. 331–80.

—— ' "What man artow?": Authorial Self-Definition in *The Tale of Sir Thopas* and *The Tale of Melibee*', *Studies in the Age of Chaucer*, 11, pp. 117–75.

—— (1991), *Chaucer and the Subject of History* (Madison, Wis., and London: Routledge).

Pearsall, Derek (1984), 'Epidemic Irony in Modern Appreciations of the *Canterbury Tales*', the J. A. W. Bennett Memorial Lecture, Perugia, 1982–3, in Boitani, Piero and Torti, Anna (eds), *Medieval and Pseudo-Medieval Literature* (Tübingen and Cambridge: D. S. Brewer, 1984), pp. 79–89.

—— (1985), *The Canterbury Tales* (London: Allen and Unwin).

—— (1992), *The Life of Geoffrey Chaucer: A Critical Biography* (Oxford: Blackwell).

—— (1997), 'Pre-empting Closure in *The Canterbury Tales*: Old Endings, New Beginnings', in *Essays in Ricardian Literature in Honour of J. A. Burrow*, ed. Minnis, A. J., Morse, Charlotte C., Turville-Petre, Thorlac (Oxford: Clarendon Press, 1997), pp. 23–38.

Phillips, Helen (1995), 'Chaucer and Jean Le Fèvre', *Archiv*, 232, 23–36.

Platt, Colin (1996), *King Death: The Black Death and its Aftermath in Late-Medieval England* (London: UCL Press).

Pratt, J. H. (1987), 'Was Chaucer's Knight Really a Mercenary?', *Chaucer Review*, 22.

Rex, Richard (1995), *The Sins of Madame Eglantine and Other Essays on Chaucer* (Newark, N.J.: University of Delaware Press; London: Associated Presses).

Riddy, Felicity (1993), ' "Women Talking about the Things of God": a Late Medieval Sub-culture', in Meale, Carole M. (ed.), *Women and Literature in Britain, 1150–1500* (Cambridge: Cambridge University Press, 1993), pp. 104–27.

——— (1994), 'Engendering Pity in the *Franklin's Tale*', in Evans and Johnson (1994), pp. 54–71.

Rigby, S. H. (1996), *Chaucer in Context: Society, Allegory and Gender*, Manchester Medieval Studies (Manchester: Manchester University Press).

Robertson, D. W. (1962), *A Preface to Chaucer: Studies in Medieval Perspectives* (Princeton, N.J.: Princeton University Press).

Robertson, Elizabeth (1990), 'Aspects of Female Piety in the *Prioress's Tale*', in Benson and Robertson (1990), pp. 145–60.

Rogerson, Margaret (1999), 'The Wife of Bath: Standup Comic', *Sydney Studies in English*, 24, pp. 3–20.

The Romance of the Rose, by Guillaume de Lorris and Jean de Meun, ed. Lecoy, Felix, 3 vols, CFMA (Paris: Champion, 1965); trans. Horgan, Frances (Oxford and New York: Oxford University Press, 1994).

Saul, Nigel (1983), 'The Social Status of Chaucer's Franklin: a Reconsideration', *Medium Aevum*, 52:1, pp. 10–26.

——— (1992), 'Chaucer and Gentility', in Hanawalt, Barbara (ed.), *Chaucer's England: Literature in Historical Context*, Medieval Studies at Minnesota, vol. 4 (Minneapolis: University of Minnesota Press, 1992), pp. 41–58.

——— (1995) 'Richard II and the Vocabulary of Kingship', *English Historical Review*, 110).

——— (1997), *Richard II*, Yale English Monarchs (New Haven and London: Yale University Press).

Scattergood, V. J. (1974), 'The Manciple's Way of Speaking', *Essays in Criticism*, 24, pp. 124–46.

Schoeck, Richard J, and Taylor, Jerome (eds) (1960), *Chaucer Criticism: An Anthology*, vol. 1: *The Canterbury Tales* (Notre Dame, Ind.: University of Notre Dame Press).

Shepherd, Geoffrey (1974), 'Religion and Philosophy in Chaucer', in Brewer, Derek (ed.), *Geoffrey Chaucer: The Writer and his Background* (Woodbridge: D. S. Brewer, 1974), pp. 262–89.

Strauss, Barrie Ruth (1997), 'The Subversive Discourse of the Wife of Bath: Phallocentric Discourse and the Imprisonment of Criticism', in Allen and Axiotis (1997), pp. 126–44.

Strohm, Paul (989), *Social Chaucer* (Cambridge, Mass.: Harvard University Press).

——— (1992), *Huchon's Arrow: The Social Imagination of Fourteenth-Century Texts* (Princeton: Princeton University Press.

Swanson, R. N. (1995), *Religion and Devotion in Europe c.1215–c.1515*, Cambridge Medieval Textbooks (Cambridge: Cambridge University Press).

Thrupp, S. L. (1948), *The Merchant Class of Medieval London* (Ann Arbor: University of Michigan Press).

Twycross, Meg (1990), ' "As the Sun with his Beams When He is Most Bright" ', *Medieval English Theatre*, 12, pp. 34–79.

Wagenknecht, Edward (ed.) (1959), *Chaucer: Modern Essays in Criticism* (New York: Oxford University Press).

Wallace, David (1997), *Chaucerian Polity: Absolutist Lineages and Associational Forms in England and Italy* (Stanford, Cal.: Stanford University Press).

Wasserman, Julian N., and Blanch, Robert J. (ed.)(1986), *Chaucer in the Eighties* (Syracuse, N.Y.: Syracuse University Press).

Whittock, Trevor (1968), *A Reading of the Canterbury Tales* (Cambridge: Cambridge University Press).

Wogan-Browne, Jocelyn (1994), 'The Virgin's Tale', in Evans and Johnson (1994), pp. 163–94.

—— and Burgess, Glyn S. (1996), *Virgin Lives and Holy Deaths: Two Exemplary Biographies for Anglo-Norman Women* (London: Everyman).

Wordsworth, William, and Coleridge, S. T., *Wordsworth and Coleridge: Lyrical Ballads*, ed. Brett, R. L., and Jones, A. R. (London: Methuen, 1963).

York Plays (1963) (New York: Russel and Russel, 1963; repr. of 1885).

Index

Bold type indicates an extended study. Critics' and authors' names are indexed but not the names of editors or compilers.